Haunted Liverpool 30

Tom Slemen

The Tom Slemen Press

Copyright © 2018 Tom Slemen

All rights reserved.

ISBN-10: 1727212851
ISBN-13: **978-1727212853**

CONTENTS

The Faceless Bride	1
Two Tales of Two Cults	7
Anfield Cemetery's Unknown Ghost	32
The Devil's Arms	39
Strange Cases of Possession	47
Nick Nock Nothin'	67
Don't Speak Ill of the Dead	80
Three Conscience Ghosts	91
Ghost Dad	101
Unearthly Powers	109
The Demon in the Pool	136
Walton's Peeping Lady	142
The Pink Witch	147
The Case of the Suave Abductor	160

The Christmas Ring Mystery	172
The Waltzing Matchmaker	180
Tales of the Far Out	184
The Mystery of Toy Farm	208
I Dream of Olga	219
The Odd Couple	226
Timewalker	235
The Tickler	241
The Women of the Wood	250
The Dwellers in the Void	260
The Familiar Girl	265
X the Unknown	271
Nosy Parker	291
A Sign from the Depths	296
The Clock of Owls	300
Some Strange Omens of Death	324

Two Haunted Sleepovers   330

The Ubiquitous Night Maiden   348

THE FACELESS BRIDE

One warm evening in May 1966, a 22-year-old Knotty Ash woman named Hattie Woods was returning from London on the train. She'd been for an interview for the job of a secretary at the Westminster offices of IBM (the multinational technology company), but she had a feeling she hadn't landed the job. She'd know in a few days by letter. Hattie was due to marry Peter in a fortnight and he had made it crystal clear that he wanted her to be a 'housebound' housewife, tied to the home and all of the usual domestic duties that entailed. He also wanted her to have three children (ideally two boys and a girl), and to see less of her old friends. Hattie loved Peter, but she wanted to work and have a measure of independency in the marriage. Anyway, Hattie was thinking about Peter's unreasonable demands as the train travelled down that tunnel which leads to Lime Street Station, and as the carriage passed under Russell Street, Hattie was startled to see a woman in a white wedding dress glowing ghostly in the blackness beyond the windows. The sighting lasted seconds as the decelerating train rolled past the apparition. An old woman sitting next to Hattie saw the figure too. 'Did you see that?' Hattie asked the old lady, who smiled and nodded, then said: 'You're going to be married. She's been seen for years. She's got no face.'

'I *am* getting married too,' gasped Hattie, 'in two weeks.'

The old woman said: 'If you see her, and a man is in the carriage with you and he sees her too, you're going to marry him. That's what I've been told over the years, anyway.'

'Oh, really?' said Hattie with a puzzled look. 'What a strange superstition.'

Three days later, Hattie travelled to Manchester by train for an interview as a script editor at Granada TV, and as the train pulled out of Lime Street and passed through the tunnel, Hattie – and a man who looked about 25 years of age sitting next to her – both saw the ghostly bride. 'What on earth was that?' the man exclaimed, and with wide eyes he turned to Hattie and asked: 'Did you see her?'

Hattie nodded. 'It's a ghost. I saw her three days ago.' Hattie did not tell him about the unusual superstition associated with the ghost in case the passenger thought she was hinting at some romantic relationship.

Throughout the hour-long journey to Manchester, the man sitting next to Hattie introduced himself as Jeff Swift, a singer-songwriter who was on his way to audition for a Manchester band. Hattie told him she was going for a job interview too, and he wished her well. On that short journey between the two cities, Hattie and Jeff really hit it off. Hattie was usually a bit shy talking to people she didn't really know –

especially men – but she felt so relaxed talking to Jeff, and felt as if she had known him for years. She desperately wanted to see him again, but when the train reached Manchester Piccadilly the two young people went their separate ways. Hattie discovered script-editing was not her thing, and she told her interviewer as much, and she then left the offices of Granada Television. She walked through a drizzle to the train station, and as she waited for the train back to Liverpool, she heard someone call her name behind her. It was Jeff. He stood there with his guitar case in his hand with a big infectious smile on his face.

'Oh, Hello there,' Hattie beamed a big grin at the musician.

'They said they'd let me know but I could tell they didn't like me,' he told Hattie.

'Oh, I thought you'd passed the audition with that big smile on your face,' said Hattie.

'No, that was because I saw *you* standing there,' Jeff replied, with a slight blush. They boarded the train to Liverpool, and just over an hour later, as they left Lime Street Station, Jeff begged Hattie to go for a 'little drink' with him. Hattie agreed to go for just one drink in the Crown Hotel. When the drinkers in there saw Jeff's guitar case, they persuaded him to open it and Jeff did, and soon he was strumming away and everybody started singing along to the songs of Jeff's repertoire, which included hits by The Beatles, Herman's Hermits, the Kinks and the Rolling Stones. After a couple of drinks, Hattie even did a duet with Jeff of the Tom Jones hit, *It's Not Unusual* - and every drinker applauded because the harmonies were amazing. Many pubs later, Hattie noticed it was getting dark outside and she felt so choked up when she told Jeff she'd have to be making her way home.

'Hattie, I *have* to see you again,' Jeff told her, and she could see he had a tear in his eye.

Hattie left the pub in tears and Jeff went after her. He grabbed her wrist and turned her to face him. 'What's wrong? What have I done?' he asked.

'Jeff, I'm getting married in just under two weeks' time, and this – this is wrong,' she said, wiping her tears with her fingers.

Jeff took his handkerchief from the top pocket of his jacket and slowly handed it to Hattie as he asked, 'Married? You didn't say – '

'I know, and I should have Jeff, but – ' Hattie struggled to finish the sentence.

'But what?' he wanted to know.

Hattie lunged into him, and she pressed her face against his chest as she sobbed. She was saying things but Jeff couldn't understand a word she was saying because of her sobbing. He dried her eyes and took her across the road to the Punch and Judy Café.

'We need to talk,' Jeff told her, and he sat Hattie down at a table and went to order two coffees. He came back and asked Hattie why she had no engagement ring on.

'The ring's in H Samuel getting repaired; one of the stones fell out of it,' she explained, and unconsciously felt the third finger of her left hand.

'Do you love him?' Jeff asked, and glanced to his right at the bustle of night life beyond the window.

Hattie looked at the red Formica tabletop and in an almost inaudible whisper she said, 'I don't know.'

'You must know,' said Jeff, his voice sounding

laconic because his throat was so constricted with sadness, 'you either do or you don't.'

Hattie was so choked up she could only shrug at the question.

'Maybe we should just be friends – ' Jeff was saying when Hattie cried out: 'No!' and her hands shot across the table and grabbed his fist. They went from café to café, talking things through, and ended up at Joe's Café on Duke Street, a place that never closed, and by the time they left the premises the sky had turned to Turkish blue and the fresh morning air was alive with the sweet birdsong of the dawn chorus. Hattie could imagine the turmoil at her home in Knotty Ash, and she felt so selfish for staying out, but she realised she had fallen in love with Jeff in such a short span of time, and for the first time in her life she felt free. Jeff was so funny, loving, charismatic and open-minded – and more modern-minded than Peter. Jeff had even said in one conversation that women shouldn't have to give up their surname when they marry.

And so, after much soul-searching, Hattie decided she couldn't go through with that wedding. Peter coldly told her there were more fishes in the sea, and Hattie's parents warned her that a dreamer with a guitar would not be able to support her financially. Jeff and Hattie got married at a registry office on Mount Pleasant and went to live in a flat in what is now known as the Georgian district of Liverpool. They struggled for years, with Hattie working as a poorly-paid secretary to a department store and Jeff earning money from a job as a school caretaker. But they stayed together, and one afternoon in 1970, a curious thing happened. Hattie had to go to the funeral of a relative in Manchester, and upon her return to Liverpool on the train, she found herself seated next to a handsome man who kept taking furtive sidelong glances at her. As the train approached Lime Street via that tunnel, Hattie just knew she'd see that faceless bride again, and so she squeezed her eyes shut, and sure enough, she heard the man next to her say, 'What on earth was that?'

Hattie kept her eyes closed for a little longer, and she heard the woman in the seat facing her say, 'She had on a wedding dress!' 'Yes, that's right,' said the man next to Hattie, 'and she looked as if she was lit up. How extraordinary; an actual ghost.' He turned and asked Hattie: 'Did *you* see her?'

'No, I didn't thank God!' Hattie replied, and got up off the seat as the train rolled on sparking wheels into Lime Street Station.

I still get the occasional report of the faceless bride in the tunnel, but I have no idea who she is, or how she exerts that strange influence which can apparently bind the hearts of two strangers.

TWO TALES OF TWO CULTS

On the Friday evening of 6 May 1955, 13-year-old Tina Edwards and 14-year-old Dean Clark, both hopelessly in love with one another, tried to elope (albeit rather unrealistically) to Gretna Green, but the parents of the couple got wind of the plans and they were waiting at Birkenhead Central when Tina and Dean arrived, so the teenage lovers turned and fled and decided to hide in a church all night until they could make another escape attempt in the morning. This was Dean's idea. They eventually found a suitably deserted church after walking for miles, and they hid under benches and waited and waited as they embraced and kissed, and eventually a hard silence fell upon the cavernous interior of the house of God. It looked as if Dean's plan could work. The hidden juveniles heard the heavy oaken doors of the church being locked and bolted, followed by soft footfalls and jingling keys. The lights went out and a vestry door slammed and its echoes reflected off the walls as the eerie plaster statues stood like miniature sentinels in the moonlight filtering through the stained glass windows. Full of caution, Tina and Dean slowly got up and sat on the bench with their satchels at their feet, and Dean looked at the altar and in a low guarded voice he whispered, "We should be getting married at an altar like that. Why won't they just let us be?'

'Oh Dean, I love you so much,' Tina kissed him and snuggled her head under his chin.

The young romantics kissed for a while, then out came the bottles of lemonade and chocolate bars and salmon paste sandwiches stashed away for the train journey to Dumfriesshire, where runaways could be joined in marriage with no questions asked – or so Dean had heard. When the snacks and lemonade were gone, the teens tried to sleep on the benches, but they were too cold and hard. 1955 was the year it snowed in May, so Tina and Dean had to sleep with the hoods of their coats up. At some point, around 10pm, Tina and Dean woke up. Unable to get back to sleep they walked around the nave, and Dean even preached his undying love for Tina from the pulpit, but by midnight, the intendeds started yawning and so they dozed off on the pews using their satchels as rough pillows.

They were awakened sometime after 3am. Tina rubbed her eyes and thought she was dreaming. A crowd of about thirty people dressed like monks in hooded robes came into the candlelit church wheeling a bizarre tall statue of a winged man with horns. The right claw-like hand of the statue pointed up and its other hand pointed down. This sounds like a description of Pazuzu – an ancient Mesopotamian demon. The castors on the base of the statue squealed harshly as it was steered to the altar rail by two robed men. Tina and Dean hid on the floor and peeped over the benches at the weird proceedings; this was no

Christian Mass – so what was going on?

In addition to the candles that had already been lit around the place, five huge black candles were lit at the base of the weird statue, and a man in a strange boxlike hood with two eyeholes went onto the altar and began the 'service'. He wore an upside-down Celtic cross on the chest of his vestments and he swore and used blasphemous words that scared the teenagers. He spoke of the Devil being the saviour of mankind, and the officiating speaker bragged that he could easily murder without ever being captured because he was shielded by occult forces. Some of the unholy congregation cheered when he made this statement. Eventually a naked couple appeared at the statue of the demon. They did not wear hoods and Tina and Dean could see the couple were in their early twenties. What followed seemed to be some sort of satanic parody of a marriage ceremony, only the couple carried out sex acts on one another during the service. When the hooded man on the altar declared, 'I now pronounce you man and wife in the eyes of Satan,' the massive shadow of a man with horns was cast on the walls of the altar, and this really frightened Tina, because she could not see what was casting the shadow. By now, the church was filled with sulphuric and sweet-smelling incense, and it was making Tina want to cough.

At the end of the twisted marriage service, all of the people present – including the man on the altar - removed their hoods, and Dean recognised a teacher he knew, a bank manager who was a friend of his father, and Tina recognised adults she knew. The priest on the altar wore horned-rim spectacles and had reddish-blonde hair with a distinctive widow's peak. Overcome with the stifling fumes of the intoxicating incense, Tina coughed out loud, and she and Dean ran as fast as they could to the side entrance of the church – where the ritualists had come in to the nave. The door the teens came to at the end of a corridor was bolted but not locked. Dean drew back the bolt on the door in the nick of time and he and a screaming Tina fled into the moonlit streets. The teenagers were chased by the robed Satanists for quite a distance until Dean waved to a passing police patrol car. The Devil worshippers then turned and ran and were soon lost to sight. The police didn't believe a word of the teens' story and Tina and Dean were sternly told to go home immediately. No one believed Tina and Dean, but for many years they received anonymous letters warning them to say nothing about the "Mass" or they'd be killed and no one would ever find their bodies. Tina also received threatening telephone calls in the dead of night, years after the incident, when she had moved to Liverpool, and the voice was always the same: gruff and menacing, and the caller seemed to know when Tina was alone. Most self-proclaimed modern Satanists will tell you that they do not wish anyone any harm, but the mysterious hooded spokesman of the band of hooded cultists in that Wirral church in 1955 spoke gloatingly of murder and other evil acts, so he might have represented some splinter group of Devil worshippers.

We now move sixteen years into the future to the Liverpool of 1971 as we look at another case of a strange menacing cult. Florence Champerty of Mossley Hill was a pretty 18-year-old blonde lady with a charming personality and a selfless nature, and she had many friends of both sexes. Florence was a very down-to-earth girl looking for work in the summer of 1971, and her mind was solely concerned with finding the money to buy some outfits, as she was a very fashion-conscious girl, who, as her mother often quipped, "was all with it". Her mind was certainly not concerned with the murky world of the supernatural as she walked along Allerton Road on her way to do a bit of shopping. Florence fancied working in a shop, and she had made enquires downtown in the stores of the city centre, but had heard nothing so far. She went to buy a box of cakes for her Nan and mum from Clooks the confectioners on Allerton Road, and whilst there she had asked the woman behind the counter if there were any vacancies going; there weren't, but the woman in the shop said she'd let her know if any vacancies arose. Florence also made enquiries at Cleggs the dry-cleaners, the Pet and Garden Store, and Ellie Langford the florist, all to no avail. Florence did some shopping, and then, around 3pm she made her way homewards, which meant turning onto Green Lane. A woman sprung out from the bus shelter on the lane and grabbed Florence's arm, giving her quite a start. The woman looked about thirty, and she had wild staring pale blue eyes with dark bags under them, as well as straggly black hair that was greasy and long, and her ears protruded from this slicked mess of oily rat tales. She wore a long white raincoat with a belt tied around her exceedingly tiny waist, and as this petite but strong woman dragged Florence into the bus shelter, the teenager dropped the box of cakes, and she crossly asked the stranger what she was doing.

'They want you!' the woman said, her eyes bulging, and Florence could see the fear in them. She let go of Florence, and as the girl stooped to pick up the white cardboard box, the apparently deranged woman replied: 'They're everywhere!' and she looked out the windows of the shelter behind her and angled her head sideways for a moment, as if she thought someone might be listening.

Florence had a face flushed with anger as she lifted the lid of the string-tied box a few millimetres to see that the cakes were intact. 'What *are* you talking about?' she asked this public nuisance.

The woman grasped the sleeve of the teenager, tugged it hard three times and in a low voice she said: 'I know you think that I'm some crank, but I'm not. I've got all my marbles believe me. Now listen, I was over by the pet shop before when you were asking for a job – '

'Oh,' Florence was spooked by the way the woman had told her this, and it vindicated what she was already thinking: that this woman was not only a nutcase, she was a dangerous one who'd been following her. 'Look, I've got to go,' Florence firmly told her, 'I'm in a hurry.' And she left the bus shelter.

The woman followed her and walked in front of her. 'Just hear me out, and tell your mum and dad, love. These people are a big organisation; they're everywhere, and they can just take people off the streets like that!' The woman snapped her fingers.

Florence slowed a little, and thought about how this woman had been watching her at the pet shop earlier. If she was mentally unstable and happened to have a knife, she could kill and merely be thrown in a mental hospital, Florence thought with a shudder.

The stranger continued. 'They either go for women who are run-down – like I was after I'd had my baby, or they go for the young girls walking about with their heads in the clouds.'

'Look, you better leave me alone or I'll report you!' Florence warned the woman, and then she started to walk faster, but the woman trotted after her.

'If you only knew,' the woman told the teen in a voice that sounded broken with sadness, 'I'm trying to stop you becoming another victim.'

'I'll do it; I'll go to the police station on Rose Lane!' Florence raised her voice even higher. 'Get away from me!'

'Do you know what they'll do to you, eh?' the unbalanced woman asked, but Florence suddenly took off as fast as a professional sprinter when the starting pistol is fired. She left the kooky woman far behind her, and only looked back once to see her standing out stark as a bright spot in that white raincoat 200 yards away. Florence lived on Menlove Gardens North, and she hurried home, constantly looking back in case the disturbed woman saw where she lived. Once inside her home, Florence told her mother about the woman grabbing her at the bus stop and the strange things she had said about people who were out to get her. 'Ah, she's more to be pitied, Flo,' said Mrs Champerty. 'Go and sit down and I'll make you a nice cup of tea.'

'I'm too hot for tea, Mum,' said Florence, fanning her face with her hand, 'I'll have a glass of cream soda with ice.'

Florence took her coat off and went into the living room, where her Nan was sitting in her usual armchair reading *Woman's Own*. Florence told her about the 'head-case' who had tried to convince her that people were after her, and Nan said, 'Maybe she's escaped from somewhere. You don't know who's knocking about in this day and age. Next time you go out shopping, take one of your friends with you.'

'They're all working or at college, Nan,' Florence told her with a wistful look. She wished she had a job too. She wasn't even signing on at the moment and her father was always telling her money didn't grow on trees. She'd used the little money she'd got for her 18th birthday to buy things in the past week and it'd soon be gone.

On the following day at 2pm, Florence thought she'd visit a few shops on Penny Lane and Smithdown Road to see if there were any vacancies going. She started her quest for a job by visiting a popular shop on Penny Lane named Cunningham's, which sold all sorts of provisions and groceries, but before Florence reached the shop, she was startled to hear a car horn beeping to her left. She turned to see a white car crawling along on the wrong side of the road, and the driver – who was looking at her with the side window wound down – was *that* woman – the one who had overeagerly accosted her on Green Lane – or so it appeared initially. Florence thought the person was wearing some mask of that woman's face, because the eyes looked wrong – they were very dark brown, whereas that woman had had pale blue eyes. 'Excuse me, love!' the driver shouted, and Florence thought the voice did not sound like that of the 'loco' woman – this voice sounded more well-spoken and deeper.

'I'm sorry about yesterday, but I'd had a little too

much to drink. Bye now!' she said, and the car steadily picked up speed and accelerated up Penny Lane until it disappeared over the hump in the road. This incident spooked Florence somewhat. She went to Cunningham's, discovered there were no vacancies going, and then she went straight home to tell her mother of the strange incident.

'Oh Florence, why would someone be wearing a mask and be pretending to be that nutty woman?' her mother asked with a grin as she cleaned the cooker.

'Mum, I don't know,' Florence admitted, sitting at the kitchen table eating a doughnut, 'that's why I'm telling you about it; I thought you'd know why!'

'Oh you make a mystery out of everything, Flo,' said Mrs Champerty, and then she paused and stopped cleaning the cooker. She turned to her daughter and said, 'Oh, and here's a real mystery for you: your mate Donna snubbed me this morning.'

'Who? Donna?' Florence asked. Donna was her best friend.

Mrs Champerty nodded slowly. 'Yes, I let on to her and she looked down and walked straight past me. I was going in the post office and she was coming out.'

'She probably hadn't noticed you, mum,' Florence reasoned, 'Donna walks round in a daydream.'

Mrs Champerty shook her head and applied a cloth soaked with Flash to the cooker door. 'No, she saw me alright, and I thought you and her might have had a fall-out or something.'

Florence telephoned Donna to see if everything was alright. The girl's mother answered and said Donna wasn't feeling well. A few days after this, Donna passed Florence in the street without acknowledging her. Florence shouted after: 'Donna? What's wrong?' but she got no answer. Donna walked on without looking back. Over the course of the next few weeks, all of Florence's other friends also became distant, and acted as if they'd found out some ghastly secret about her, and their behaviour really baffled and upset the girl. 'Mum, why are they being like this?' she asked her mother one day, and then she burst into tears.

'I haven't a clue, pet,' said Mrs Champerty, embracing her daughter and stroking her head. 'Do you want me to go and see Donna's mum about this? Maybe someone's been spreading lies about you.'

'No, don't go and see her, it'll only make things worse,' said Florence, shaking her head at her mum's bosom.

When Florence's father Colin heard about the way his daughter's friends were giving her the cold shoulder, he decided to take her on a drive up to Southport to cheer her up. Florence wasn't at all keen, but her dad cajoled her into going along, and that day, the girl received quite a shock. As the car taking her to Southport was travelling up Queens Drive, just a few minutes from Florence's home, the lights turned to red at the Woolton Road junction, and Colin Champerty slowed his vehicle. To his left he noticed a crowd on the pavement and Florence, seated on the left side of the car in the front passenger seat, had a better view of this knot of people. She saw they were gathered around the body of a woman lying on her back – and she had on a white raincoat. It was the woman who had jumped out on her from the Green Lane bus shelter. She had her eyes open but she wasn't moving. Colin saw that one of the people in the crowd was a friend of his named Terry, who now ran a shop on this road.

'Dad! That's the woman – the one who grabbed me on Green Lane!' Florence wound down the side window and looked out at the crowd.

The lights changed to green, and Colin drove on slowly, but the impatient driver behind him sounded his car's horn. 'Really?' Mr Champerty said.

'Yes, she looked as if she was dead!' Florence strained her neck looking back at the crowd as the car continued up Queens Drive. 'What happened to her?' said Florence, turning to her father as if he should know.

'I'll ask Terry,' said her father, glancing at the crowd in his wing mirror, 'he's a mate of mine; he was in that crowd. I'll probably see him in the pub later.'

Seeing that woman, possibly dead, put the kibosh on any fun to be had up at Southport. It was as if a great sun-eclipsing menace had cast its shadow over everything that day. On the following morning at breakfast, Colin was surprised to see that his daughter was up early, and she asked him if he'd seen his friend Terry.

'Yeah, he said that woman had collapsed,' her father told her with a solemn look, 'and one of the people was a first aider but he said she'd passed away.'

'Oh my God,' gasped Florence, 'what did she die of?'

'I don't know, love,' her father shrugged and shook his head, 'they'll do one of those post mortem things and find out.'

'What do *you* think it's been?' Florence pressed him for an answer.

'I haven't a clue love,' her dad confessed, 'could be a

seizure or drugs, or natural causes even. I don't know.' He said, then poured milk on his cornflakes and said, 'Anyway, let me have my breakfast now; I'm already late. I'm only in work half day today so I'll see you this savvy.'

That afternoon, Florence told her mother what she thought had happened concerning the woman who had died. 'Mum, I think someone killed her because she knew something.'

'Knew *what*?' her mother asked with a perplexed look.

Florence explained her outlandish theory. 'She was trying to warn me about something – something bad, and then that person I saw on Penny Lane tried to cover up by wearing a mask so she'd look like that woman. Whoever that person was, they tried to convince me that the woman's claims had all been down to drink, but then they got rid of her somehow to silence her for good.'

'You're going worse,' said Mrs Champerty. 'That's called paranoia, Flo. That woman – God rest her soul – was not all there, and you're reading things into the stuff she came out with.'

'No, there's definitely something going on, Mum,' Florence insisted. 'And why are all my friends snubbing me and acting weird?'

'What's *that* got to do with all this?' Mrs Champerty's voice went up in pitch as she posed the question.

'I don't know, but I just have a feeling something weird's going on,' Florence replied.'

'Florence, you need to go back to bed,' her mother told her after looking at the puffy bags under her daughter's normally bright eyes. 'You've been up all night and it's all because of these fair-weather friends of yours and that silly woman. I know she's passed away and I feel bad for saying it but the poor lady obviously had mental problems.'

'I don't want to go to bed, I'm not even tired,' protested Florence, 'but I think I need to go for a walk to clear my head.'

'Your mum's right love,' her father chipped in, 'go back to bed for a few hours and then perhaps if you feel up to it you can go down to the labour exchange – and get that unemployment benefit thing sorted out.'

'Oh leave her,' Mrs Champerty dismissed her husband's advice with a downward wave of her hand, 'I don't need any keep off her. She'll have a job soon.'

That morning, Florence visited the labour exchange – soon to be known as a 'job centre' – and on her way to the building she noticed that a white car was moving along at almost a walking pace, moving parallel to her as she walked along. It looked exactly like the white car that been cruising up Penny Lane, driven by the woman with the obvious mask. This time a red-haired man was at the wheel, and he kept taking glances at Florence. As soon as Florence got within a few yards of the entrance door of the labour exchange, the man with the red hair took off in his car, and Florence was only too glad to get into the building. She registered her details with a clerk and was given forms to fill in, and she took them home. She told her mother about the man in the white car looking at her, and Mrs Champerty, who was in the middle of doing some ironing, sighed and said, 'Flo, you're really worrying me with this paranoia. No one is out to get you or looking at you. If you don't pull yourself together you'll have to go and see the doctor.'

This warning frightened Florence. 'Mum, I'm not paranoid – these things are really happening.'

'I don't want to hear another word about this,' her mother told her, and accidentally touched her finger with the side of the hot iron. She cried in pain and then shouted to a startled Flo: 'Fill those forms in and shut up about all this rubbish!'

Flo turned and went into the hallway and put on her coat.

'Where are you going?' her mother appeared in the doorway of the living room, and was already regretting the harsh words. She put her mildly burnt finger to her mouth just to justify the outburst.

Without a word of reply, Florence opened the front door and left, slamming the door behind her. Within a few minutes Florence was on Menlove Avenue, and she had no particular destination in mind, but ended up in Calderstones Park. She walked towards the boating lake when she had a feeling of being watched. Florence turned and saw that red-haired man; the one who had been following her in the white car. He was smiling and had his hand in his inside jacket pocket as he walked towards her. For a moment, Florence could not move her legs; she was paralysed with shock – but then she suddenly ran off, back towards the entrance of the park. She noticed a man step from behind the thick trunk of a tree to her left. He had on a white suit and wore sunglasses. He started to run towards Florence. The girl drew a sharp intake of breath and stopped. She turned and saw the red-haired man – he was running to her. She ran to her right – and another man, much taller than the other two, emerged from behind a tree, and he wore a dark brown jacket and green trousers. He started running in her direction. Florence screamed to a couple in the distance: 'Help! Help me!'

The couple were about a hundred yards away and Florence saw the pale spots of their faces as they turned towards her. They looked at the distressed girl, but then turned away and walked on. Florence somehow ran around the red-haired man, and as she passed him she heard him shout: 'We won't harm you Florence!'

The girl heard nothing but her own heavy panting and stifled cries as she raced towards the gates of Calderstones Park. She expected another man to step out from behind one of the towering pillars of the gate piers, but her exit was clear. She heard faint voices behind her as she rushed out onto Calderstones Road. Florence fled up Harthill Road, and she saw an old neighbour, a Mrs Greenhall, walking her poodle, and the girl was in two minds as to whether she should tell her about her three pursuers or whether she should just run past her. What protection could an old woman like Mrs Greenhall provide her with? The thought flashed through the teenager's mind, and she ran on past the woman and her dog, and she heard Mrs Greenhall shout something to her. Florence looked back, and she saw that white car – the one that had followed her near the labour exchange. It was coming her way, and behind it, further down the road, the man in the white suit with the shades appeared as he came running around the corner. Florence was almost knocked over by a car as she sprinted across Menlove Avenue. She reached her home on Menlove Gardens

North, and being unable to find the door-key, she hammered on the knocker. She heard her mother shouting, 'Alright, alright!'

As soon as Mrs Champerty opened the door her daughter barged in and almost knocked her over. Florence closed the door, fumbled with the catch on the lock and slid it down, then crouched and slid the bolt on.

'Florence, what are you doing?' her puzzled mother asked. She saw the redness of her daughter's face as she stood up and the droplets of sweat rolling down her cheeks with her tears.

'Three men tried to get me in the park! They're coming to get me,' Florence told her mother, panting heavily, and pushing past her to get to the telephone on the hall table.

'Who are you calling?' Mrs Champerty asked, following Florence closely, suspecting that the paranoia was now out of control.

'The police – ' gasped Florence, 'the police. They're trying to kidnap me or kill me!'

There was a noise at the front door and the letterbox clanked.

Florence screamed.

'It's the postman! Will you please stop this?' Mrs Champerty yelled at her daughter and went to pick up the telephone bill from the mat. As she returned to her daughter, intending to take the telephone handset from her, she heard her say into the mouthpiece, 'Police please!'

'Stop that!' Mrs Champerty reached for the handset but Florence turned her back on her mother and continued speaking to the operator: 'Yes, police!'

Her mother started to wrestle the handset out of her daughter's clutch, and when Florence turned and yelled, 'Get off!' her mother slapped her face hard. The girl's hair flew across her face with the impact, and then she stood there in shock for a moment, wide-eyed with her mouth open, and Mrs Champerty took the handset from her and slammed it down.

'That's it, Florence! You're going to see the doctor in the morning!' she roared at her daughter, 'And you can run off if you want but you can't run away from this problem! And it *is* a problem!'

Florence burst into tears and ran upstairs to her room. Later that day, her mother came into her room and said, 'Florence, the doctor's receptionist has just kindly telephoned me to say someone's cancelled an appointment tomorrow morning at ten, and Dr Craddock will see you instead. This is only for your own good.'

Florence lay on her bed, face to the wall. She said nothing, but her mother could see her long eyelashes flickering, so she wasn't asleep.

'I'm sorry I hit you, but you scared me, Flo. You know I love you.'

Florence started to sniffle and sob.

On the following morning, just after ten, Dr Craddock listened to Florence's long account of how she was being followed, and how the woman who had tried to warn her about 'some sort of kidnap thing' had been found dead. The girl really did think that the medical man would believe her and tell her to take the matter up with the police, but instead he just smiled and nodded throughout the account, and then he paused, scratched his chin, and said, 'I'm not a psychiatrist. Let's just get that clear Mrs Champerty,' and he looked at Florence's mother and asked, 'Do you want a specialist to look at Florence?'

'How do you mean? A specialist in what?' the concerned mother said, fearing the worst.

'A psychiatrist,' said Dr Craddock, 'I mean, I could prescribe a mild sedative to calm Florence down, but that's not really addressing the root cause of this paranoia – '

Florence took issue with this diagnosis. 'It's not paranoia!'

'Florence!' Mrs Champerty chided her daughter, 'Let Dr Craddock speak. I'm sorry doctor; you were saying.'

The doctor turned to Florence and smiled. 'You're not nuts or anything and it's pretty common in teenagers, especially when they've withdrawn from a group of friends.'

'I didn't withdraw,' Florence interposed, 'they left me.'

'What you have related to me Florence fits the classic profile of this type of paranoia,' said the doctor, looking at his scribbled notes, 'unwarranted suspicions of being hounded and followed, of impostors covering things up, and the harbouring of unjustified suspicions about the motives of friends. These are just a few of the symptoms one would associate with this condition. It may pass in time – it usually does in juveniles.' Craddock then turned to Florence's mother and said: 'I could refer you to a psychiatrist, or you could leave it in abeyance for now and see if it dies down; it really is up to you.'

'Can I see how things are for say – a week or so,

doctor?' Mrs Champerty asked.

Dr Craddock nodded slowly and said, 'Yes, of course. See that Florence gets enough sleep, and ideally, if she is occupied – perhaps by finding employment – this condition will lessen considerably until she returns to normality.'

'Thank you doctor,' said Mrs Champerty, and she and Florence left the surgery. Florence said the doctor didn't know what he was talking about and assured her mother she wasn't going mad. In the days that followed that visit to the doctor's, Florence claimed that she had been followed around the city centre as she shopped by a weird-looking woman in a headscarf, and the teen also claimed that the telephone was bugged. She heard clicks on it and even voices, and when she called her father to the telephone and he heard the voices, he said it was just a crossed line – an electrical fault which had allowed her to hear someone else's conversation. The faint voices of two men stopped as he stated this to Florence.

'They were talking about me, Dad, I could hear them mention my name,' said Florence, taking the handset off her father and listening to the earpiece. All she heard now was the usual purring sound.

'Florence, it's a lovely June day,' said her father with tiredness in his voice, 'why don't you go and sunbathe in the garden or I'll take you out somewhere – New Brighton or even Wales while I still have a few days off.'

'No, I'm not really in the mood thanks,' she replied, replacing the handset on the cradle, then went up the stairs to her room.

'Well, I think I'll go for a drive, just to get out. All

this paranoia lark is driving me spare,' said Colin Champerty, and he walked into the living room, where his wife was reading a morning newspaper, and he asked: 'Do you fancy a day out, love?'

'I've got a lot of washing to get through,' his wife said.

Florence halted on the landing and listened.

'Oh leave the washing, love,' said her father, 'let's go out. We can bring your mum with us if you want.'

'No, it's Tuesday – she'll be visiting her friend Margaret today in Wavertree. Maybe we could go to Southport again,' Florence's mother suggested, 'I love shopping on Lord Street.'

'Well it'll just be you and me – Florence doesn't want to go out,' Colin told his wife.

'Can we trust her here on her own?' Mrs Champerty whispered to her husband.

'What do you mean, "Can we trust her on her own"?' Florence shouted from the upstairs landing.

'I'm just concerned about you, that's all,' her mum shouted back to her.

'I'll be alright, stop worrying!' Florence shouted back, and went to her room.

Her father came upstairs and asked her to come with him and her mum to Southport but Florence said she wasn't in the mood. She said she'd rather relax and read a book and perhaps watch the first round of the Ladies' Singles at Wimbledon on the telly. In the end her father gave up and Florence's parents left the house about one in the afternoon.

Around two that afternoon, Florence got in the shower. After a minute or so she thought she heard a noise, but decided it was someone mowing the lawn in one of the neighbouring gardens. The shower curtain flew back, and that red-headed man who had chased Florence in Calderstones Park stood there with two other men the girl had never seen before. Florence screamed but the red-headed intruder clamped his hand over her mouth and she felt hands grabbing at her arms. They pulled her out of the shower and out of the bathroom, and she tried to break free of their gripping hands but she was dragged to the bedroom, where the trio held her down on the bed. Florence thought she was about to be raped. The red-head produced what looked like an oxygen face mask with a rubber tube leading from it to a small canister. As soon as this mask was pressed over Florence's screaming face, she inhaled something with a very sweet sickly aroma, and after struggling for what seemed like a minute, she passed out.

She awoke and thought she was blind. Blackness surrounded her, and when she tried to get up her forehead hit something hard. Her frantic hands searched about and she realised she was in some sort of box – or a coffin.

The terrified girl began to hyperventilate and she couldn't even cry out as fear engulfed her. Then she heard an electronic whirring sound to her left, followed by a pause. Then the same sound was heard to her right. The blackness became a dazzling light as the lid was lifted off the box she was in. Florence realised she was naked and began to cry as she sat up in what turned out to be a coffin. She was indoors but she could not tell where she was because of the bright torch being directed into her eyes. A monotone voice said, 'We've got you at last. A virgin for – ' and the word that followed sounded unintelligible to Florence.

'Who are you?' the teenager asked, 'What do you want with me?'

There was no reply, and as Florence shielded her eyes from the light with her hand, she caught a glimpse of about six men or more, mostly in silhouette, standing around her. One of them grabbed her wrists and held them together, while another person tied a blindfold tightly around her head. She felt the cold metal of handcuffs being snapped on her, and then she felt something being attached to her ankles. Florence was lifted out of the coffin and taken outdoors, where she felt the cold air. She was taken into a vehicle – the back of a van perhaps, and the journey lasted minutes. The terrified teenager was carried from the vehicle and she felt herself being placed on damp grass. The shackles and handcuffs were taken off, but not the blindfold, and Florence felt her wrists being tied to something. Her legs were pulled wide open and each ankle was also tied with something that felt like rough rope. The blindfold was then removed, and Florence saw that she was either in woodland or a park and it was night-time. She had been tied to four wooden stakes driven into the ground, and all around her were trees and those strangers she had glimpsed earlier, and they were all wearing hooded robes. The fear Florence felt made her head swim, and she looked at the night sky between the trees and saw a red spot. Mars was bright that night – the night of the Summer Solstice – but it was a moonless night, and the stars glowed steady, far away from the light-pollution of streetlamps. 'Oh Jesus, please help me,' Florence whispered to the heavens, and a few of the robed men standing around laughed. Florence thought she was going to be raped and possibly murdered, perhaps as a sacrifice to something evil. The girl was so afraid, she wet herself.

Then came the faint sound of a dog barking and someone shouting: 'Come here! Rex! Rex, come here!'

The figures all turned to look at something beyond the two trees Florence's feet were pointing at. Florence lifted her head as far as she could, and saw an Alsatian dog running in her direction between those trees.

'Shoot it!' cried one of the hooded strangers.

'No, let's go!' said another one of the weird figures.

A tall man in a white tee shirt and jeans came running after the dog, which was now growling at one of the robed abductors.

'What's going on here?' the man asked, and then he cried at the dog: 'Seize! Get them Rex!'

There was a loud crack as one of the figures fired a pistol into the night sky to scare off the dog, but the Alsatian merely ran away in a curve which brought it back to the group as they started to back away.

Florence heard the sound of running and a garble of excited voices which became fainter with their footfalls. The Alsatian came over and licked Florence's face, then poked its cold wet nose into her eye and she yelped with fear.

'Rex! Stop that!' said its owner, and he knelt by Florence and asked, 'You okay? What did they do to you?'

Florence burst into tears.

In the distance, the engine of some vehicle thrummed, followed by the sounds of crunching cogs from a mistimed gear change. The vehicle then tore off into the night.

The man who had inadvertently come to the rescue was a 23-year-old student named Dennis, and he informed Florence that she was in Calderstones Park. He carefully untied her from the stakes, then took off his white tee shirt and put it on the girl. It was so long and baggy it almost went down to her knees. He escorted Florence home to Menlove Gardens North, where the girl's parents were overjoyed to see her when they opened the door. Her mother and father had found the house deserted with the shower still running when they had returned home at 5pm, and they'd realised something very strange had happened when a neighbour said a hearse with a coffin had backed into the driveway of the house. Three men had gained access to the house and taken that coffin indoors. They had obviously placed the naked anesthetized Florence in that coffin and driven away. The neighbour who had seen the hearse, old Mrs Greenhall, thought someone had passed away at the house. The police were informed and Florence was given an examination to see if she had possibly been raped while she had been anesthetized, but thankfully she hadn't.

Florence's parents apologised to their daughter for doubting her claims of being followed and dismissing her as a teenager on the brink of a nervous breakdown because she'd fallen out with her friends. Florence's account of the robed men pinning her down in the park with her legs apart was apparently not taken seriously by the police, even though Dennis backed up the girl's testimony, and the culprits who had abducted the girl from her home were never found. For a few months after the traumatic incident, Florence felt as if those mysterious people were still watching her, but eventually the paranoia wore off, and a strange thing took place; the girl's friends started to talk to her again. Just why they had abandoned her in the first place remained a mystery, as none of her mates could explain why they'd given her the cold shoulder treatment; it was as if something had manipulated their minds to make them avoid Florence. A week after the harrowing incident, Florence started to date Dennis, the student who had rescued her from a fate that did not bear thinking about, and she eventually married him. I gave a very shortened version of this story many years ago on a local radio programme, and received many calls at the radio station from people of all walks of life who assured me that there were occultists about who targeted vulnerable people – mostly females – for occult reasons, namely sacrifice. Some callers even claimed that a few local unsolved murders were the work of these occultists, and that they usually carried out the rituals in December - at the time of the Winter Solstice - or June, at the time of the Summer Solstice. Tuesday, June 22nd, 1971, the day Florence was allegedly abducted, was also the Summer Solstice. I don't want any of my readers to become paranoid because of this story; the chances of you becoming a target for some local cult are probably very remote, but be aware all the same, and if a friend tells you he or she has been followed by persons unknown either on foot or in a car, do not dismiss the claims as paranoia – the real cause may be something much more sinister...

ANFIELD CEMETERY'S UNKNOWN GHOST

On the humid Saturday night of 16 June 1973, four students, George, Pete, Alan and Jim, were sitting in the kitchen of the flat they shared at a house on Anfield's Bingley Road, drinking a crate of sherry that had been delivered to the house by mistake. The topic of conversation among the students was absent flatmate Mike and his new girlfriend Janina.

'How did an ugly-mug like Mike get a beauty like Janina?' asked a squiffy George, drinking a pint glass full of sherry.

Pete smiled and said, 'You sound jealous George; you should be glad for old Mike; he's been celibate for over a year.'

'No, Georgie's right,' said Jim, 'Janina should be with someone better; someone who's handsome and knows how to dress – and dance. Someone like me.' He burped.

'We need to make a holy show of him,' said Alan, pouring himself a generous measure of Emva Cream, 'we need to take him down a peg. Mike thinks he's a right Don Juan, he does. He was showing me a copy of the *Kama Sutra* and saying he'd tried all the positions. He's really getting on my wick.'

'I've got an idea,' said George, his glazed eyes wide with excitement. 'Mike is terrified of the supernatural isn't he? Remember how he ran out the place when we did the Ouija?'

'Yes?' said an intrigued Alan. He went and sat on the arm of the sumptuous armchair George was slouched in.

'Tonight, Mike will come back here with Janina, and then after he's bored us all with every detail of his night out, he'll walk his beloved to her home on Bodmin Road. Now, he was moaning to me that Janina makes him take a short cut through Anfield Cemetery – as she thinks its romantic, and there's a big full moon tonight.'

'So what's the plan?' asked Jim.

'I'll put flour on my face and wear a white sheet and lay in wait for him!' said Georgie, 'He'll have a heart attack when I jump out on him from behind a gravestone!'

'Can I come with you?' Alan asked with a beaming face.

George shook his head. 'No, you'd give the game away laughing, Alan, and you're sloshed mate. No, I'll go alone and give him the biggest scare of his life. I bet he runs off and leaves Janina!'

They all thought the prank would be a scream, and when Mike came in with Janina from a night out, George slipped out the house via the backyard door with the white sheet folded into a neat bundle and a face covered in flour. He had put black shoe polish on his nose to add to the illusion of decomposition. Five minutes later he was in position behind an obelisk in moonlit Anfield Cemetery, near to the Priory Road entrance. George had his head partly covered by the white sheet so it looked like the hood of a shroud. Mike and Janina would be coming through here any minute after a glass of sherry, and then he would walk out on him making the best groaning sound he could produce. In this setting with this moonlight, Mike's imagination would run riot and he'd think he was being confronted by an apparition. George wondered how the lovely Janina would react...

'Who were *you*?' said a woman's voice behind George, and he turned, startled, to see a lady of about fifty in a dark fleece coat. She wore a headscarf, tied under her chin in a bow, and a pair of dark-rimmed glasses, and the beady eyes behind the lenses of those spectacles looked lifeless. Before Mike could speak, this woman nodded to a gravestone to her left and said: 'I'm resting there.'

George screamed profanities at what he perceived to be a ghost, and the woman's eyes widened with shock – and then she vanished. George threw off the sheet and fled, and upon leaping over the low wall of the cemetery he landed awkwardly in his drunken state and sprained his ankle. Mike and Janina encountered him limping along in agony, with his face powdered with flour and his nose daubed with shoe polish, and when he told them about the ghost, Mike thought he was just trying to scare him. Mike and Janina escorted the injured George back to the house, and then the couple walked through the cemetery as planned, holding hands. Janina noticed George's discarded white sheet draped over a gravestone and pointed to it, and Mike thought it was something standing there for a moment and received quite a start. The couple walked on, kissing and after Mike had seen Janina to the doorstep on her house on Bodmin Road, he went to his student digs on Bingley Road via Priory Road rather than take

34

a short cut through Anfield Cemetery on his own.

The ghost of the spectacled woman in the headscarf has been seen many times, both day and night at the cemetery, but so far, her identity remains unknown. I once interviewed a hackney cab driver who told me how he had noticed the ghost standing near to him one sunny afternoon in 2011 as he put flowers on his mother's grave. He had remarked upon the weather being too hot, and the woman in the headscarf had replied, 'I'll always be cold. Be thankful you can feel the sun on you.'

She then vanished in front of the cabby's eyes. The taxi driver was more stunned than scared. He had never believed in ghosts and so he couldn't take it all in for a moment. He walked slowly from his mother's grave and looked about, hoping he'd see the woman again, but he never did, and he has been to visit his mother's grave many times since that afternoon, but he still hasn't seen her. I mentioned this ghost on BBC Radio Merseyside's *Billy Butler Show* one afternoon and my brief description of the apparition elicited quite a response. One caller, an Old Swan woman named Marie, told a particularly gruesome tale about a ghost that matched the description of the carnate spirit encountered by the taxi driver in 2011 and the student in 1973. One sultry Sunday afternoon around 3pm in August 1998 Marie was visiting the grave of her aunt at Anfield Cemetery to place flowers in a grave vase when she noticed the shadow of someone moving slowly across the well-kept grass to her right. Marie turned to see a woman in a headscarf and glasses almost creeping up on her, and she thought it odd that this woman was wearing a heavy dark furry jacket on such a hot August afternoon. The woman halted, and wore an expression of surprise on her face, and Marie said, 'Hiya.'

The woman didn't reply for a while, and Marie was very nervous because she wondered why this woman, who looked as if she was in her mid-fifties, had been creeping towards her. She considered the possibility that the woman was mentally unbalanced.

The woman suddenly said, 'She's still asleep – you never see her.'

'Sorry?' Marie queried, unsure what the woman was talking about.

The spectacled lady nodded to the gravestone of Marie's auntie and said, 'Her, in there. She's one of the sleeping ones.'

'Oh,' Marie muttered, and was now convinced the stranger was batty.

'Some of us know we've popped off but some don't know or won't accept it, like,' said the woman, 'and others stay asleep – like her in there.' She nodded to the gravestone of Marie's aunt.

'You been visiting too?' Marie asked the woman, trying to make conversation.

'I live here,' said the woman.

Marie gave a false chuckle and looked about, ready to leave. A weird and frightening notion suddenly arose in Marie's mind; that the woman was a ghost. She turned away from her, and then she slowly walked away.

'Yeah, you guessed right,' said the woman behind her, and Marie felt all of the little hairs on the nape of her neck go rising up, and although there was a pounding heat being beamed down from that sun in the clear blue sky, Marie felt a cold shiver down her spine as she walked on. Marie heard the weird woman shout out something to her but she could not make out the words. Marie left via the exit on Priory Road, near to the lodge, where there was a little green metal plaque on a gate which read: 'Commonwealth War Graves".

When Marie got outside, the road was unusually quiet, even for a Sunday afternoon. About twenty yards from the Priory Road gates of the cemetery, there is a grid set into the gutter of the road, a couple of yards from a bus stop. There was a head on this grid – and it was the head of that woman, still wrapped in her headscarf but not wearing her glasses. The eyes of the disembodied head were closed, and Marie, who was now reeling from shock, could see slight traces of blood. Then near to the bus stop, Marie saw the headless body of the woman in that dark fleecy coat with its arms bent at unnatural angles. Mari started to run at this point, and she saw a youth of about twenty coming towards her. Marie told him what she had just seen behind her, and the youth went to have a look at the body and the head, but he saw nothing. Marie thought she was going insane and she told her doctor. The doctor said, 'Marie, you're not seeing things. I've had other patients in here tell me they have seen her over the years. You didn't hear it from me but I think you saw a ghost.'

This suggests that the woman was possibly knocked down outside the cemetery, and with such force, she was decapitated – but I cannot yet find any record of a gruesome accident on Priory Road, but there have been many fatalities on that road over the decades concerning adults and children who were knocked down by cars and a few buses. A diligent researcher may be able to record all of the graves on the Priory Road side of the cemetery and see if any of those buried there met a violent death involving decapitation. I have looked, but may have missed out a few of the graves there, and some may not have grave markers, so the answer may lie in the burial records of the cemetery. Whatever the cause of the woman's death, it might have somehow left her earthbound. Hopefully we may know the tragic history of Anfield's unknown ghost one day.

THE DEVIL'S ARMS

Sid and Joan Greene left the Johnson's house in Southport at 2.30am that Sunday morning on 10 June 1979. The forty-something Garston couple were in good spirits after a very enjoyable night out. Joan had refused every alcoholic drink at her friend's 20th wedding anniversary party because Sid had promised he wouldn't drink as he would be driving the car back to Liverpool – but when Joan kissed him in the car she smelt brandy on his breath and went ballistic. 'You sly selfish get!' she shrieked, 'I went without drink all night because of you! And you heard what Jack said about the police lying in wait to catch drink-drivers. You'll get nicked now!'

'Oh put a sock in it you nagging ninny! Jack was the one who practically forced me to have one for the road!' said Sid. 'We'll go home via the back roads!'

'That'll take hours,' moaned Joan, and so, under the full moon, the Morris Oxford went on a meandering journey through the Lancashire night.

Joan wasn't talking now, so Sid put the car radio on and easy listening music on BBC Radio 2's *You and the Night and the Music* programme warmed the cold silence a little.

'Jack insisted on me having a brandy,' said a guilty Sid. 'You're allowed so many units – '

'Just drive,' said Joan, coldly, and she looked out the

window at the vast expanse of moonlit fields on this warm summer morning.

'No one asked you not to drink either,' Sid went on, 'you should have had a few.'

'It's called loyalty – something you wouldn't understand,' was Joan's icy reply.

Somewhere in Great Altcar, off Lord Sefton Way, Sid spotted a huge mock Tudor pub all lit up, and he slowed the car, then reversed. The sign on the gatepost to the sweeping drive said: "Open Till Three – Late supper served".

Sid smiled at his wife, and she looked away as he said: 'We might just be in time for me to have a few black coffees to flush the brandy out my blood, and they reckon scoff's good for getting alcohol out the system don't they?'

'It said in *Reader's Digest* that only time and lots of water can get alcohol out the human body,' said Joan, and she added: 'It's just an excuse to eat with you.'

Sid drove the Oxford up the drive and promised: 'I'll get you a triple orange gin and tonic to make up, love, and we'll see if they do your favourite – shepherd's pie.'

'Oh Sid, let's just get home,' said Joan, 'it's too late to be eating and drinking.'

'No, come on love, I owe you one,' said Sid.

'Well wait till we get home,' said Joan with a giggle, and Sid chuckled.

'Hey, look at these motors,' said Sid, nodding at the vehicles in a parking bay on the shadowy side of the inn where the moon's rays were blocked. There were Bentleys, a Rolls Royce and a Lotus 7 sports car parked there. 'Must be an upmarket joint, this,' Sid reasoned, and he got out the car with Joan. Joan went over to the Elizabethan windows and got on her tiptoes to look in. She could see crowds milling about inside. 'It's packed, Sid,' she said, 'we'll never get served.'

'We will, come on, ' Sid pushed the door open and stood aside to let his wife enter before him. The usual aroma of tobacco and hops greeted the noses of the couple. Sid pulled a vestibule door with windows engraved with arabesque designs, and right away he could see that the place was heaving with people of all ages and classes; scantily-clad young ladies, businessmen in striped suits, tanned-faced farmers in their tweeds, then Sid's heart somersaulted when he saw a policeman in conversation at the far end of the room.

'Bleedin' marvellous isn't it?' he said out the side of his mouth to Joan, who had also noticed the constable. 'I go miles out of my way to avoid the law and there's a PC Plod in here having a bevy.'

'Oh Sid, you'll be alright,' Joan tried to reassure him, 'All those cars out there must be driven by some of the drinkers in here. He'd have to breathalyse everyone.'

'Stop that,' said Sid, turning to his wife. He felt her stroke his backside. 'There are people about.'

'Stop what?' Joan returned a puzzled look.

Sid realised the willowy blonde walking past with a packet of crisps in her hand was the culprit. 'Oh, nothing love,' he said to his wife, and guided her through the crowd to the bar.

The barman had long sideburns and rosy cheeks and seemed very jovial, and in a Lancashire brogue he said to Sid and Joan, 'What a lovely couple. Not from round here are you? Haven't seen you two round here before, like.'

'No, we're from a little fishing village down the road called Liverpool,' joked Sid, and the landlord smiled and asked: 'What can I get you and your lovely wife, sir?'

'Do you do coffee?' Joan butted in as Sid uttered the first syllable of reply. 'Only he can't drink because he's driving, you see. I'll have a gin and tonic. With ice.'

'Yes, we'll get a pot of coffee on, my dear,' said the barman. 'My name's Nick by the way. A single gin or double?'

'Triple,' said Sid, and he smiled as Joan tried to protest, then added, 'Oh, and do you do shepherd's pie by any chance – Nick?'

'Sid, no!' Joan blushed.

Nick closed his eyes, slowly nodded, then opened them and said: 'Of course – made with lamb, like. And garden peas – and any extra veg?'

'Nah, just peas'll do,' said Sid, and he took his wallet out. 'The pie's for the missus'.

'Pay later when you're done, sir,' said Nick. 'Do *you* want anything to eat with your black coffee, sir?'

'I could murder a pork pie – just on its own,' said Sid.

'Sid!' Joan smiled and shook her head.

'I think there's a free table over there,' Nick tilted his head back and looked down his nose as he pointed to a table in the corner.

'Will we have time to eat all this?' asked Sid, looking at his watch and seeing that it was a quarter to three.

'We're open till four now, squire,' Nick said, and he turned and walked through a doorway behind the bar.

Joan sat at the table in the corner and looked up at the oak beams criss-crossing the low ceiling. A shapely young lady smiled and winked at Sid and he got talking to her, until Joan dragged him to their table. Joan had something to say to her husband.

'Sid, there's something odd about this place,' said Joan, eyeing the guests.

Sid rolled his eyes, 'How? It's a lovely joint this,' he said. 'What's odd is the fact that we found a decent boozer with a good landlord who's open till four. You don't get stay-behinds in Liverpool like that.'

A jukebox started playing the Commodores' hit *Three Times a Lady*.

A handsome young man came over to the couple's table and asked Joan if she'd dance with him but Sid said, 'She's with me – hop it!'

Joan said: 'Sid, I told you – they're too friendly in here; doesn't seem right, somehow.'

'Nah, it's just high jinks because they're all drinking and having a good time,' said Sid, and then he smiled and tapped Joan's hand. 'Look who's leaving; good riddance.'

The policeman was pushing against the vestibule door on his way out.

'Sid, haven't you got a bad feeling about this place?' Joan asked her husband, and then she noticed he was looking at the bare legs of a girl young enough to be his daughter.

'No, but I've had a few *good* feelings,' he said, all tongue in cheek.

'Sid, I'm serious,' said Joan, and her hand clasped her husband's fist on the table top. 'It's like a sixth sense with me; I just know when something's not quite right.'

'Oh will you give over, Joan? You're giving me the creeps,' said Sid, shaking his head.

The blonde lady who had touched Sid's derriere earlier was walking past the table, and she suddenly halted and turned to look at him. She gave a little wave, then continued on her way.

'Cor – ' grunted Sid, unaware for a moment that he was with his wife, and then he said, 'Cor, is that the time?' looking at the clock above the bar. It was ten minutes to three. 'Can't wait for my pie – lots of brown Cheerio sauce on it.'

'Sid, that Nick's eyes – ' Joan suddenly remarked, then hesitated to say more.

'What about them?'

'Well, they looked really cold,' said Joan. 'People with brown eyes usually have a warmth in them, but *his* eyes seemed almost devoid of any feeling.'

'Turn it in, Joan,' said Sid screwing his face up as if he was in pain. He sat and talked about football, and Joan didn't listen to a word. The jukebox played the Blondie song *Sunday Girl* and Sid said, 'That's your song, love. You're my Sunday girl.' And then he kissed her. As the song ended, the clock over the bar struck three. It chimed three times – and everyone stopped dead. Dancing stopped, conversations ceased. People who had been drinking placed their glasses on table tops and the bar counter. Joan and Sid saw that the guests now had waxen faces, like shop mannequins, and they stood there stock-still. The barman came over with a sinister smile, and he kept his hands behind his back. His eyes seemed luminous. Sid thought it was just a trick of the light for a moment – a reflection –

but no – light was being emitted by Nick's eyes. What did he have behind his back? Sid wondered with a shudder. He and Joan just sensed something bad was about to happen, and so they got up from the table and ran out of the inn as the landlord shouted something at them. Joan later said it sounded like something which included the c-word. Sid jumped in the car and unlocked the front passenger door as Joan yanked frantically on the handle. Joan fell into the Morris Oxford and told her husband, 'Get out of here Sid!'

As Sid started the car, he saw the headlights of the Bentleys, the Rolls Royce and that Lotus 7 sports car come on – even though the vehicle had no one at their wheels. Sid drove off as his wife cried: 'I knew there was something odd about that place!'

The driverless cars followed the couple down Lord Sefton Way, and when Sid looked in his mirrors and said the cars were giving chase, Joan screamed. The cars pursuing Sid and Joan never caught up, but tailed them for almost three miles, when their headlights went off and they vanished into the darkness near Downholland Cross. Over an hour later, Sid and Joan reached their home on Garston's Lovelace Road. Over a scotch and gin, they tried to make sense of the terrifying incident at that inn in West Lancashire, but they could not explain it in any logical way. The couple were determined to get to the bottom of the supernatural mystery and they bravely returned to Lord Sefton Way a week later and saw that the inn was gone; there was just a field where that mock Tudor pub had stood. A passing elderly farmer saw the couple standing there and he remarked, 'I take it you visited the Devil's Arms then? It appears round here now and then.'

'The Devil's Arms?' Sid said, taken aback by the old farmer's words.

'Aye, ' said the farmer with a nod, and his wise eyes turned to look at the exact spot where he himself had seen the phantom establishment a few years ago. 'It has been seen by so many over the years, and they say some who went in there never came back. The police think they are just missing persons, but the other fellah down below has them – Old Nick.'

The mention of the name 'Nick' struck a chord in the minds of Sid and Joan, for they recalled the name of the landlord of that vanished pub. It wasn't long before Sid and Joan were travelling back to Liverpool, and they never ventured anywhere near Lord Sefton Way again.

STRANGE CASES OF POSSESSION

One night around 11pm in May 1958, a 34-year-old Liverpool woman named Sherry returned from the pub with her 55-year-old partner, Stan. Upstairs at her terraced house on Birkenhead's Craven Street, Sherry's 10-year-old son Craig listened as his mum and her fellah laughed and chatted. The boy had been left alone at the house on many occasions while his mother frequented the pubs, and a couple of years ago, when Craig was aged just eight, his mother had left him alone at his former home in Toxteth one night, when three men broke in and robbed the coin-operated gas and electricity meters. They had even taken the copper hot water tank (which would earn them a few bob at the local scrap dealer's yard), and Craig had to escape the criminal trio by climbing out of his bedroom window and climbing down a pipe into the back yard. On this night, Craig expected his mother to at least come up to his room with a bottle of lemonade and a packet of crisps from the pub, but instead she burst into song downstairs in the parlour. She started to sing the Connie Francis hit of that month *Who's Sorry Now?* as Stan laughed and added his out-of-tune vocals to the song.

Then there were three slow knocks at the front door, and Craig heard the singing stop. 'Who's that?' Sherry asked.

'Well let's open the bleedin' door and find out!' cried Stan, full of drunken bravado. 'I haven't got X-Ray eyes woman!'

'Stan, be careful – you don't know who it is!' Sherry cautioned him.

'Of course I don't know who it is you silly mare,' chuckled Stan, heading for the door.

Craig got out of bed, went to his bedroom door and opened it a few inches. He heard the door downstairs being opened, followed by his mother exclaiming: 'Ooh!'

'Oh God, no!' Stan cried, his voice laced with fear.

Then came the sound of echoing laughter – the laughter of more than one person, and Craig could hear his mum's shrieks, followed by a hard silence which allowed the boy to hear the clock downstairs on the mantelpiece ticking. He then heard the front door slamming shut, and he cautiously went downstairs to see that the parlour light was off, and the only light filtering into the room was from the kitchen. Craig saw Stan standing there, facing the drawn curtains, but the boy thought his mother was standing in a very strange posture. Her head was tilted sideways, to the right, and her arms at her sides were behind her back. Her hands were pointing back, towards the kitchen floor.

'Mum?' Craig went round her to look at her face, and saw that her mouth was wide open with the tongue protruding and her eyes were white and bulging; they had no irises in them, as if the eyeballs had rolled back. Stan's eyes were the same, and the two figures stood as motionless as statues. The unnatural expressions of the couple, their bulging white eyes and their inertness naturally scared Craig, and then the boy jumped when Stan started to make a strange jabbering sound. Sherry then made a whining noise and started to drool, and when Craig touched her and asked, 'Mum are you sick?' she swore at him in coarse language he had never heard, and it didn't even sound like her voice – it sounded like some old man impersonating his mother. Stan's body then tilted backwards by about thirty degrees, yet he remained rigid and did not topple over. Craig ran out of the house in tears and went to the home of a neighbour, and she in turn attracted the attention of two policemen who were on their beat on Craven Street. Even the hard-boiled coppers were spooked by the blank eyes of the couple and the way Stan was apparently defying gravity with his backward tilt – and then the policemen and two neighbours saw strange long shadows of figures appear on the walls of the parlour, and these shadows were cast by people that no one could see. The shadows had risen up from the floor and appeared to be projected by figures performing a strange dance.

Sherry's arms started to thrash about, and she hit one of the policemen in the face with such force, he was knocked across the room and landed on the sofa. A medical student living a few doors away heard of the strange events unfolding in the house, and he visited and told the policemen that the couple looked as if they had some contagious fever, as both of them were now sweating profusely. The student advised the police to take Sherry and Stan to the New Ferry Isolation Hospital, but he was told by one of the constables to mind his own business. One of the neighbours ran to the house of a Catholic priest, and convinced him to come at once and see a case of possession. At this time, the Catholic Church was the only denomination of Christianity to have a Rite of Exorcism, and the priest told the policemen that this rite would have to be carried out in order to reclaim the souls of Stan and Sherry. The police refused the request at first and two more constables arrived. The four policemen could not make Stan budge; it was as if his feet were stuck to the floor at that strange backward angle. The gibberish Stan spoke was construed as "tongues" – the voices of demons – by the priest, and he said this was a very serious and life-threatening form of possession. He warned the police that the demons possessing the couple could possess anyone present if they wished. At one point a Church of England reverend and a Methodist minister turned up and they, with the Catholic priest, prayed openly (against the wishes of the police) until Sherry and Stan collapsed. The couple was taken away and never recovered from the strange ordeal, and it is said they were both committed to mental hospitals, as their bizarre and violent behaviour was deemed a danger to the public. Craig was put in the care of his aunt in Flint when his biological father in Widnes refused to look after him. There were rumours that Sherry had been dabbling with an Ouija board before the strange incident, but this seems to have been pure conjecture, and whatever called at the house on Craven Street that evening in May 1958 remains a mystery to this day. Some form of possession seems to have taken place there, and such cases of demonic takeovers of the human mind and body still occasionally take place in the 21st century. At a house on Brodie Avenue, in

2017, Stefan and Jaz (short for Jasmin) a married couple in their early thirties, had their lives turned upside down by a case of possession that came out of the blue. Stefan had no interest in the supernatural and similarly, Jaz was a very down-to-earth person; an agnostic who did not believe in the paranormal and had no time for so-called New Age matters. One morning in February 2017, Stefan was awakened in his double bed by what he could only describe as a type of harsh, almost guttural whispering. He turned to his right, and there, silhouetted in profile against the nickel-grey predawn light diffusing through the curtains was his wife Jaz, sitting up in the bed. Now, sometimes when Jaz couldn't sleep, she would prop herself up with four pillows and listen to tracks on Spotify or YouTube with earphones plugged into her iPad, and she would sing along in a whispering voice so as not to wake up Stefan, and he thought that was what he was hearing at first. He got up to go to the toilet, and he padded across to the door and opened it, admitting the light from the landing which was always left on at night. That light revealed a very unsettling scene. Jaz was sitting up and she was not listening to any music on the iPad. She was just sitting there, and at first, Stefan thought she was looking straight ahead, but when he walked back to the bed to take a closer look at his wife, he saw that her eyes had rolled back and he could see nothing but white eyeballs – her green irises were not there. She was swearing and using a very offensive word over and over, and it was in a raspy-sounding voice that made Stefan's flesh creep. He slowly reached out with his right hand and shook Jaz gently by her shoulder, and she stopped talking and her eyes rolled back to normal. She jumped and seemed startled, as if her husband had shaken her from her sleep, and she looked at Stefan and asked, 'Was I talking in my sleep?'

He nodded with a very concerned expression, then said, 'I'm just going the toilet; then I'll tell you what you were doing.'

He turned the light on in the bedroom and went to have a wee and then he washed his hands at the basin and rushed back into the bedroom – and to his horror he saw that Jaz was ranting in that raspy voice again, and her eyes had rolled back in her head again.

'Jaz, what's wrong?' he asked, and he felt his chest jolt about with heavy palpitations.

'Your bastard brother!' she suddenly said in that gasping, almost laryngitic voice, and then she smiled and reached behind her to grab the four pillows under her. She swore and threw them off the bed. She fell onto her back, tossed the heavy duvet off her, and then she started to breathe heavily. She wore a pink tee shirt and a white pair of knickers, and as she lay there, her bosom rose and fell with a slow undulating motion.

'Are you okay Jaz? Babe?' Stefan queried, so naturally full of concern. He wasn't sure whether his wife had suffered some stroke, or if she had taken drugs. He was about to touch her, hoping to rouse her from this ghastly state, when the bed started to rise and fall. Stefan couldn't believe his eyes. He looked down and saw the bed leave the carpet. It rose about six inches then slowly fell, so that the whole bed looked as if it was rising on a wave at sea, and those long heavy breathing noises Jaz made were perfectly synchronized with the rising and falling of the levitating bed. Now and then she would say, 'Poor Liam,' and laugh. Liam was Stefan's younger brother. Why on earth was Jaz mentioning him?

Sensing something evil was at work in the bedroom, Stefan suddenly cried out: 'In the name of Jesus, stop this!'

The bed immediately fell to the floor and Jaz let out a long high-pitched scream, then howled in pain and writhed on the bed as if she was in agony. She sat up, put her hand to her mouth, then got off the bed and ran past the hands of her husband as he tried to reach for her. The girl was violently sick down the toilet. Stefan came into the toilet and tried to hug her but she pushed him away and went to the wash basin. She slid open the mirrored door of the wall-mounted cabinet, found her electric toothbrush, and then she grabbed a tube of Colgate and unscrewed its cap. With shaking hands she applied the paste to the toothbrush bristles and turned it on. Stefan was talking all the time through this, asking her what was going on. He didn't know it, but Jaz had almost choked as hydrochloric acid had shot up from her stomach as she had retched and now she had to get the awful burning taste from her mouth and teeth. She gargled and spat out, and then she tried to talk as she gasped for air. 'Liam!' she said, breathing heavily as she spoke as if she was suffocating. 'Liam!'

'What about him?' Stefan asked, puzzled, and very worried.

'He's going to die! You've got to call him and stop him!' said Jaz, and she dropped the toothbrush in the sink and her hands grabbed at the forearms of her husband.

'You're not making sense!' Stefan shouted, raising his voice through nerves rather than anger.

'He'll crash on his motorbike!' shrieked Jaz, and then she fainted, and Stefan caught her. He dragged her from the toilet to the bed and she started kicking out and her arms started flailing about.

'Jaz! What the hell is wrong with you?' Stefan cried, but then she stopped thrashing about and smiled, and then she opened her eyes and asked, 'Did it happen again?'

'I'm calling an ambulance, love!' Stefan told his wife, and he reached for his mobile phone on the bedside cabinet, but Jaz shouted: 'No! Call Liam before it's too late! He's going to crash!'

Thinking he might calm his hysterical wife down by calling his brother – who lived down in London – Stefan navigated through the menu on his phone till he found Liam's number. He called it, but an automated voice stated: 'Sorry, the person you are calling is not available.'

'Keep calling, Stefan, keep calling!' Jaz urged him.

Stefan could not get through to his brother, and he asked Jaz how she felt. She told him she felt as if something weird had come into her.

'I don't understand.' Said Stefan, holding his wife's hand, 'how do you mean?'

'Something horrible and cold is inside me, and it won't go,' Jaz told her husband. Stefan then noticed long scratch-marks across his wife's back, at right angles to her spine. They looked as if they were red-raw, and Stefan recalled how Jaz had short fingernails; she could not have scratched herself in her sleep, and

Stefan was a habitual nail-biter who had even shorter nails than his partner.

'My head is banging,' said Jaz, rubbing her forehead with her palm. 'Could you get me a few paracetamol and some water please, love?' she asked, and Stefan rushed downstairs to get the painkillers and a glass of mineral water from the fridge's dispenser. When he returned to the bedroom he was relieved to see that Jaz had not slipped into that weird state where she spoke in that creepy croaky voice. Stefan's mobile chimed as someone called him. He looked at the screen and saw it was his older brother Dougie. Stefan quickly accepted the call from his brother.

Dougie couldn't seem to get his words out for a moment, and then he said: 'Stefan, our Liam's had a crash on his scooter – a bad crash – and he's critical. He's in hospital. Me Mam and Dad are going down to London to see him; do you want me to take you down?'

Jaz could hear every word coming from the phone, and she threw her hands to her face and her eyes bulged with shock.

Hours later, Stefan and Jaz, and the rest of his family stood around the bed where his kid brother Liam lay on some sort of life support machine, and the ventilator acting as Liam's lungs made that very same sound that Jaz had made hours earlier when something had possessed her in her bed, and Stefan could feel his wife squeezing his hand as they both heard that slow mechanical noise. Liam died three times, and then, through some miracle as Jaz started to pray out loud, his heartbeat returned, and the young man pulled through. As the bleep of the recovered heartbeat echoed through the small hospital ward, Jaz felt that cold icy entity leave her body, and she burst into tears. Jaz had not been to church since the day she had been married, and although she and Stefan were Church of England, Jaz had an urge to become a Catholic. She went to the nearest Roman Catholic church to have a word with the priest about her wishes, and shortly afterwards she began her Catholic Education Classes at the church until she was officially accepted into the faith. Only then did Jaz feel safe from the thing that had briefly possessed her. Why the entity chose Jaz remains a mystery to her, but a priest told her that possession can literally come out of the blue, and on many occasions, beings that might be demons targeted the most pious people as well as hard-line atheists. We next travel 66 years back in time to take a look at another case of possession, and this time, the thing that was doing the possessing put in a physical appearance, and other terrifying phenomena were also witnessed.

A few years ago, an old Wirral man named Dominic passed away, and weeks before he died he told me a story I had been chasing for over a decade – the strange exorcism of a wealthy man's daughter at Rock Ferry. I had heard fragmentary details of this strange episode, but Dominic had worked at the house where the exorcism had taken place as a butler and had witnessed the horrifying events there firsthand. The story then: in the summer of 1951, a successful exporter named Douglas resided at a rather gothic-looking villa in Rock Park, Rock Ferry, situated on the riverfront. The villa, like many of the other listed buildings in the area, was constructed from blocks of sandstone excavated from Storeton quarry in the 1840s, and this ancient stone allegedly triggered the supernatural incident which took place in the villa in June 1951. A window cleaner named Albert Johnson noted the 'snake' carved into one of the sandstone blocks of the house one morning next to the upstairs window of a bedroom where Douglas's 22-year-old daughter Gillian slept. Gillian leaned out of her window and ran her fingers over the bas relief snake, and a friend of her father – a Llandudno businessman named Campbell who held an interest in palaeontology – had a look at the snake in the stone and declared: 'That is a most unusual fossil and it should be removed and donated to a museum!'

Gillian would not hear of it, and said the snake would be her lucky totem. Gillian later told her close friend Wendy that she had been having a lot of luck since she started stroking that stone snake outside her window. Gillian showed Wendy the snake and stroked it as she said, 'I want Stirling to be my husband and I want to have his baby.'

Stirling was a dashing young Liverpool man who worked for the girl's father, and Wendy said that wishing on a fossil smacked of paganism. That evening, Gillian doubled up with crippling stomach cramps and the family physician Dr Maple was sent for. He saw that Gillian's stomach had ballooned to such an extent, she looked like a pregnant woman about to give birth. Then the physician felt the little kicks, and he recoiled in shock. He asked Gillian: 'Are you pregnant, my dear?'

Gillian shook her head and cried in agony, and then her 'water broke'. The doctor went outside the room and cried to the butler Dominic: 'Summon the midwife!' He then went to fetch some towels from the bathroom to soak up the birthing fluids.

The old midwife delivered something that looked like a baby, but it didn't feel real, and it was as white as snow. It moved but had no heartbeat, and the midwife made the sign of the cross and left the house, convinced she had delivered a devil. The 'baby' – which had large black domed eyes and a very unsettling grin - walked about the room, and Dr Maple then noticed the way Gillian's behaviour had undergone a sea change. She swore loudly, spat at him, and began to rant about the church. Maple left the room and told the girl's father a priest was needed, for Gillian seemed to be possessed. Seeing his daughter in convulsions upon her bed, and hearing the awful blasphemies she was screeching, Maple sent the butler Dominic to find a vicar or priest to deal with this terrifying condition afflicting Gillian. Dominic was gone for some time, as most of the reverends he talked to refused to come out to tackle the alleged possession. A Catholic priest – Father Fausto – and a nun named Sister Raphael – arrived at the house. Fausto was a visiting Catalonian priest who brought a Gladstone bag crammed with the tools of the exorcist's trade, and he was even equipped with chains and ropes to restrain Gillian whilst in the throes of possession. Douglas was instructed to stay away from his daughter while the exorcism got underway, but Dominic the butler was posted outside the bedroom door. Sister Raphael prayed at the foot of the bed and after bounding Gillian to the bed in chains, Father Fausto began the Rite of Exorcism. The 'baby' entity fell down in the corner and withered until a pool of sticky white liquid remained. Fausto asked the demon to give its name, and Gillian said, 'Jack the Ripper' and laughed hysterically.

'In the name of Jesus Christ you will give me your name, demon!' Fausto cried. Gillian's mouth opened wide and out came a huge snake – which spoke. It cracked macabre jokes and tried to undermine the priest's faith by telling him about contradictory passages in the Bible.

'Your name is Nahash isn't it?' Faust asked with a smile. The snake hissed and snapped its jaws at him. 'The old serpent from the Garden of Eden!' Faust bravely laughed, and he dipped the aspergillum (a silver rod with a brush at the end) in a small bucket of holy water, then flicked it at the ancient serpent. The entity writhed and screamed in agony with bulging red eyes as if the priest was splashing the creature with acid. One of the chains binding Gillian to the bedstead snapped and whipped through the air, just missing the nun. There was a loud crash outside the door. Dominic could not believe his eyes. It looked like a horse covered in blood, as if it had just come from the knacker's yard, and it was blocking the stairs. A minute later this supernatural apport vanished. The 'serpent' slid out of Gillian's mouth and hid under the bed, but it was never found, and the young lady eventually returned to normal. The block of sandstone with the fossilised snake was removed from the building and returned to Storeton quarry. Its present whereabouts are unknown. Gillian attended church every Sunday after the possession, and later married Stirling. She occasionally suffered nightmares about the serpent until the day she died. The serpent seems to be an archetype found in most of the earth's cultures, but the most notable one is the sinister creature described in the Book of Genesis. This serpent was able to speak and tempted Eve into eating the fruit from a tree God implicitly told her not to eat from – the Tree of the Knowledge of Good and Evil. Eve then gives Adam some of the forbidden fruit, which is nowadays visualised as an apple. The serpent is believed by most modern theologians to be the Devil in disguise, as there are two passages in the Book of Revelation which call the 'Serpent of Old' Satan. Other thinkers believe that the serpent in Genesis is merely a symbol of human curiosity. Likewise, the 'serpent' which emerged from the mouth of Gillian in the 1951 possession case remains an enigma. Was it the Devil or was it an ectoplasmic emission, just like the baby she secreted through some pseudo-birth?

Possession of the human mind may take many forms, ranging from possession by devils to possession by the Holy Spirit (which is a good thing), and even in ancient Buddhist scriptures we read of dangerous entities known as "seizers" who take over the minds of children. There have also been alleged cases of possession by aliens, and beings from other dimensions. Sometimes there is a thin line between the alien and the spiritual being, and a case that springs to mind immediately in this respect is "Lam" – the name the accomplished occultist Aleister Crowley gave to an entity he made contact with in 1918. Crowley drew many portraits of Lam and they all look identical to artists' impressions of the so-called classic Grey aliens who are allegedly carrying out abductions of humans and animals as well as insidious infiltrations of people's minds. Lam has the large egg-shaped cranium (with no visible ears) and the elfin pointed chin and large dark eyes of the greys, but Crowley encountered Lam back in 1918, nearly thirty years before the Modern UFO Era and sixty years before the greys were first reported. Crowley said that Lam had come through a rip (which he called "a rent") in the very fabric of space-time which the magician had caused during a potent ritual. A much overlooked form of possession is that by the Fay – also known as Faeries (mostly spelled today as "Fairies").

Many of us believed in fairies when we were young – and I still do. They are known by many names – "the dwellers by the border", The Fay, Tylwyth Teg – Welsh for "Fair Family" and over on Wirral their ancient name was the Poldies. You must never underestimate the power of the fairies – they are not like Disney's Tinkerbell, and if you get on the wrong side of them, they will unleash terrifying forms of retribution that makes the Cosa Nostra seem like a bunch of mischievous kids. They are made up of several races and their sizes range from a few inches to about three feet. There are specific spots all over the north west where the fairies have their territory, and a witch once showed me an ancient map charting unheard-of boroughs of the Little Folk with names like Rath (which stretches from Anfield to Edge Hill), Fairyknowe (most of Knowsley), and Sithe-Barrow (Wavertree to Hale). May is the month when most of the fairies go crazy as they pay homage to the Goddess of the Green (whose name I cannot reveal), and you may notice an increase in 'paranormal' goings on in this month. In May 1942, there was an incident in Ormskirk where a 17-year-old member of the Home Guard named Neville went to investigate reports of strange lights in a wood with an older member of the Local Defence Volunteers named Gordon. The general consensus at the time was that a spy was signalling to the pilots of German bombers with a torch. As the two Home Guard men passed a cottage, they saw an old woman putting a tray of "fairy cakes" on a table in her garden. Neville rather fancied eating the cakes with their pink icing, as it was a rarity to eat such sugary delicacies because of wartime rationing, and so he asked the elderly lady for one of the cupcakes and she told the young man that the cakes were for the fairies, and 'not for human consumption'.

Neville and Gordon visited the wood, and found no evidence of any spy at work, and when they embarked on the journey back to HQ, the soldiers passed the cottage and saw the pink-icing-topped fairy cakes on the table. The old woman was nowhere to be seen, and Neville couldn't help himself. Gordon warned Neville he could be punished by the captain of the unit for theft as he gathered all the cakes in his two hands, but the teenager had a very sweet tooth, and he ate two of the cakes, one straight after the other, and said they tasted delicious. Neville offered one of the fairy cakes to Gordon, but his colleague shook his head and said he'd have no luck if he did. About five minutes later, Neville seems to have suffered what we would now term as a panic attack, and he ran off making strange yelping noises. Gordon, being an old man, could not keep up with the freaked-out youth, and he returned to HQ and told the captain what had happened. A search was launched but no one could find Neville. The woods were searched twice, all to no avail. The sergeant of the Home Guard went to see the old woman who had left the cakes out and asked her if she had put any narcotic substance in them. The old woman, regarded as a witch by two local farmers, said she had made the cakes with the usual ingredients – self-raising flour, butter, castor sugar, eggs, milk, vanilla extract, as well as some herbs she was not allowed to identify, but none of them were poisonous.

On the following morning, Neville was found by a farmer, a mile south of Burscough. He was in a field of wheat singing and dancing, with a daisy chain round his neck, a plucked rose protruding from the barrel of his rifle, and a sparrow chirping on his shoulder. In his hand he held a huge sunflower, and butterflies fluttered around him. There was enchanting flute music coming from somewhere close. Neville was singing a very strange-sounding song, and the words were nonsensical. Then the farmer saw what he took to be children at first, wading through the wheat; they had skin as white as alabaster, and the faces of cherubs. A girl with huge bright blue eyes said, 'Hello!' and she was followed by three other boys her size. She wore pink, but they wore green tunics – and pointed hats. The farmer then realised who they were: the Little Folk - and he fled. Neville changed from being a gung-ho soldier to a pacifist who ended up jailed as a conscientious objector. Some say he ended his days in a mental hospital after WWII, his mind turned by the faeries. Till the day he died, Neville refused to speak about that day in May. It is said that in the woods in Ormskirk where the lights were seen a phantom flautist is still occasionally heard, and the tune this unseen person plays can drive you mad because it is so catchy. It leaves those unfortunate enough to hear it unable to sleep because they cannot drive the melody out of their minds, which seems like a severe form of the modern-day 'earworm' nuisance, in which pop tunes play continually in the mind's ear of those afflicted for days, making it impossible for the 'infected' person to focus on anything. There was a case reported to me years ago about a telephone engineer named Geoff, who, while repairing a telephone line on Ramsbrook Lane in the Village of Hale, saw a long file of little people coming down the lane as he was up a telegraph pole. At first the engineer thought they were children dressed in red and green one-piece suits and 'odd-looking hats' as he described them, but as they passed by below, Geoff could see they were much too small to be children; the figures were all about a foot in height. They marched by, going north, then passed through a hedgerow and were lost to sight. Geoff descended the pole and told an old woman coming up the lane what he had seen, and she told him they were the "Ferishers" – and advised Geoff to never confront them or they'd take over his mind and make him do anything they wished. She told Geoff that many senseless murders over the years had been carried out by people who had been acting under the influence of the Ferishers, a very powerful race of faerie that had come over from the eastern counties after being disturbed by the English Civil War (1642-1651). The old woman said that being "fairy-struck" could leave a person permanently insane, and then she walked on down the lane. A week later, Geoff and another, older engineer named Roger were fixing a fault a mile north of the last one, at the north end of Ramsbrook Lane, and Geoff was up the telegraph pole while Roger was sitting in the GPO van, reading a newspaper. It was a rainy day, and Geoff was working away fixing wires when he saw the same file of little people coming up the lane. He shouted down to Roger, 'Roger! Look down the lane!'

'What in blue blazes are they?' Roger asked, seeing the tiny people dressed in red and green drawing nearer.

'Roger! Stay in the van! Don't say anything to them!' Geoff warned, but Roger got out the van and stood there, dumbfounded.

'What are they? They're like bleeding dolls!' Roger shouted back to his friend without taking his eyes off the advancing troop of little men.

'Roger! Get back in the van!' Geoff cried.

Roger stepped aside, and then the figures slowed as they neared him. Their faces looked full of mischief and to Roger's eyes, he thought the little people had faces of far eastern appearance. Roger started laughing at the size of the odd 'midgets' and then they all stopped.

One of the little men pointed at Roger, and he heard a crackling sound which reminded him of the sizzling noise a high-tension electric spark produces when it jumps across two metal contacts.

Roger passed out and fell to the ground, knocking his forehead on the tarmac. Geoff was a little scared at the way his friend had been knocked out by the pointed finger of the Ferisher, and he kept perfectly still as the rain lashed his face, and the file of faeries continued on their way up the lane until they again vanished into a hedgerow. What happened next was unbelievable. Roger got to his feet and began to remove all of his clothes as if he was going for a swim, and then he ran off naked across a field. Geoff descended the telegraph pole and tried to chase after his deranged colleague but soon lost him. The police finally tackled Roger outside a cottage where he had been looking through the windows at two old spinsters. When Roger 'came to' he had no memory of his naked romp through the outskirts of Hale, and when he was taken into custody he kept bursting into laughter for no reason and laughed so much, he experienced respiratory problems. Geoff told the police what had happened to his friend and they asked him if he and Roger had been taking drugs. Eventually, after about five months, Roger's sanity returned, but by then he had lost his job and his wife, as she had left him after he had been arrested for his bizarre and disgusting behaviour in Hale. Geoff never deserted his friend, knowing Roger was not to blame for his 'insane' actions. Roger said he had felt as if someone with a childish and very wicked sense of humour had been controlling his every action that day in Hale. Roger chillingly told his friend that, had the weird mind manipulator willed him to kill himself, he would have done it without a second thought, and Roger somehow knew that many others who had been mere puppets to the overpowering mind had done just that over the years.

NICK NOCK NOTHIN'

On the morning of Friday 30 June 1995, a 50-year-old man named David Gravett left his detached home on Woodhey Road, Bebington and was driven by a friend to Manchester Airport where he jetted off to a fortnight-long Sunrise Travel holiday in Sydney for £569. Gravett was going to stay with his brother down under, and his 19-year-old niece Kelly was assigned look after his house while he was away. David hadn't seen Kelly since she was 17 and recalled how quiet and sensible she'd been, and he'd asked his sister to give her daughter Kelly the keys to the flat once he'd left for Manchester Airport. What Uncle David didn't know was that Kelly had undergone quite a change since he'd last seen her. She'd discovered boys, alcohol and had a penchant for throwing long parties in other people's houses which often ended with the police being called out because of the decibel disturbances. David's sister worked nights, otherwise she would have looked after the house, and she warned her daughter not to betray the trust of Uncle David by throwing wild parties at his place. Kelly promised she'd behave and just spend most of the days at the house watching TV, listening to her CDs (at a reasonable volume) and catching up on some good books. However, on that first evening at David's five-bedroom house, Kelly phoned around, calling friends and a few ex-boyfriends, and inviting them all to her 'house-warming party' – which was to be 'a small affair' – and sixteen people turned up. Uncle David had cable TV, and he had a huge TV wired to cable in his spacious upstairs study, so The Box and MTV music channels were a must, and Greg, one of Kelly's former boyfriends, cheekily raided Uncle David's wine cellar shortly after his arrival at the Bebington house. Kelly's two best friends, Imogen and Laura, took over the kitchen and made chicken curry for everyone. Uncle David's study was soon a right mess, with couple's kissing on the expensive chesterfield sofa and one girl even broke the antique globe of the world by trying to sit on it. Someone put The Prodigy album, *Music for the Jilted Generation* on Kelly's ghetto blaster and by midnight the police were hammering on the door after complaints from neighbours about the sound levels. By one in the morning, things had quietened down a bit, but only because everyone was drunk on what was left of Uncle David's wine cellar, and someone told a ghost story out of the blue. This led to Laura suggesting an Ouija session, and one of the lads present was so spooked by the suggestion he left, as he said he'd had a very bad experience messing with an Ouija board a few years ago. Imogen cut out twenty-six squares of paper with the letters of the alphabet and ten squares of paper for the numerals zero to nine. A wine glass was upended on the low round coffee table and then fifteen teenaged hands rested on the base of this glass for a moment, then in a serious voice, Laura intoned, 'Spirits, please move the glass if you are there, and answer our questions. Thank you.'

There were giggles and raspberries were blown, but then Kelly brought in three lit candles and placed them around the study before dimming the lights. Predictably, people pushed the glass about at first and laughed, and some of the dabblers became bored with the proceedings and garbled messages from the glass and they gave up and mellowed out as they ate snacks and watched the MTV videos on the muted telly. A dozen people continued to try and seriously use the upturned glass to contact the dead, and suddenly, the wine glass slid about on the coffee table, and Laura was ready with Kelly's eyebrow pencil to take down the message. The letters which came up spelled 'Nick Nock Nothin'.

'Are you sure it spelled that out, Laura?' Kelly asked her friend, looking at the bizarre three words.

'Yeah, that's what the spirit dictated, Kel,' Laura assured her.

'What does it mean?' Greg asked, and suddenly the lights and TV went off.

Kelly asked if anyone knew how to fix fuses and two lads went into the hall in search of the fuse box. The sitters meanwhile, were intrigued by the nonsensical message, and Kelly looked up into the air and asked: 'Are you Nick Nock?'

The glass flew to the letters, 'Y-E-S'.

'Do you have any more messages Nick Nock?' Kelly asked.

The glass seemed to almost lift off the table by a few inches, and then it slid about, and spelled the message 'You All Die'.

This scary message halted the proceedings and

everyone took their hand off the glass, and that glass turned itself the right way up, vibrated as if a HGV was rumbling past the house, and then it emitted a weird ringing sound. It sounded as if someone had wet their index finger and were rubbing it in a circular motion along the rim of the glass. The two sash windows of the second-floor study opened on their own, and bottles, glasses, plates – anything that was not bolted down – flew out the window, including an expensive looking lamp, and although it's cord was ripped from the wall, its bulb unaccountably burned bright as it floated out the window. Everyone ran out of the room, but when Kelly tried to run, she felt herself being dragged backwards – through the open window. She screamed as she toppled back over the window sill and then she fell in what felt like slow motion, and landed in the front garden thirty-odd feet below with only a slight thud. Her ghetto blaster, and some of her belongings that she'd brought to the house fell around her in slow motion. Kelly felt her arms and legs and ribcage, and could not believe she was unhurt after such a fall from the third-floor window. Within a year, everybody who had attended that Ouija session had died from accidents and various illnesses, and only Kelly survived. The identity of "Nick Nock Nothing" remained a mystery and David Gravett was perplexed by the poltergeist phenomenon because he had lived at the house for ten years and had never once seen anything remotely supernatural while he was there. What's particularly interesting about this case beyond the poltergeist activity and the 'transportation' of Kelly from her uncle's study to the front garden is the *name* of the Ouija spirit, for unbeknownst to Kelly, a spirit which went under that same name – "Nick Nock Nothin'" – had been reported over in Liverpool thirty years before.

The Ouija session in October1965 arose one rainy Sunday afternoon during idle talk about ghosts and witchcraft. The place was a fourth-storey flat in a tenement known as Myrtle House, situated on the border between Edge Hill and Toxteth, and the loafers sitting about in front of the gas fire sipping tea and smoking cigarettes were two sisters in their early twenties named Denise and Anne, and six similarly aged male friends who included Denise's boyfriend Tony and Anne's fiancé Rodney. Tony claimed that there was a life after death and that he'd seen a ghost when he was a kid, and Rodney said the supernatural was a load of rubbish. 'Once you're dead, you're dead – that's it!' was Rodney's blunt uncompromising view. Anne said an old woman she used to work with at a textile factory in town was a witch, and Denise said she had a friend named Mona who was into witchcraft, and used real spells to get boyfriends. Rodney laughed at the claims of the girls and said, 'It's all a big loaf of hokum.'

Tony told his sceptical friend he was wrong and suggested they should draw the curtains and try and contact spirits with the upturned glass. Everyone but Rodney thought it was a good idea. 'Ah, I don't know if that's a good idea, mate,' said a worried-looking Rodney, 'you know, with it being Sunday and that, like.'

'Ah, so you don't believe in witchcraft and spirits and all that but you believe in all the things the Bible says, eh?' said Tony with a grin.

'Yeah, I do,' Rodney replied, 'and I'm not ashamed to say so either.'

'So you believe that Jonah lived in the belly of a whale for three days and three nights?' Tony asked him, and puffed on his rolled up cigarette.

'Oh just shut up Tony,' Rodney grimaced and shook his head, 'you're turning into a heathen mate. You'll know it when you're brown bread mate. Straight down into the pit of Hell you'll go mate.' Rodney traced Tony's metaphysical trajectory into Hades in the air with his finger and gave a whistle at the gestured descent.

A toy blackboard used by Anne's kid brother was used as the Ouija board, and Tony drew a wonky circle made of all the letters of the alphabet and all of the numbers from zero to nine. A four-inch-tall whiskey glass was taken from the kitchen and turned upside down on the blackboard.

Curtains were drawn in the living room and no candles could be found so Tony stuck two wax crayons in the top of an ornamental brass candlestick and lit their labels. The ad hoc crayon candles produced a good light.

'Now, here are a few quick rules for using the Ouija,' Tony told the seven sitters (Rodney refused to participate in the 'ritual' and sat in a corner). 'First, don't ever skit at the spirit or taunt it or joke with it, or you'll know it, and never ask the spirit when anyone is going to die – just don't alright? Don't mention God. I'm not even going to explain why, but just don't, and if the spirit starts spelling out "ABCDEFG" or "12345" just stop immediately and say "Goodbye spirit" because it means it's an evil spirit and it's about to jump into someone.'

'Maybe we should just leave this alone – ' said Anne. Her large dark eyes looked so afraid in the light of the burning crayons.

'We'll be alright Anne,' said Tony, confidently, 'so, let's get on with this.'

Everyone waited and there was a tense pause. Rodney could be heard tutting disapproval in the corner.

Tony looked up at the shade of the light on the ceiling and announced: 'Spirits of the next world, I acknowledge you are there; please come and speak to this assembly through the glass. Thankyou!'

Tony placed his index fingertip on the base of the upturned whiskey glass, and the others gathered around the blackboard on the table did the same. The glass remained stationary for about five seconds, and then it moved side to side. Denise smiled, thinking someone was pushing it.

'Spirit, what is your name? And are you a good spirit?' were Tony's questions as he watched the glass move.

He noted the letters the rim of the glass touched, and he and Anne tried to read out the letters at the same time, so Tony told Anne to be quiet; he was the leader of the session. The name spelled out seemed to be 'NIKNOK NOTIN'. Then the word 'YIP' – perhaps the vernacular for 'yes'.

'Has anyone here got a question for – ' Tony tried to pronounce the odd name the glass had produced, then opted for 'the spirit' instead.

Everyone seemed too scared to pose a question, so Tony said, 'Will Rodney marry soon?'

'Hey, piss off Tony!' came Rodney's voice from the dark corner of the room, 'Don't be bringing me into this, and I thought you said you shouldn't joke with the spirit?'

'I'm not joking with the spirit,' Tony was saying, when the glass started spelling out the bizarre message: 'CAYK KILL ABCDEFG'.

'Right! Goodbye spirit! Spirit depart in the name of the Trinity!' Tony said in a voice that sounded full of fear, and he rushed from the table and lunged at the light switch. He switched on the light, and then he went to open the curtains.

Anne screamed as she looked at the blackboard. The glass was dancing on the board and no one was touching it.

'In the name of the Trinity depart!' Tony shouted at the animated whiskey glass, and it stopped moving, fell on its side, and rolled in a semi-circle.

'I *told* you not to dabble with that thing!' Rodney yelled as he gripped Tony by the lapels of his jacket. 'And you had to mention my name! I'm going to church tonight!'

'What did that message mean about cayk kill?' Denise asked, 'Was it trying to spell out the words "cake kill"? Doesn't make sense.'

'It was a bad spirit,' said Tony, pushing Rodney away from him, 'and when it started going through the alphabet I ended the session.'

'Look at my hand,' said Rodney, holding his trembling palm out, 'that's thanks to you, that!' he looked at Tony and gritted his teeth.

'Have a drink, love,' said Anne, and she told one of Tony's friend's to pour Rodney a small neat whiskey, and then she hugged him and as she placed her head against his chest she could hear his heart pounding. She never knew her fiancé was scared of the supernatural.

'Are you sure someone wasn't just pushing that glass about?' Denise asked Tony with a lopsided smirk.

Tony shook his head vigorously and said, 'You saw the glass dance about Denise, how could anyone do a trick like that? They couldn't do that in the Magic Circle. It was a bad spirit, but it's gone now.'

'Here you go, nervy,' said one of Tony's mates, handing Rodney a glass of neat whiskey.

Rodney didn't even say thanks; he grabbed the drink and knocked it back in one go.

'Rodney – you didn't just drink out *that* glass, did you?' Tony asked him.

'It was the only glass I could find,' said the man who had served the drink to Tony.

'Why? Why? What will happen if it was?' Rodney asked Tony, and his eyes bulged as he looked at the empty glass.

'You're supposed to wash the glass or put it away and never use it again,' Tony replied. 'You'll be okay, though,' he added, and sounded and looked uncertain of his words.

Rodney lunged at his friend and the other men present had to drag him off Tony.

'If anything happens to me now – ' Rodney was saying, when Tony stormed out of the flat, followed by his girlfriend Denise and his friends. Anne calmed Rodney down, saying that the whole thing had been down to imagination, but Rodney was that on edge, he jumped as the makeshift crayon candles loudly sputtered and died. Anne went to the seven o'clock mass with her fiancé that night at St Anne's, and afterwards she stayed over at Rodney's flat on Grove Street. Anne woke up at around 3am and heard Rodney talking faintly in his sleep. He was saying what sounded like, 'Nick Nock nothing', Nick Nock nothing,' over and over, until Anne shook him awake. Rodney pushed her away and sat up in the bed, gasping for air. He said he'd had a vivid dream of a pitch black shadow of a man with glowing blue eyes leaning over him. For three nights in a row, Rodney had nightmares about the silhouetted man with the bright blue eyes, and he'd always awake sweating with his heart pounding away. And then he was visited by an old flame named Josie one afternoon. She stood on the top step at the front door, and she had a white box in her hand tied with string. She seemed sincere as she said, 'Congratulations Rod. I heard you got engaged to Anne and you're getting married. I made you two a cake. I got the recipe out the *Constance Spry Cookery Book*; it's made of – '

'I'm not interested in what it's made out of – beat it!' Rodney told her.

'Don't be like that, Rod,' said Josie, 'I'm not trying to get back with you or anything – I've got a boyfriend now. I just thought it would be a civilized gesture.'

'I don't want any cake off you and I don't want you coming anywhere near me,' said Rodney, 'you two-timed me and said all kinds about me behind my back, so off you pop, love.'

'Rod, just have a look at all the work I put into this cake,' Josie started untying the string which bound the white box, and she sniffled as if she was about to cry.

Rodney sighed as she lifted the lid of the box and thrust the elaborate cake with its large cursive words 'Congratulations Rodney and Ann' in white piping on pink icing.

'There's an "e" at the end of Anne's name,' said Rodney with a slight smile.

'Oh, I didn't know,' said Josie, and a tear rolled from her eye, down her blushing cheek, then landed on the icing.

The tear on the cake finally did it. In a slow and determined voice fraught with mounting anger, Rodney said: 'I think you'd better go before I lose my temper, Josie. I don't know what's going on in that brain of yours and I don't want to know, but I don't ever want to see you again. Just keep away!'

'You ungrateful bastard!' Josie lifted the cake out of the box and into the air for a moment, ready to hit Rodney in the face with it but he pushed her backwards and she fell down the three steps and the cake landed on the pavement in a smashed heap before she landed on her back, winding herself.

Passers-by slowed down when they saw the splattered cake on the pavement and Josie getting to her feet, trying to shout at Rodney without an ounce of breath in her lungs. He slammed the door and walked back to his flat upstairs, and he heard the letterbox flap open and a voice of a passer-by who shouted: 'That was pretty brave of you, pal! Pushing over a girl! Come out and try and do that to me you big shithouse!'

Rodney swore at the interferer and went into his room, slamming the door behind him. He heard the commotion outside, and when it had finally calmed down, he sat and tried to read *The Catcher in the Rye* but his mind kept harking back to the tear dripping on that cake. Rodney made himself a cup of Nescafé instant coffee in the kitchenette, and returned to the paperback, and about half an hour later he heard a girl scream outside. He went to the window, wondering if barmy Josie had returned, but instead he saw a girl crouched over a black and white mongrel dog that was lying next to the remains of that cake. It looked as if it was dead with its tongue hanging out.

Three young lads slowed as they walked past the girl and one of them asked what the matter was.

'My dog's dead,' said the girl, prodding the inert animal's head with her fingers. 'I think he's been poisoned.'

'That's sly that,' one of the young men said, and he crouched down and he also tried to rouse the dog by patting its back, but it wouldn't move. The unconscious animal suddenly had its last wee, and a boy standing nearby screwed up his cherubic face and said, 'Ee-yacka!'

In a flash, Rodney realised that the dog had eaten part of the cake, and that cake – the one Josie had wanted him and Anne to eat – had been laced with some poison. He felt sick. And then he recalled that cryptic message during the Ouija session, when Tony had asked the spirit: "Will Rodney marry soon?"

The spirit had spelt out something that seemed to say: 'Cake kill'. Now Rodney went cold inside. He left the house and went to see his priest, Father Keating, and the old clergyman had the patience to listen to the young man's rambling story. He blessed Rodney, and told him to come to the church around eleven in the morning. On his way to the church on the following morning, Rodney was told by an old school-friend that his ex Josie had hanged herself on a long rope tied to the top of a stair rail five flights up. The drop of fifty feet had been that long, the girl's intestines had burst out of her vagina and she had almost been decapitated. When a very distressed Rodney turned up at the priest's house, there was a younger priest with Father Keating, and this man of the cloth performed an exorcism on Rodney. Rodney fainted half way through the Rite of Exorcism, and when he came round, he was told by Father Keating that an 'unclean spirit' had left him. The priest who had performed the exorcism tried to obtain the name of the spirit, but it refused to reveal it, and Rodney attended church for many years, till he passed away from a short illness in the 1990s. I have a feeling the spirit was the same one that would later manifest itself at the Ouija session at Bebington in 1995. I gave a short version of this story on BBC Radio Merseyside a few years ago and many people contacted me after the programme saying they had heard stories about the same entity which called itself 'Nick Nock Nothin'. This name will not be the proper name of the demon (if that is what it actually is) but just an invented nickname to throw off any occultists or priests who would try to use the real name of the entity to drive it out of its victim. In the world of the occult, using the name of a person in a spell or rite makes the spell much more effective. I hope this is the last we shall hear of Nick Nock Nothin' – whatever it is...

DON'T SPEAK ILL OF THE DEAD

There is an old superstition that states: 'Don't speak ill of the dead" for it is an old belief that those who criticise or unfairly defame departed souls will be visited by them and may also receive bad luck as punishment. An old ancient Latin phrase that refers to this superstition runs: De mortuis nihil nisi bonum – "Of the dead [say] nothing but good".

The following eerie story took place in 1995 at a house in Kensington, less than fifty yards from the Coach & Horses pub, which was open at that time on Low Hill. Ten university students had a house-warming party at the terraced dwelling that they'd started to collectively rent in Kensington, and the party went on till around half-past two in the morning, when they all went to their rooms. A student named Toria – a 21-year-old from a well-to-do family in Chester, went to bed with her boyfriend Mike, who hailed from Old Swan. Their room was on the ground floor. Mike was studying modern history and political science at uni, and he was, by his own admission a Marxist with leanings towards anarchy, whereas Toria was a member of the Conservative Party and believed that Capitalism was the only realistic political system, and at university she was reading economics, business studies, and already held an accountancy diploma. Mike said she had the right name – Toria – with her pro-Tory fanaticism, but he loved her all the same. Toria's dream was to found her own bank, and years before Bitcoin was conceptualized in the early 21st century, Toria talked about a hypothetical 'global artificial currency that could be digital in nature' – in other words, a cryptocurrency. The couple lay in bed on this morning around 2.45am, slightly tipsy, and somehow they got into an argument about politics, and Mike extolled the philosophy of Marx and Toria praised the father of Capitalism – Adam Smith, and at one point in the debate, Mike asked Toria: 'So, you are saying that poor people have no one to blame but themselves for being poor?'

'In a way, yes I am!' she replied, and the argument became so heated, a student name Ron Clive knocked on the couple's door and told them to continue their political debate in the morning because their heated discussion could be heard all over the house. Mike and Toria refused to make up, and slept facing away from one another. At around 4am, Toria awoke to the sound of children's voices. At first she thought it was outside in the street, but then she felt cold hands on her leg, which was resting on top of the duvet, and she sat up, startled, to see that a blue glow was illuminating the room. Surrounding the bed was a crowd of ragged-looking children, many of them wearing cloth caps, and some had dirty faces. Toria realised they were ghosts. She turned to tell Mike but he was face down and fast asleep. A ghostly boy with reddish hair at the end of the bed suddenly said, 'They killed us in that house,' and then he and the crowd surrounding the bed vanished as groans echoed and faded. Toria shook Mike awake and told him about the ghosts and he said she'd had a nightmare. Toria knew she had been wide awake and had not been dreaming. I have a feeling those boys were ghosts from West Derby workhouse, which stood near to the students' house on Kensington in Victorian times, and the spirits of the destitute children might have been stirred up by Toria's assertion about the poor having only themselves to blame for their poverty. If this is so, then it is a classic case of speaking ill of the dead and the ensuing evocation of spirits that have returned from beyond the grave because they were besmirched.

In 1972 a 40-year-old Walton car mechanic named Kevin started to date a beautiful 20-year-old woman named Patrice after meeting her in the She club on Victoria Street. Everyone called Kevin a cradle-snatcher because Patrice was half his age but the couple got on well despite the age difference. Patrice was a trainee nurse at Walton Hospital, and she lived near her place of work at the family home – an up-market detached residence - on Stuart Road. Kevin lived in a small terraced house on Northcote Road, a road which no longer exists today. A fortnight into the relationship, Kevin pestered Patrice to come back to his place, and he had only one thing on his mind – he wanted to bed his young girlfriend, and after taking her to a restaurant in the city centre, the couple went for a drink in the Philharmonic Hotel, and then they got a taxi to Kevin's home on Northcote Road. Kevin and Patrice went straight to bed, and after about ten minutes of kissing and embracing, Kevin had to go to the toilet (after drinking so much all night), and while he was gone, Patrice had the strangest feeling of being watched. She also felt as if the eyes on her belonged to a female, and she was so freaked out by the uncanny 'presence' she got up and turned on the main light. When Kevin came back from the toilet he asked Patrice why she'd put the light on when the bedside lamp was already on. She never told him about the presence she had sensed, but after Kevin turned the light off and got into the bed, Patrice said: 'Kevin, you mentioned your old girlfriend Delia earlier on in the pub, but you never told me how you and her split up.'

'Oh, well,' Kevin muttered, and then seemed lost for words for a moment. 'She left me. Yeah, left me, and that was that. I never heard from her again.'

'Left you as in just up and went?' Patrice asked, as Kevin tried to remove her knickers. 'Stop that, Kevin.'

'Oh God, what does it matter?' Kevin said, drawing back to his side of the bed in a sulky manner. 'Delia's gone, and now I have you – she's all in the past and the past is dead and gone.'

'But why did she just leave you? Was it for someone else?' Patrice asked, and she lay sideways now, resting on her right elbow as she looked at Kevin.

'She was a two-timer,' a po-faced Kevin said, looking at the ceiling, 'she went where the grass was greener. She'd been seeing him for some time behind my back, but, as I said, it's the past; it's *now* I'm concerned with; us.'

'I'm sorry,' Patrice said, and she moved closer to Kevin and they hugged and kissed, and then they made love, and as soon as the act was over, Kevin rolled onto his back and started snoring. After ten minutes, the snoring stopped, and a silence fell on the bedroom. Kevin got up and left the room to go to the toilet. As soon as he left, that uncanny presence manifested itself again. Patrice became so afraid of the unseen woman she could sense, she closed her eyes and tried to fall asleep, but she couldn't drop off; she was always like this after she'd been drinking. Alcohol seemed to delay the nodding-off mechanism with Patrice. She opened her eyes when she heard a noise in the room. She had not imagined it; something had made a noise by the door. Patrice tried to will herself to sleep again and closed her eyes.

She felt a slight breath near the left side of her face. She knew it was not a draught but the exhalation of something that was not of this world, and Patrice's heart palpitated with fear. She knew that if she opened her eyes she'd find a ghost looking at her face close up. She couldn't help herself though, and she opened her eyes.

The hideous face of a woman was inches away from Patrice's face. Straight away she noticed the apparition's bulging bloodshot eyes and the dark rings around them. Those eyes, glimpsed in that brief moment, seemed full of hate.

Patrice tried to scream, and tried to shout for Kevin, but her throat just couldn't produce any noise. She was so utterly scared, she felt weak and faint.

'Get out of my bed!' said the naked, almost skeletal woman leaning over Patrice, and as her left hand reached out and grabbed the pillow the nurse's head was resting on, Patrice saw the blood streaming from the deep dark-red cut to the figure's wrist. The pillow was yanked away with such force, it twisted Patrice's head and in turn twisted her neck, and she was later in agony with a whiplash-like injury. The pillow was thrown towards the window, where it hit the curtains and fell, and then the naked woman let out a scream and lunged at Patrice, who pulled the covers over herself in a reflex defence action.

Then silence.

The bedroom door squeaked open and then the mattress rocked as Kevin got back into the bed, and he tried to pull the covers off Patrice but was unable to do so because her fingers were gripping them.

'Pat? What's up?' he asked, wondering if she was messing about. 'What's that doing over there?' he said, noticing the candy-striped pillow on the floor beneath the window.

Patrice emerged from the bedclothes with wide scared eyes that looked around as if searching for something. 'Where is she?' she asked Kevin, and sat up, and then her bottom lip twitched.

'Where's who? What are you on about?' Kevin asked her, and followed her line of sight, which led to the door.

Patrice recalled the other shocking details she had noticed besides the cut wrist; the other wrist was cut, and the woman had blood coming from a cut to her neck that had dripped down between her breasts. Her ribcage stuck out like a washboard, and those eyes; they had been bulging out of their dark sockets.

'A *ghost* attacked me!' Patrice said, getting her words out at last.

'What?' Kevin laughed out this questioning word.

'I'm serious! A woman with a cut throat and cut wrists! She told me to get out of *her* bed! She threw that pillow over there!'

'It's been a nightmare Pat – ' Kevin started to say but Patrice leaped out of the bed and put the light on. 'I'm not staying here – this place is haunted, and I've got a good idea who's doing the haunting!'

Kevin gave a weak impression of being amused but the forced smile didn't agree with the fear in his eyes. 'Oh don't be daft! You had a bleedin' nightmare you soft cow!'

'It was Delia, wasn't it?' Patrice asked, hesitating for a moment with her bra on back to front so she could link its hook and eye.

'You're round the friggin' bend, you are – Delia?' was Kevin's reaction, and he tried to act surprised at the suggestion but Patrice could see that the name of his ex had struck a chord.

She continued getting dressed and then, despite him begging her to stay, she left and walked home to Stuart Road. She had no doubts about being wrong about the ghost's identity, and when Patrice told her mother what had happened, the strange story was passed on to neighbours and spread, and then a few days later, Patrice's mother came into her daughter's room one morning and said, 'Hey, I hope you don't mind, love, but I told Mrs Sutton about that thing that attacked you in Kevin's place – '

'Oh mum, you didn't tell everyone did you?' groaned Patrice.

'No, listen love, Mrs Sutton said that Kevin's girlfriend committed suicide by cutting her wrists in the bath, and then she cut her own throat, and er – '

'What!' Patrice shrank in horror at this claim.

'Yes, but listen: his girlfriend, er what was her name?' her mother touched her forehead in frustration as she tried to recall the name, but Patrice supplied it.

'Delia?'

'Yes! That's what Mrs Sutton said – Delia – yes, she was having a terrible time with that fellah – Kevin – because he was always having affairs behind her back, and in the end he told her to get out of his house and he threw her out and even had the lock changed, but she got into the house somehow and killed herself.'

That was it. Patrice immediately 'chucked' Kevin and told him why. He said the story wasn't true and that Delia had been the one who had been unfaithful, and that she had committed suicide because he had told her he was leaving her. However, as the months went by, Patrice heard the same version of the story as told by Mrs Sutton – that Kevin was a womaniser who had tried to evict Delia, and the girl had ended her life in a very gruesome manner. Not long afterwards, Kevin was with another woman, a 30-year-old lady who worked in a local factory in Walton. This woman didn't last long with Kevin, and there were rumours that the ghost of Delia had again intervened and haunted the latest squeeze, but of course, these were just rumours and it's difficult to say why the relationship didn't last. When Patrice told her Nan what had happened, the elderly Waltonian said, 'He spoke ill of the dead you see love, and he was telling lies about the poor woman. That's why she returned from the grave; it must have ruffled her. That Delia must have turned in her grave with the lies he was spouting.'

We now move 9 years into the future from 1972, to December 12, 1981. Blizzards had just swept the country and Merseyside County Council was criticised by the Automobile Association for the inadequate gritting of the region's roads. There had been scores of accidents on the black-iced roads of Merseyside and the fifteen main highways into Liverpool had become almost impassable because of glass-hard ice covered in layers of new snowfall. People were nominated as "snow wardens" to organise the clearance of snowdrifts on the roads and pavements in the arctic chaos, and strong easterly winds brought even more snow, so that at one point in these subzero conditions, giant blocks of ice coursed along the sewers of Liverpool like subterranean icebergs. On this Saturday night that December in 1981, a hackney cab driver named Peter Hadley-Wallis put on his tracksuit bottoms, and then he put his jeans on over them, and he had on two pairs of socks under his Doc Marten boots. He wore layers of tee shirts under a Slazenger sweater, and he put a parka on as well. It was all play-acting, of course, but only he knew that.

'Life must go on, love,' Peter told his wife Joanne as he headed into the hallway of his Wavertree home, 'and there are young people out there right now trying to get home from clubs, and I have to earn my bread and butter.'

Joanne shouted after him as he reached the door. 'Peter, the fellah on the radio has just said people should stay indoors unless their journey's necessary!'

Without turning he went to the snow-covered cab in his driveway shouting: 'My journey *is* necessary – I don't want people to die of pneumonia waiting for a taxi in this weather. Don't wait up love, get some sleep!'

Of course, Peter wasn't in the least concerned about stranded clubbers in town, he was going to see the other woman – a 22-year-old student named Mandy, often referred to as his "bit on the side" in conversations with other cabbies at the taxi-driver's café on Bolton Street.

The hackney cab wouldn't start at first, and Peter's wife knocked on the side driver's window with a smiling face. Peter wound the window down and narkily asked, 'What? What?'

'Peter, that's a sign,' said Joanne, closing one eye as a snowflake stuck to her eyelash. 'Come on love, come and get some supper and see how things are in the morning.'

'You're turning into another Mary!' he growled, and tried the ignition again without success. 'She was like this; couldn't move for her! Don't start all that love!'

'I'm just concerned about you, that's all,' Joanne told him, and the sting in her heart was worse than the nettling stings of the subzero cold on her face. 'Don't compare me to Mary.'

Peter tried the engine and again and this time it came to life and thrummed. 'I'm sorry Jo girl, you're nothing like Mary, here giz a kiss!' Peter said, and puckered his lips.

Joanne leaned forward and kissed him.

'Stop worrying, I'll soon be back love,' Peter told her as the cab inched forwards, 'and watch the cat doesn't get out in this weather or we'll need to thaw him out with a blow torch. Ta ra love!'

As Peter drove up ice-slicked Smithdown Road through the start of another blizzard, he found the thoroughfare deserted, and then he noticed someone beyond the squealing windscreen wipers standing in a long white robe. This barmy person was facing away from Peter, and he beeped his horn and carefully drove around someone he assumed to be a drunken student messing about. Then he saw the face of the person in that flowing white robe. It was Mary, the wife he had lost to cancer twenty years ago. She was in the burial shroud he had seen her in at the undertaker's chapel of repose with that hood, and she leaned into the offside window, and although it was closed, he heard Mary say: 'Don't cheat on Joanne the way you cheated on me.'

The eyes of the ghost were red and looked so sad, and before a spooked Peter could accelerate away, Mary vanished. She'd been buried in the cemetery close by – Toxteth Park Cemetery - in 1970. After getting over the shock of the visitation, Peter's heart broke as he recalled the many affairs that had ruined his first marriage, and he turned the cab around and drove home. He knew that he had somehow brought his first wife back by speaking ill about her. She had not fenced him in at all and stopped him from going out – she had merely tried to stop him from embarking on so many of those affairs which had finally broken her down. He felt that all of that stress Mary had been under because of the infidelities had contributed to her awful terminal disease. Peter remained faithful to Joanne until he passed away, twenty years later. I don't think this case is a typical example of a dead person returning because she was slandered; I think Mary felt some sympathy towards Peter's present wife and had returned to wake the cabby up to his selfish behaviour.

THREE CONSCIENCE GHOSTS

Back in the days when the January sales were actually held in January, a certain well-known department store in Liverpool was visited by someone not of this world. The ghost had visited the store nine days previously (on Christmas Eve) and had filled what looked like a green burlap sack with various toys. The store detectives had moved in on what they assumed to be a real flesh-and-blood shoplifter, only to be greeted by thin air when they pounced. I know from first-hand experience what happens to non-believers in ghosts when they actually meet one – they invariably go into shock – and the store detectives were left doubting their own sanity, and they were unable to report the spooky shoplifter of course – or they'd risk being dismissed for drinking on duty. Rupert Hanley from menswear had been off that Christmas Eve and laughed at the whispered rumours about the ghost. 'There're no such things as ghosts and if there were, what would a ghost want with toys? To play with them in his coffin?' he had chuckled in the store's canteen at the superstitious girls from the lingerie department. And then, on New Year's Day 1966, the store doors were thrown open, and among the throng of bargain hunters, Rupert saw with his own eyes a man in ragged clothes with a ghastly pale face, and he held a green sack. Into the sack he stuffed boxes of Airfix model kits, dolls, Subbuteo sets, model trains and their tracks,

Mousetrap and Monopoly board games...

'Mrs Batt! Is that the man the store detectives were talking about?' Rupert hid behind the formidable head of the perfume counter, and she marched over to the scruffy, bearded shoplifter. 'He might be a ghost, Mrs Batt, be careful!' said Hanley, following her gingerly. She dismissed his ludicrous suggestion, and to the tatty pilferer, she snarled: 'And what do you think you're doing?'

In a rich deep voice the man answered: 'I am requisitioning these playthings for the poor children of this city! These bagatelles shall not be missed!'

'Thief!' Mrs Batt cried out, and noticed the store detectives watching, but they seemed afraid and never came to her aid. The bedraggled man then said, 'I must do good you see, for I was once as iron-hearted as you!' And he vanished, along with the sack. Mr Hanley yelped and backed away. And I have many stories from that time, of poor children across Liverpool, finding brand new toys on their beds in the wee small hours, left there perhaps by that ragged Robin Hood from beyond. The unknown ghost was seen on many more occasions in the department store, especially around Christmas, and the head of the store saw the scruffily-dressed intruder from the next world on several occasions, and instead of being scared of the apparition, the ghost somehow evoked a feeling of charity towards the poorer people of the city in the heart of the department store's senior manager, and it moved him to donate money and even buy toys at the store for the impoverished local children. I call these entities - which affect the moral sense for the better in the minds of those who perceive them – as conscience ghosts.

They come in all forms – not just as figures but as symbols in some cases, but they all have a ghostly quality about them, and one of the most sinister conscience ghosts in my files has to be the Prenton Mummy. I have a record of an encounter with this curious entity dating back to 1894. The ghastly-looking apparition of a man covered in bandages from head to toe appeared at Number 2 Gerald Road, the palatial Prenton residence of one Charles Aldridge, a renowned architect and president of the Liverpool Architectural Society, and certainly not a man who was prone to seeing ghosts. Mr Aldridge had been working late, drawing up a detailed blueprint, and was now ascending the stairs to his bedroom at around 2am on the Wednesday morning of February 14 with an oil lamp, when he saw a motionless figure on the landing above. Naturally, the architect was startled by what he initially assumed to be a burglar, but then, by the feeble light of the lamp, he saw that the intruder was swathed in yellowish bandages which coiled about his entire body, and as Aldridge halted on the steps, he noticed the stark-looking eyes staring out two holes in the bandaged head, and then he saw the ragged mouth, with a fringe of frayed strands, open and close as the mummy spoke. 'I have no heart! Look!' the strange bandaged trespasser shouted in a very deep and unsettling voice, and his mitten-like hands fumbled at the ragged and stained gauze of his chest and pulled at the fabric to reveal a hole with something red inside. Mr Aldridge felt faint at the sight of the gaping aperture. 'But I am dead! You are living and you also have no heart!'

Somehow, Charles Aldridge knew what this terrifying phantom was referring to; he had just cruelly dumped a woman he had been having an affair with after he had persuaded her to break off her engagement with her fiancé. The figure in bandages made a growling sound and dashed forwards down the stairs, and the architect turned and fled. He couldn't get out of the house because the servants had long locked up, so he hid in the pantry, and thankfully the thing did not enter there. Mr Aldridge never saw the bandaged monstrosity after that, but upon mentioning the ghost to an elderly friend, he was told that the thing had been seen in the area for years, and no one knew whose ghost it was, but on its previous manifestations it had always said something similar about those it haunted having no heart. I gave a brief summary of the Aldridge incident on a local television programme, and afterwards received three emails and many letters from viewers who had either heard of the heartless mummy or had encountered it themselves. One of the latter was a man in his sixties named Brian who had been a hackney cab driver in his younger days. In February 1969, at around 6.30 am, he was driving up Gerald Road, on his way to pick up an old woman in Prenton, when he heard a weird deep voice in the back of the vehicle. Brian looked into his rear view mirror and saw the head and shoulders of someone sitting in the rear seat of the hackney, and the presence of this person startled the cabby. He switched on the interior light, and saw what seems to have been the very same ghost seen 75 years before on that same road. It was a grotesque mummy – a figure wrapped in dirty stained bandages, and the dark eyes of the thing were twinkling through the two torn holes in the tightly-wound gauze strips. The mouth was a torn open hole with stringy strands hanging from its edges. This hole moved as the unearthly hitcher spoke in what Brian could only describe as a groaning voice. 'I have no heart,' the creepy figure moaned, 'and neither do you, and you deserve to die!'

Brian swore out of pure fear, and started to brake, and yet, as the taxi came to a screeching halt, the resulting inertia did not affect the 'mummy' – it did not lurch forward as any normal solid object would have done. Brian was feeling for the crowbar he kept under his seat in case he was ever held up by a robber, and in the mounting panic as his hands searched for the ad hoc weapon, the bandaged figure in the rear seat shoved its mitten of a hand deep into its chest, and it spoke in a guttural manner, saying 'No heart!'

Brian found the crowbar, lifted it to strike the sinister entity, but caught the rear view mirror with it and shattered it. He slung the crowbar at the horrific figure and it glanced off its head, bounced off the seat, and fell to the floor of the vehicle. As Brian wrestled with his seatbelt and tried to get out of the taxi, he heard the menacing phantasm say: 'You left her in Liverpool to die on the streets!'

And then that bizarre and frightening man vanished into thin air. Brian knew what the ghost was referring to, and the fear in him turned to shame. Yesterday he had dumped his pregnant dog on the Landing Stage at Liverpool, and he had managed to get back on the ferry without her. As the ferry had moved away, the abandoned dog had spotted him, and it howled and whined at him. Brian's conscience was pricked so much, he drove to Liverpool and after hours of searching he found the dog he had deserted, and took her back. That strange bandaged being was last seen in a certain bedroom in Prenton one night in 2003, and maybe it is still being seen, but the identity and history of the ghost, how it came to lose its heart, and why it pricks the conscience of the living, remains a mystery. An apparition known as the "Cross of Honesty" also remains a mystery. This tiny glowing white Greek cross was first seen by a Fazakerley woman named Rose when she was just a 9-year-old girl. On that first occasion in 1955, Rose had stolen a tiny doll from the house of a girl named Julie who lived next door but one, and she had gone into her back garden to play with the doll when Rose's Nan remarked, 'Isn't that a lovely little doll?' and Rose nodded. The tiny blonde doll was dressed up in the traditional outfit of the Netherlands, which included yellow clogs, dark blue calf length dress, white apron and the usual Dutch cap.

'Did your mum buy you that, Rose?' Nana asked.

Rose blushed and looked down at the grass in the back garden, and nodded. She was lying of course, and then the child looked away, unable to face her grandmother, and looked at a corner of the clear blue eastern sky where the dusk was approaching – and the girl saw a cross hanging there. It was not like the Christian cross, which has a horizontal beam that is shorter than the vertical one; this one was looked like the plus symbol (+) because the horizontal and vertical beams were the same size. The cross seemed to have a silvery glint to it.

'Nanny, what's that?' Rose pointed to the stationary cross in the sky.

'You can see that too, then?' said the child's grandma with a surprised look, and she replied, 'Well that's the Cross of Honesty, love, and when you tell a fib or deceive, or do something you know is wrong, it appears as a sign for you to be honest.'

'Oh,' said Rose, knowing what the cross meant in her case, and she turned to her Nan and said, 'I took the doll out of Julie's house because I like it, and I didn't think Julie still wanted it.'

'Did you now?' Nan asked her. 'Well, you'll have to take it back then, Rose; stealing is wrong. Go and take it back.'

With a lump in her throat and a protruding bottom lip, Rose returned to Julie's house and she posted the little Dutch girl doll through the letterbox. She returned to the back garden and saw that the intriguing cross had vanished from the sky. Rose soon forgot about the cross, and when she mentioned it to her mother later that day, her mum said she'd just seen a plane and that her Nan was pulling her leg. Two years later, Rose was walking home from school one afternoon in November when she saw an elderly neighbour of hers who she only knew as Mr Barron, accidentally drop a pound note as he was putting money away in his wallet. The old man was in front of Rose, and she looked about, and seeing no one was around, she picked up the crisp pound note and clutched it in her hand. In those days, a pound could keep a child in sweets and comics for nearly a month. A 1957 £1 has the purchasing power of £23 in 2018 money when adjustments are made for inflation and other factors. Rose's first thought as to go to the sweet shop, but on her way she happened to glance up at a break in the clouds – and there, suspended in a piece of blue sky was that cross again. Rose went cold inside when she recalled what that Greek cross meant – it was telling her she was being dishonest. Rose ran after Mr Barron and when she had caught up with the old man she tapped him on the arm and he was very surprised - and very impressed – at the girl's honesty. He was so impressed he gave Rose half a crown as a reward for her honesty. The girl looked up at the sky but the patch of blue had vanished, and with it that mysterious cross. Rose ran home and told her Nan what had happened, and her grandmother praised her and said she had first seen that cross when she was a little girl. She couldn't explain how it knew when dishonest things were being done, but she hadn't seen it for nearly fifty years, but the old woman didn't say what she had done to make it appear all those years back.

The years rolled on, and Rose's beloved Nan passed away in 1966. In 1967, 21-year-old Rose started work in the Sayers cake factory on Lorenzo Drive, Norris Green, and it was the real first proper paying job Rose had had, and when she got her wages she gave her "keep" to her mum and spent the rest on clothes and shoes, and she started to go out to pubs. She met a man who was much older than her named Len, and started to date him. Len would come to pick Rose up from her home every Thursday and Saturday, and he began to pester her to sleep with him. Then Rose was told by a friend at Sayers that Len was a married man with two children, and Rose refused to believe this at first, but she finally confronted Len one night as he came to pick her up in his car. Len drove Rose to a milk bar in the city centre and finally admitted he *was* married but said that his wife had met someone and was only staying with him for the sake of the kids. She was very near to leaving him, Len said, and suspected she'd run off with the children. He then begged Rose to stay with him for the night at a hotel on Mount Pleasant. Rose really loved Len, and although her heart told her to leave him because he was married, she agreed to go to the hotel, and she knew it was inevitable that she'd end up sleeping with him. As the car pulled up outside the hotel on Mount Pleasant, Len said, 'What's that?' and he pointed to something beyond the windshield. It was a glowing cross. It looked about the size of a thumbnail when the arm is extended, and it was hanging in the starry sky. Rose instantly recognised the 'Cross of Honesty' – and immediately she thought of her Nan. The couple got out the car, and Len went into the hotel first, and as he did, Rose ran off in tears. She knew she could not go with a man who was cheating on his wife; he was married and in her eyes, it was wrong to go with a married man, even though many girls her age would have no qualms about committing adultery in this age of so-called Free Love. She heard Len shouting after her, and she hid in an alleyway near the Wellington Rooms and watched Len run past towards the top of Mount Pleasant. Rose then made her way home and told her mother what had happened, but she did not mention the enigmatic cross which always pricked her conscience. Rose later discovered that Len's wife doted on him, and that Len was in fact a serial womaniser who used the same sob story on all of his 'conquests' about his wife wanting to leave him. After that night, Rose never saw the glimmering cross in the sky, and she has no idea what it was, but she does believe that it made her a better person.

GHOST DAD

I've had quite a few reports of ghostly parents over the years. The bond between parents and their offspring is naturally very strong, and in some cases it transcends death itself. This chapter is concerned with a story of a ghostly father, and when I found it in my files, I found notes with the account about other ghostly fathers. A pharmacist in Aintree named Richard told me how, when he was nineteen, he lost his father one Saturday as they both walked to a football game. Richard's dad - William – suddenly collapsed and died from congestive heart failure. William had a constant cough which never seemed to clear up, and a swelling of the ankles – both possible signs of the heart condition, and he had smoked around forty Woodbines a day. Richard was naturally devastated by the death of his father, and about a week after the funeral, Richard woke up at half-past-three one morning at the family home on Altway, Aintree, and feeling thirsty, he went downstairs to the kitchen for a drink of water. As he walked along the hall, he noticed that there was a thin line of light at the bottom of the closed living room door, so Richard assumed his mother had absent-mindedly left the light on in that room. He opened the door and looked in, and Richard received the biggest shock of his life. His father was sitting there in an armchair to the right of the fire surround, and he was smoking as he sat there looking at the wall to his son's left, apparently unaware of Richard's presence.

'Dad,' Richard gasped, and his father turned towards him, as if in surprise, and he smiled, took a puff of his Woodbine, and then stubbed it out in the dark glass ashtray on a bookshelf next to the fire surround. Thinking he was dreaming, Richard closed his eyes and then he looked back – and his father had vanished. Richard went over to the armchair where his late father had been sitting and he felt the leather cushion; it was warm. He looked at the glass ashtray on the bookshelf and saw the crumpled stump of the filterless Woodbine cigarette there. The aroma of that cigarette still hung in the air. Richard wanted to tell his mother straight away about the supernatural visit, but sensibly waited until the morning, and he expected his mother to say that he'd been dreaming, but instead she told him a curious thing. She didn't smoke, and neither did Richard or his 12-year-old sister, and yet Richard's mum had been finding the stumps of Woodbines in the old ashtray used by her husband, and she had also been noticing the smell of tobacco around the house. Richard said nothing about these strange goings-on to his sister, but she said she had seen her father at the end of the garden one afternoon after she returned from school. He had gone into the shed – a place where her father often went to dabble with his hobby, which was electronics – and yet that shed had been locked. This case is typical of the many I have received, and to me it seems to suggest that the deceased father puts in an appearance to reassure his family that he's okay in the life hereafter. Another case referred to in my file along with the aforementioned one is that concerning a 5-year-old child in 1988 by the name of Cheri, who went missing on two occasions, weeks apart, from her home in West Derby. Cheri's 25-year-old mother Sandra was visited by social workers because neighbours had seen how Cheri was allowed to play unsupervised in the front garden of her home and had wandered off on some occasions until one of the neighbours brought her back. On the two occasions when the girl vanished for over an hour, she returned tight-lipped and would not say where she had been, but Sandra noted Cheri's lips were pink and smelled of candy floss. On the third occasion the girl was seen in the company of a man at a fairground near Croxteth Hall, and when Cheri reappeared back at her house, Sandra yelled at her daughter and asked her who had taken her. The answer the child gave was not accepted by her mother. 'Daddy took me out,' the girl said. Sandra had not told her daughter that her father had died the year before from cancer. Sandra hardly knew the father – a man named Ken – and did not want to upset Cheri. Other people later came forward to say that they had seen Ken with Cheri, at the local shops and also at the fairground, but Sandra said they must have been mistaken because her husband was dead. Ken had no brothers who looked like him, so Sandra thought some sinister man was at large who had taken Cheri for some seedy reason that did not bear thinking about. However, one day, Cheri was playing in the hallway, and she told her mum she wanted to play in the garden, but Sandra, mindful of the threats the social workers had made to take the little girl into care, accompanied Cheri into the garden. Not long afterwards, Cheri shouted, 'Mummy! There's Daddy!'

Standing at the gate was Sandra's deceased husband, Ken. He held a large "Lucky Bag" in his hand, and he tried to hand it to her over the gate, but Sandra was so scared, she picked up Cheri and ran inside with the child. When Sandra looked out the window, she saw that her late husband had vanished. The Lucky Bag was picked up by Cheri when the child was allowed back out again about fifteen minutes later. As Cheri grew up, she would always dream of her father and she always felt as if he was around her, especially when she was in any danger. It was as if the father had returned from the grave to see his beloved child grow up. Twenty-five years before the return of Ken to see his child, another father seems to have come back from the mysterious life beyond - in this case, to save his son...

On a fogbound Liverpool night in October 1963, a disembodied voice whispered in the ears of small-time gangster Mickey King as he walked to the doors of the Lion Tavern on Moorfields. It sounded like his late father, Charlie King, calling his name.

'Mickey... Mickey...'

Spooked somewhat, Mickey looked around, and he saw only the faint ghostly outline of an old tramp with his bearded woolly-haired head bowed, shuffling towards an alleyway in the icy sodden fog. A foghorn groaned on the Mersey and echoed throughout Moorfields, and then Mickey went into Lion alehouse and his old mate - another local hoodlum named Billy

Baker remarked: 'Alright, Mickey, you look white as a sheet as if you've seen a ghost or summit.'

Mickey returned a painful smile, and just said, 'It's a bit raw out there.' He was very superstitious and didn't mention the ghost, and he was grateful of the brandy Baker bought him. A minute later as Mickey finished the stomach-warming brandy, Baker turned his bald head to Mickey and in a hushed voice he said, 'Listen mate, I'm not sure if you already know, but there's word going round that Fowler's been having it away with your girl.'

Mickey shot an enraged look at Baker, swore under his breath, and through gritted teeth asked: 'What?'

'I'm sorry mate, and it's even worse than you think,' laughed Baker, and he laughed more out of nerves than his offbeat sense of humour, but Mickey went for his throat and the few drinkers in the bar recoiled in horror, for most of them knew about Mickey's brutal reputation.

'If this is your idea of a joke – ' Mickey's large hands closed around Baker's narrow neck.

'No! It isn't!' Baker gasped, trying to dislodge what felt like cast iron hands from his throat. 'I'm just telling you what you're going to hear sooner or later!'

Mickey calmed down and they went to a private corner of the tavern to hear the 'gen'.

'Fowler's become that besotted by Lorette, he wants to marry her and he wants you out the way first, and he wants your little business as well.'

'Where did you hear all this?' Mickey asked, lighting a cigarette.

'It's all over the manor, Mickey,' said Baker, 'I wasn't sure if you already knew.'

'No, I didn't know,' said Mickey, 'because there'd be an *occurrence* if I did know, like.'

'What are you gonna do, mate?' Baker enquired. 'I'm right behind you, whatever you have in mind.'

'I'll have a word with her first,' Mickey replied, and he inhaled slowly as if he was keeping some great inner demon of temper at bay.

Mickey confronted his wife that night and asked her if she was having an affair. She denied it at first, then burst into tears and threw herself face-down on the bed. Mickey got his old army revolver, loaded it, telephoned Baker at his usual watering hole on Lime Street, and told him: 'You better not be pissed because you're required to drive me to Fowler's house on Catharine Street, pronto.' And then Mickey hung up.

Twenty minutes later, as Baker steered the car carrying Mickey along Hope Street, a strange thing happened. Mickey heard his dad's voice call him again, and he glanced in the rear-view mirror – and there was the familiar round face of his late father. 'Don't be a mug, son, Baker's setting you up,' said the ghost.

Mickey's wide shocked eyes travelled from the rear view mirror to Baker's face as the latter was reading the road through the windscreen. Baker had not reacted to the presence of the ghost – it was as if only Mickey could hear and see his father's ghost, and the voice of the apparition was crystal clear. The ghost said: 'Fowler's blackmailing Baker you see son, and Baker wants you to do Fowler in. Lorette *is* seeing someone, son,' said the phantom, 'but it's not Alfie Fowler. Throw that gun in the Mersey, son, I don't want to see you hang.'

And then the ghost of Charlie King was gone, and

his words echoed in his son's mind.

'Billy, has Fowler got something on you, mate?' Mickey asked, and he saw a telltale twitch in Billy Baker's face.

'Eh? No, why?' asked a surprised-looking Baker.

'Pull over here a mo, Billy,' Mickey said, and he got out the car and walked to the Pier Head, where he tossed the revolver into the river. He walked back to the car whistling and Billy said, 'Did you throw that shooter in the drink?'

'Take me home, Billy boy,' said Mickey, getting into the car. He slammed the car door hard as he sat there with a slight smile on his face. 'There's been a change of plan you see.'

Billy Baker drove him home and Mickey had it out with Lorette. She said she'd been seeing Mickey's older brother Danny. She hadn't slept with him, but he'd taken her out to a few nice restaurants and it was about to get serious.

'You're never home Mickey, and I get lonely,' she told him, 'Most girls in my situation would have well blown you out.'

'I admit I have been neglecting you, girl,' said Mickey, and he looked into her eyes and for once she did not see the usual steel-blue emotionless eyes drilling through her; Mickey actually looked as if he was genuinely sorry, and there was warmth in those eyes. 'Lorette, you'll have to give Danny the big elbow then,' Mickey said with a smile and raised eyebrows, 'and we'll hit the town later. Let's go and get you some decent dresses.' Mickey took Lorette to a Jewish dressmaker named Manny, who had a warehouse at the back of London Road, and Lorette came home with seven outfits. Mickey painted the town red with his girl, and eventually he turned his back on crime, and then he married Lorette. Each night, Mickey said a little prayer of thanks to his father for saving him from the gallows.

UNEARTHLY POWERS

A high percentage of children possess the talent of Extra Sensory Perception (ESP) and unlike adults, kids, being very open-minded towards the subject of the paranormal, never question or try to rationalise the ESP faculty. Some children have had some very strange powers of the psychic kind. There was a case reported in Liverpool in the 1970s where a 9-year-old boy named Bobby was apparently using telekinesis (the ability to move and levitate objects at a distance through the sheer power of the mind) to make chocolate bars and tubes of Smarties fly from behind a sweetshop counter and sail out the door to him. The shopkeeper, Mr Johnson, thought his premises – situated in the Old Swan area - were haunted at first, but then he realised that the 'poltergeist activity' only took place when Bobby was in the immediate vicinity, and on one occasion Mr Johnson saw a box of Maltesers glide through the air from his shelf, fly through the doorway of his shop, and land in the waiting cupped hands of young Bobby, who then ran away down the street. Mr Johnson had a word with the boy's mother, and she in turn told Bobby's stern father, who gave the boy a hiding for pilfering. The parents of Bobby did not view the strange skill of their son with even the slightest scientific curiosity; instead they thought the telekinesis power had something to do with spirits and the Devil. A priest was called in and he blamed the parents for not attending church and for being too lackadaisical regarding discipline towards their children. Within months, Bobby was an altar boy, and fearing an eternity in the furnaces of Hell, he became too scared to use the power he once regarded as a very handy gift, and eventually the incredible faculty deserted him for good.

In the early 1970s, 48-year-old window cleaner Ian Emerson bought a used car from Georegeson Brothers in Anfield, and as he drove home to Kensington, Ian stopped at a set of traffic lights and the driver in the next lane – a friend named Charlie Howard - wound down his window and told him Billy Pickitt, a notorious burglar was being buried at Anfield in the afternoon at 3pm. Two months ago, Pickitt had burgled Ian's house and amongst the items he had taken were Ian's treasured collection of silver cups won for various sporting events when he was a kid. As soon as he got home, Ian told his wife Hilda he was going to break into Pickett's shed (where he was known to keep his loot) when the burglar's funeral was taking place and get the cups back.

'You're obsessed with those cups, Ian, let it go!' Hilda chided him, but Ian was determined to get his beloved cups back.

'This is my only chance to get my cups back,' he told his wife. 'My dad was so proud of me when I won some of those cups, and that toe rag took them. I don't mind robbers who screw big factories and banks that are insured for theft, but robbing from your own class is barley as far as I'm concerned. I want them cups passed onto my grandkids, like an heirloom.'

'You're going to risk getting nicked, just to get those bleedin' old cups back? They're only silver-plated as well I'm sorry to tell you!' Hilda's eyes looked even bigger than normal as they bulged with anger, contrasted against her flushed face.

Ian smiled and shook his head. 'I won't get nicked, Hilda – no one will see me – talk about Raffles; I'll sneak into that garden of his and I'll have my stuff out that shed before you can say –'

'Walton Prison!' Hilda interposed and gritted her teeth.

'Don't start jinxing me,' said Ian, as the colour drained from his face, 'Start believing in me will you?'

'This shower around here will have a field day gossiping if you get done for house-breaking,' Hilda told him, her arms folded now as she stood in front of the gas fire. 'It'll be all over the *Echo*; I'll be stigmatised.'

'Will you stop jinxing me you bleedin' Jonah!' seethed Ian. 'Look love, I'll knock at Pickitt's house a few times first, and when there's no answer I'll know no one's in. They'll all be out paying their respects and biding their time at the funeral service so they can all go and get pissed at the nearest boozer. I'll soon be back here with the cups.'

'Ian, I've had enough - I am washing my hands of you,' Hilda announced, and she swung around and walked off into the kitchen.

'The birds I turned down to stay with you!' Ian shouted after her, 'Some of them would have been really loyal; some of them would have come with me on this job. And I K.B'd them for you!'

Hilda slammed the kitchen door on Ian. He then heard her singing *Gonna Get Along Without You Now* as she ran a tap.

To the cat, slouching on his armchair, Ian said: 'You've got the right idea, lad; just have your fun with the opposite sex and then piss off before they get their claws into you!'

Ian donned a woollen hat and an old donkey jacket with the black leather strip across the upper back – the coat Ian had worn during his happy days as a coalman – before gas and electric heating made open fires a thing of the past. He took an old satchel from the cubby hole under the stairs and then he said goodbye to the indifferent cat and left the house via the backyard. He caught the bus to Anfield within minutes and after a short walk he arrived on the road where Pickett's house stood at 2.30pm. From the cover of a bus shelter he watched the funeral cortege waiting to leave. "Big Ben" Cochrane – who had been Pickett's partner in crime - locked the front door of the house and got in a limo – and then Ian sneaked from the bus shelter and knocked at the door. He waited. No one answered. He knocked again, and then he pushed the letterbox flap inwards and looked in at the empty hallway. The place seemed deserted. Ian looked about, and then he went to the side of Pickitt's house and tried the door to the back garden. It was bolted as he expected it to be. Ian looked left and right, and there wasn't a soul about. He threw the satchel containing a crowbar over the back garden fence, and then he climbed that fence and he was so out of shape, it was almost a near-death experience. He dropped into the garden, wheezing and fighting for his breath as he saw spots and floaters swimming about before his eyes. 'So far, so good,' he gasped, complimenting himself as he got a bit nervy. Something wet touched his left thumb.

He turned to see a huge young black Alsatian dog sniffing his hand. He froze, for Ian was terrified of dogs.

'Ah, hello there!' he said to the guard dog, and he felt sweat trickle down his torso from his armpits and his left eye started to twitch. The young dog barked at Ian and then it rolled on its back and panted. Ian started speaking the type of gibberish he usually spoke to babies, and the dog followed him as he walked in slow motion to his satchel.

The dog started barking and Ian froze and said, 'Don't make me do you in!' even though he knew very well that he didn't have the guts to harm the animal. Luckily for him, the dog was barking at a ginger cat that was perched on the high fence on the other side of the garden. Ian dashed to the shed and used a crowbar to remove the padlock. The dog was still barking furiously at the cat, which seemed to be taunting it. Ian saw a switch and flicked it, and a light came on in the shed, revealing boxes and tins full of the spoils of many burglaries. Ian smiled as he spotted the row of silver cups on a shelf – they were *his* cups! He stuffed them in the satchel, along with a Huntley and Palmer biscuit tin full of jewellery. He knew very well that Big Ben Cochrane and the other vultures would be straight into this shed after they'd had their bevies at the pub. Getting out the garden was easy; Ian simply slid two bolts off on the back garden door, waved to the worst guard dog in Liverpool (who looked at him in a quizzical way with its head tilted to one side), and then he walked half a mile to a bus stop, continually glancing over his shoulder. He waited ages for a bus back to Kensington, and when one arrived, he rushed onto the vehicle, and an old man advised him to leave his satchel in the luggage rack.

'Nah, it's okay mate,' said Ian, 'it's only light,' and then he dropped it and an almighty clanking sound turned everyone's head on the bottom deck.

Ian sat with the satchel to his left – in the 'window seat' – and he smiled as the bus trundled on. He pictured Hilda's face when she saw all that jewellery, but he also knew she'd complicate the situation somehow; she'd probably tell him he'd been followed by Special Branch. Ten minutes later, something wiped the smile clean off the window cleaner's face.

Two stops on, Big Ben Cochrane got on the bus and sat behind Ian. Ian's stomach somersaulted as he heard Cochrane, inches behind him, chatting to a woman the crook obviously knew. 'Hiya Margie,' Big Ben said to the woman sitting in the window seat. 'I was supposed to be paying my respects to Billy Pickitt when they planted him in Anfield, but his missus started having a go at me, saying I should be the one getting planted and blaming me for Billy's heart attack.'

'No!' gasped Margie, 'Fancy saying that. God, you were like a brother to Billy.'

'I was Margie,' said Ben, 'And well, a few others there started mouthing off and you know me, Margie, I'm not into violence, but one of them called me a word I won't repeat in front of a lady, and I had to put him away, and he went in the hole.'

'No! Oh Ben, haven't they got any respect any more?' said Margie.

'So the priest then turns around and told me to leave, like – ' Ben was saying.

'No!' Sympathetic Margie cut in.

Big Ben continued. 'And then I'm leaving the cemetery, and the fellah who's supposed to be minding Billy's house tells me the place has been turned over.'

'No!' exclaimed Margie, sounding ever so shocked.

'Yeah,' replied Ben, 'while Billy's being buried, his place gets screwed. That's lower than a snake's belly that. I've got an idea who they were, like. Am just going to see a few people who'll give them a hiding.'

Ian's stomach started gargling when he heard the latter. Cochrane was an inquisitive man, and if he recognised Ian he'd naturally ask him about the contents of the satchel, and those cups were already clanking about as the bus went over every pothole. Ian pulled his woollen hat down as he heard Cochrane suddenly say to Margie, 'I think I *know* him.'

'Who?' Margie asked.

'Him in front of us,' Big Ben replied, and his big thick index finger tapped Ian on the shoulder. 'Oi, mate, I'm trying to place you.'

Ian broke out in a sweat and never replied, and a half-forgotten memory suddenly came out the depths of his mind; it was more like a dream than a memory, and it harked back to when he was a kid. At the age of nine, Ian discovered that he could sometimes make himself invisible. When the school-board man or street gangs were after him, he often closed his eyes tight and vanished as he pictured himself being invisible. He tried to show some of his friends how he did this 'trick' but none of them could do it, and some mates thought he had something to do with the Devil and stopped knocking round with him, so he then hid his talent, and it only seemed to work when he was in danger. He felt he could pull off that trick now, and he said a little prayer to God, asking him to make him vanish. Otherwise, Big Ben Cochrane would discover the silver cups and the biscuit tin crammed with brooches, rings and necklaces and if Ben didn't give him a good hiding himself, he'd hire someone to kill Ian. With his eyes squeezed shut, Ian started to feel a slight dizziness followed by the sensation of being as light as a feather, and then that old tingling feeling coursed down his body from his forehead to his feet. He heard Margie behind him shriek, 'Oh God! Where did he go?'

Ian left his seat and wondered if the satchel would remain visible, but apparently it wasn't, for he couldn't see it – and he couldn't see his own body. He reached out to grab the vertical chrome bar to steady himself as the bus rocked about, but his hand, which he couldn't see, missed it, and he lunged forward and the satchel whacked the right side of Big Ben Cochrane's square head.

Cochrane cried out and leaned into Margie as he shrunk away from the 'ghost' and Margie screamed.

Ian felt the bar for the red button and pressed it. The bell sounded, and the bus decelerated to a halt at the next stop. Ian got off the bus and walked thirty yards as he experienced a total feeling of unreality, as if he was in a dream. The bus moved off, and then Ian saw his shadow reappear on the pavement. He was visible again, but he felt nauseous and drained of energy.

Ian's wife didn't believe his story when he got home, and maintained that Cochrane had been that engrossed in his conversation with that woman, he had somehow not noticed Ian when he got up to leave the bus. Ian tried to perform the invisibility trick in front of his wife but he couldn't do it and the window cleaner was unable to perform the 'trick' ever again.

The occultists have been saying for centuries that the human race have hidden talents and powers they are completely ignorant of, and these abilities include invisibility, levitation, super-strength, psychometry (the 'reading' of an object's history just by holding the object in your hand), rapid self-healing of wounds, telepathy, the ability to knock people and dangerous animals out by discharging high voltages from the hands, teleportation (the translocation of the body from one place to another without passing through 3-dimensional space), fire-immunity – the ability to withstand high temperatures, as well as cold-immunity – the power to comfortably endure subzero conditions by warming the body up through pure concentrated will-power, and many other astounding capabilities. There are people who have an amazing sense of direction when they are exploring a city they've never visited before; they never get lost and their brains seem to act like compasses, sensing which way is north, whereas other individuals can get lost in a large department store. It was only recently discovered that most people have a protein called a cryptochrome in their eyes – in the retina to be exact – and this protein is capable of magnetoreception – it can detect magnetic fields – even the earth's magnetic field – the same field that makes a compass point unwaveringly along the north-south axis. A great variety of creatures – including birds, sharks, butterflies, turtles and even foxes – routinely navigate by the previously unknown sense called magnetoreception, but humans of today, who rarely have any need for this ancient sense in the modern world (with GPS SatNav devices and all sorts of electronic navigational aids) seem to have largely lost this sense. I have a feeling that there are similar proteins and miniature structures similar to cryptochromes in the human brain – probably around the parahippocampal gyrus area - that may act as some type of transceiver which can send and receive thoughts from other minds, and this structure could be responsible for the many claims of telepathy that have been made over the years. Furthermore, it is possible that our hypothetical cerebral transceiver might be sending out particles as mysterious and ghostlike as the neutrino – a weird subatomic particle first hypothesised in the 1930s but only detected in the late 1950s. A neutrino can pass through the earth in less than a second as if the planet wasn't there. The particle has hardly any mass, and if someone found a way to use neutrinos to carry conversations and texts on your mobile phone, you would always have a perfect signal – even if you were on the farside of the moon and the other person was on the Atlantic seabed on earth. A secret telepathy experiment was conducted by astronaut Edgar Mitchell during the Apollo 14 Moon mission in January 1971. Despite Mitchell being 150,000 miles from Earth on his way to the Moon, he was able to guess a sizeable percentage of numbers being mentally broadcast to him by experimental telepathic transmitters in the US. The experiment strongly suggested that telepathy is not affected by distance.

From the grand setting of a telepathy experiment conducted during a historical space mission in 1971, we come down to earth – to Kirkby in the summer of

2006 – to the bedroom of a 16-year-old girl named Kelly. The time was shortly after midnight, and Kelly was surfing the internet in her bedroom at her home in the Westvale area of Kirkby when she suddenly had a craving for picked-onion Monster Munch crisps. The desire for these crisps gradually took over the teenaged girl's mind and she decided to walk to the mini market in Westvale filling station half a mile away on Whitefield Drive to get the Monster Munch crisps. Her parents were asleep in bed and her older brother Dan was out drinking in Liverpool's city centre, but Kelly left a note on the kitchen table which simply stated: 'Dad, I've gone to the garage to get some crisps – Kelly'.

With a full moon hanging in the sky and an unusual stillness in the muggy air on this August night, the girl walked the half a mile to the filling station, bought two packets of crisps, then made her way home, when she suddenly realised that a tall man in a trilby and a long calf-length coat was walking behind her. Kelly just had a bad feeling about this man the moment she set eyes on him, so she crossed Whitefield Road and walked along near to the railings of Westvale Primary School's playing fields.

The man crossed over too. Kelly crossed back over the road – and the man did the same, so the girl started to walk faster – and the man in the trilby did the same. Kelly glanced back and saw the smiling moonlit face of the man who appeared to be stalking her. The man started whistling loudly, and Kelly wondered where everybody was; there wasn't a single car on the roads and not a soul to be seen. The man following hot on the girl's heels was gaining on Kelly, and when she got to the junction of Whitefield Road and Mercer Avenue, the man suddenly said something which sounded like, 'Bitch!' and he ran towards Kelly. The girl screamed and ran off as fast as she could up the road. About 150 yards up the road, another man – dressed exactly like the one who was chasing Kelly – came running towards her from Ingoe Lane. He looked so like her pursuer, Kelly thought it was him, and she looked back, wondering if he had somehow taken a shortcut to get ahead of her to intercept her – but she soon realised that there were two men – and they seemed to be identical twins. As they closed in on the frightened girl – one from the back and the other from the front, Kelly let out a scream, and suddenly she saw a car which came screeching around the bend as it travelled towards her from the south of Whitefield Road. Kelly wondered if the twins would kidnap her and put her in this approaching car, but with relief she saw it was her father's car. Before the twins could get to Kelly, the car pulled up alongside her and out got her father, Terry, and he was a big man and a former club bouncer. When the identical men saw Terry run to his daughter, the two of them ran up Ingoe Lane into the moonlit night and were soon lost to sight.

'Don't you ever go out on your own like that at this time of night!' Terry roared to his daughter, who was now in tears.

'I know, I know, it was a stupid thing to do,' Kelly sobbed, and she got into the car as her father looked towards Ingoe Lane, wondering if the two would-be abductors (or possibly rapists) would return. He intended to give them a hiding if they did.

When Kelly arrived home, she received a good

telling off from her mother, Pat, but then she also learned something very strange from her mother. Pat told her daughter, 'Your father awoke from a nightmare while you were out tonight, and he told me he saw two men who looked like identical twin brothers, watching you. He described them as having trilbies and long coats, and he was that ruffled by the bad dream, he went into your room to check if you were okay. Once he saw you weren't there, he panicked and he found the note you left on the table.'

This was probably a case of telepathy in which Terry somehow picked up on the two sinister brothers stalking his daughter as he slept, but there have been other local cases of telepathy reported to me which have occurred during waking hours in broad daylight, and the following story is a case in point. On the afternoon of Thursday, 1 June 1989, a multi-millionaire Liverpool businessman named Grahame Yardley-Noakes invited a promising 22-year-old secretary named Natasha Weldon to dinner at an upmarket restaurant on Liverpool's Hardman Street. Grahame thought Natasha had the skills to become his personal assistant, and he had chosen this tête-à-tête luncheon to tell her so. He rambled on about his preferred 'bevvy' at lunch - Latour Giraud's 1985 red Meursault, but decided on a dry sherry instead, and then he ordered guinea fowl breast with apples and Calvados and a side order of crisp bacon and veg. Natasha ordered a small bowl of Poke (pronounced "poki") – diced raw fish and seafood seasoned with soya sauce and tossed with minced green onion. While boss and secretary waited for their orders, the waiter served them their chosen drinks: Grahame opted for his medium-dry Amontillado and Natasha received a glass of Beaujolais, and then Grahame pulled a rolled-up copy of *The Times* from the briefcase leaning against the leg of the table and flipped through it to the crossword. 'Where is it now?' he muttered, running his thick index finger across the pied squares of the puzzle. 'Ah, yes – 21 across,' he said, with a lopsided smile, and glanced at Natasha. 'See if you can help me on this one. Fourteen letters altogether, grouped into two words of six and eight letters. Now, the cryptic clue is: "His cruel doom I'd mistaken for Lot's wife." Got that?'

Natasha nodded and thinned her olive green eyes as she focused on the clue.

'The third letter is a "D" and the fifth one is a "U" and it ends with the letter "E" – so any idea what this double word is? Have a look,' Grahame went to hand his secretary the newspaper.

'Sodium Chloride,' she told him.

'Eh? What's that got to do with someone's wife?' Grahame queried, his eyebrows knitted in perplexity at the answer.

Natasha grasped her glass of wine and gave her explanation. 'Lot was Abraham's nephew in the Bible, and his wife was turned into a pillar of salt by God because she looked back at the destruction of Sodom. She's not named in the Bible but Jewish scholars say her name was Edith. The crossword clue was part anagram of sodium chloride – "His cruel doom" – and sodium chloride is, of course, the chemical name of table salt.'

'You never cease to amaze me, Natasha,' said Grahame, and he pulled out his trusty Parker Premier

Noir and inked in the letters with a look of warm merriment on his face. 'Yes, that's the answer.'

At this point, Natasha noticed a couple seated at a table in a shady corner of the restaurant. The man was handsome, raven-haired, tanned, and about forty, and he wore a florid Batik shirt and pale brown trousers, and the woman sitting opposite him was about twenty years of age, possibly younger, and she was blonde, elfin-faced, and she wore a pink satin blouse with a bow at the cleavage, and a pleated peach-yellow dress with kitten-heeled shoes of the same colour. She had that spellbound look in her eyes as she stared at the face of the man, but Natasha thought the girl looked quite naive.

'Natasha,' said Grahame, and he voiced the name with a rising querying tone as he noticed that his secretary was looking at the couple, 'as you know, the firm is a fast-expanding business, and since the departure of Shirley Castor, I've been looking for a top PA of her calibre.'

Natasha took a sip of wine and latched onto Grahame with laser-like focus. 'Yes,' she said, and nodded.

Grahame continued. 'Now, I've been looking for someone with excellent secretarial and organisational skills who is accustomed to working at a very senior level, and I have also been looking for a candidate...'

As Natasha listened to her boss, his words seemed to fade away until they became a distant echo, and in her mind's eye, the secretary could now see the face of that man in the corner as he spoke to his young female partner. She could suddenly hear every word he was saying, and she somehow knew that his name was

Gareth Morris, and the young woman he was speaking to was Sally Wright; how could she know this? Natasha was very unnerved at being privy to this private knowledge. Gareth was saying to Sally: 'Sally, I think we should get away this Saturday. Get away from it all. There's a lovely guest house near the Great Orme called Clovelly House, and I want to take you there so we can be together without all the usual faces around us.'

'Where's the Great Horn?' Sally asked.

'Great Orme,' Gareth corrected her, 'it's in North Wales, just a short drive from Liverpool; you'll love it.'

And somehow, Natasha knew that Gareth wanted to push Sally to her death off the cliffs of the Great Orme...

'Natasha?' Grahame touched her hand across the table. 'You drifted off then – is everything okay?' her boss asked, and seemed concerned. 'Oh!' Natasha came out of the weird altered state of consciousness with a jolt, and then she looked at Grahame with look of great surprise. 'Yes, I'm sorry Grahame – I – I – ' she struggled to conjure up a plausible excuse to cover up the incredible experience of telepathy she'd just experienced.

Grahame turned and looked at the couple at the corner table who were now kissing, because he'd noticed how Natasha had seemed preoccupied with them a moment ago. 'Do you know them?' he asked.

'No, I don't – I – I – ' Natasha stammered, confused and a little upset at the impression she imagined she was giving to a boss who had been ready to promote her.

'Anyway,' said Grahame, and he smiled, paused, then

slapped his hand on the table and said: 'I'd like you to be my PA. What do you think? The salary would be five times your present one.'

'Why – yes, of course, I accept your very kind offer – er, thanks. Thank you. I'll put everything I've got into the new role.'

'Good – let's have a toast,' Grahame proposed, and Natasha leaned forward with her glass in her hand, and Grahame's sherry glass clinked her wine glass, and again, the secretary could hear the chilling thoughts of Gareth Morris as his inner voice said, 'I hope she dies when she hits the rocks. If she survived it could spell disaster.'

'To Natasha, may she be the greatest, most attentive PA ever!' joked Grahame in his toast.

There was a lag as Natasha turned her attention back to her boss from the psychopath in the corner, and she said, 'Oh yes, I'll be very attentive, ha!'

Gareth Morris snapped his fingers to the waiter and said, 'Bill.' The waiter brought the bill and Gareth paid it and tipped him and left holding hands with Sally, and Natasha watched them leave. They got into Gareth's yellow sports car, visible through the restaurant windows, and Natasha asked Grahame what type of car it was.

'Looks like a Lotus Europa,' he said, gazing at the flash vehicle. 'Had one around 1970, in red. Got rid of it though because my wife said she'd had bad dreams about me crashing in it. Should have kept it – it was a good runner; very reliable.'

The meals were served, and Grahame told Natasha she looked as if something was bothering her.

'Oh no, I'm fine, just still in shock at the new post,'

she told him, but her assertion just didn't wash with Mr Yardley-Noakes.

'Natasha, do you fancy telling me what's really bothering you?' Grahame asked, and he gave a little smile and dabbed his lips with the napkin. 'You've been my secretary since you were a teenager, and I've come to know your little mannerisms. I just know something ruffled you before, and it seemed to have something to do with that couple in the corner,' he said, indicating where Gareth and Sally had sat with his fork.

'Well, you'll probably think I'm nuts if I tell you,' Natasha told him, and then she gazed down into the bowl of Poke.

'Try me,' said Grahame, 'but I *know* you're anything but nuts, kid.'

'Okay, here goes,' said Natasha, and she sighed before she told her boss about the way she had somehow read the thoughts of the man in the corner as he addressed his girlfriend, and how she had ascertained that he was going to murder his girlfriend by pushing her off the Great Orme.

Grahame did not laugh at his personal assistant's strange claims, nor did he seem to disbelieve her; instead he asked her what names she had 'picked up' during the telepathic spell, and Natasha told him. 'Gareth Morris and Sally Wright,' she said.

'Very intriguing, this,' said Grahame, and he gave a little wave to the waiter, who came over immediately.

'Yes sir?' the waiter asked with a smile.

'Waiter, I think I know that couple who were seated over there before in the corner,' said Grahame. 'Can you possibly tell me if their names are Gareth and

Sally?'

'Just a moment, sir,' said the waiter, and as he walked away he said, 'I'll find out.' The waiter talked to a man behind a counter who looked in a large black book, and then seconds later the waiter returned and said, 'The man was Gareth Standing and the lady's name was Sally Wright.'

'Ah, that's it – Standing,' said Grahame, 'I got him mixed up with a fellow named Morris. Thanks for that waiter.'

'Maybe he's going under another name for some devious reason,' Natasha told her boss.

'Perhaps,' said Grahame, 'but you got the girl's full name correct, and I am – well, I am assuming you don't know her – '

'Never set eyes on her before in my life,' Natasha insisted, 'and I don't know how I *tuned into* his mind. It's quite unsettling really.'

'You can't read my mind can you?' joked Grahame.

'It was just a weird one-off type of thing,' said Natasha, 'but I suppose it's nothing to do with me now; I can't go to the police and tell them a man is about to kill his girlfriend because I overheard his thoughts; I'd be carted away.'

'Yes, but *we* could delve into this a little, couldn't we?' said Grahame with a slight smile on his face.

'You're not suggesting we should play gumshoes are you?' a surprised Natasha asked.

'I think it'd be quite exciting,' said Grahame. 'Now, can you remember where he said the hotel was near the Great Orme?'

'It was something that sounded like Clovelly – Clovelly House,' Natasha recalled.

'And it was definitely *this* Saturday?' Grahame asked.

Natasha slowly nodded, 'Yes, why?'

Grahame sipped some sherry, then told her the plan. 'What do you say to this: we book a room at this Clovelly House tomorrow evening – Friday – and see if they turn up. If they don't, then just look at it as a short break, but if they do, we could follow them up the Great Orme, and see how things develop – or do you think I've been watching too many telly detectives?'

'I do, Grahame,' replied Natasha, 'we could be putting our own lives in danger. I did sense that this man was an utter remorseless psychopath.'

'Oh come on,' said Grahame, almost roaring the words, 'where's your sense of adventure? Oh, and just in case you think your old boss is trying it on with you: we'll stay in one room in separate beds!'

'I hope so – I'm not that type of girl!' said Natasha with a blush.

And so on Friday evening Grahame drove Natasha almost 76 miles from Liverpool to the two-storey brown pebble-dashed guest house at the foot of Llandudno's Great Orme and they stayed in a spacious room in their separate beds. They went for a meal and a drink at the Randolph Turpin Pub, and Grahame said that if the enigmatic Gareth failed to show, he'd spend Saturday playing Crazy Golf and taking a ride on the trams up the Orme.

But on the Saturday morning at 10am, as Natasha was about to leave the guest house for a walk, she froze upon seeing the very same couple who had been in the Hardman Street restaurant. They'd obviously just arrived and each of them was carrying suitcases as they chatted to a clerk at the reception. Natasha turned and went up to tell Grahame about the arrival. He came down the stairs to the foyer and had a good look at the couple before returning back to his room with his PA. As luck would have it, Gareth and Sally took the room next door to the one where Grahame and Natasha were staying, and at two in the afternoon, Natasha heard the couple leaving the room, and she told Grahame, who was lying on his bed doing a newspaper crossword. He got up off the bed and put on a mackintosh and a trilby, and Natasha only put on a pair of large 'Jackie O' sunglasses and within the minute she and Grahame were tailing Gareth and Sally – who were heading up the road in the direction of the Great Orme.

'Slow down Natasha,' said Grahame, 'don't let them know we're following. Let them walk on a few hundred yards or they'll get suspicious.'

Natasha duly slowed down, looked towards the sea in the distance, then she slyly turned and watched the couple going further up the headland. The pursuit went on for almost two miles, and Eventually, Gareth and Sally reached a part of the domed limestone landmark where a roughly made dry stone wall a mere two feet in height lined the road named Marine Drive. The couple stepped over this wall and headed across a grassy slope that led to a clifftop. Gareth produced a camera and Grahame and Natasha saw him directing Sally towards the edge of the cliff. The girl stood with her back to the sea as Gareth appeared to take a snap.

'He's going to push her!' Natasha said, watching developments from about eighty yards away on Marine Drive.

'Yes, I think it's time we moved in on him,' said Grahame, and he stepped over the stone wall and walked towards the couple who were still unaware they were being watched.

Natasha saw Gareth taking another picture, and this time she could hear him say to Sally, 'Take a few steps back but be careful love; don't go too near that edge.'

The photograph was taken, and then Gareth stood next to Sally. He grabbed her, each hand on her shoulder, and he turned her so she faced the sea, and the girl screamed, sensing that he was going to push her. A 400 foot drop was just a few feet away.

'Hey!' yelled Grahame.

Gareth turned round, startled, and Natasha shouted: 'Gareth Morris isn't it? Or is it Gareth Standing?'

Sally was crawling away from him on all fours as she sobbed.

'We've already called the police!' Grahame bluffed, and he stooped and helped Sally to her feet.

'I'll kill myself first!' Gareth roared, and he walked to the edge of the cliff.

Natasha and Grahame took Sally up the grassy verge onto Marine Drive, and they could hear Gareth ranting but it was hard to make out just what he was saying.

'Why did he try to kill me?' Sally asked Grahame, and he shrugged and said, 'Come on love, we'll get you to the hotel and you'll be safe there.'

'Because you're having his baby, Sally,' Natasha found herself saying, and she did not know how she knew the girl was pregnant.

'How do you know I'm pregnant?' Sally asked, her eyes red and glistening with tears. She seemed puzzled. 'Who are you?'

'Gareth is married, Sally,' said Natasha, and she did not know where her words were coming from. 'He wanted to get rid of you because he doesn't want to be divorced from his wife – she's the daughter of a very rich man.'

'That can't be it!' cried Sally, 'Why didn't he ask me to have an abortion?'

'He's fed up of you, Sally' said Natasha, 'He's had his fun with you, and now you're a liability.'

Grahame was fascinated at his PA's sudden acquisition of this knowledge. He looked over at Gareth, who was still standing at the cliff edge, still threatening suicide.

When they all got back to the guest house, Sally seemed to be trying to convince herself that Gareth had not tried to push her off the edge of the cliff, and she even talked about getting back in touch with him because she feared he might have had some mental breakdown. Eventually Natasha persuaded the girl to go home with her to Liverpool. The murder attempt could not really be proven, but when Sally stopped deluding herself she decided to go to the police. Gareth was interviewed by a detective at his home and his wife discovered that he'd been having an affair with Sally. Gareth's wife left him and Gareth left Liverpool, never to be heard from again. Natasha never had any more telepathic spells, and to this day she doesn't know how she was able to read the minds of people she'd never met before.

From the mystery of telepathy, we come next to the intriguing ability of astral travel.

One inclement night in the 1990s, a 19-year-old Huyton lad named Tom came off his motorbike in torrential rain as he tried to negotiate that bend where Mab Lane swings into Deysbrook Lane in West Derby. He awoke in a hospital hours later and discovered he could hardly move without experiencing intense pain. He'd sustained broken legs and a serious back injury. The morphine enabled him to sleep, but Tom had a very weird dream; he rose out of his body and floated through the night. He could see the moonlit roads below and found himself drifting over a district he eventually discerned as Woolton. During his dreamy wandering through the skies of Woolton Tom noticed a girl at a window looking onto her back garden, and felt drawn to her. He somehow drifted into the room through the closed window, and saw she was a beautiful redhead of about eighteen. She was listening to the Bill Withers song *Lovely Day* on her hi-fi, and Tom saw her pick up a book entitled, *Still Life with Woodpecker*. The girl sat on her bed, reading the book, and her tabby cat looked up at Tom – as if it could see him.

A woman's distant voice called the girl: 'Taylor!' she shouted, and Tom watched as the girl rolled her eyes then shouted: 'What?' A blonde woman - possibly the girl's mum - came into the bedroom and began to talk to Taylor, and Tom now saw that the cat could definitely see him; its eyes followed him as he drifted across the bedroom. All of this didn't feel like a dream to Tom, and he considered the morbid possibility that he had died in his sleep at the hospital and had become some night-roaming ghost, and he naturally felt confused and a little scared. He looked at the window and floated out of it and back up into the air. He drifted through the night and eventually everything went fuzzy, and he awoke in pain in the hospital bed. On the following night, Tom found himself again floating outside of his body, and he visited Taylor and her cat in Woolton again. This time the girl was in her pyjamas and had her nose in a book about Marie Antoinette, and on this occasion the cat hissed at Tom, startling Taylor, who asked the feline what the matter was. Tom then floated back out the window and went down to the pavement. He saw the door number of Taylor's home – and also a suspicious-looking man in dark clothing who produced a crowbar and began to prise at the door. Tom found himself being drawn back to the hospital, where he awoke – and he called for a nurse and told her what he had seen.

'It's just been a lucid dream,' the nurse said, but Tom said it had been no dream, and that this was a matter of life and death. He eventually managed to persuade the nurse to call the police without giving her name. The police went to the Woolton address and caught the burglar red-handed as he forced the door open. A year later, Tom was shopping in town when he suddenly saw the girl he had inexplicably visited from his hospital bed. He approached her and asked if her name was Taylor, and the girl was naturally suspicious. Tom named the books she had been reading: *Still Life with Woodpecker* and *Marie Antoinette* by Antonia Fraser, and he mentioned the way the girl's tabby cat had hissed at him and he also mentioned the Bill Withers song Taylor had been listening to on her hi fi. The girl walked away a little spooked and she wondered if Tom had been somehow spying on her as she was in her bedroom, but the long arm of coincidence reached out to Taylor, and she later bumped into Tom at a party, and he told her about his supernatural visit to her bedroom, which intrigued her. They started to date, and Tom became her steady boyfriend for four years, and then the couple married.

The only explanation for the apparent detachment of Tom's consciousness from his body lies in a phenomenon called the Out-of-Body Experience (usually abbreviated as an OOBE in medical textbooks). The OOBE has been reported in patients undergoing operations in hospitals and it has even happened to people as they have been fast asleep. The occultist have stated for thousands of years that, besides the physical flesh and blood body, all humans possess a secondary body stowed away inside of their earthly body called the Astral Body, and this carries you and your soul off after physical death – but there are said to be well-documented techniques for coaxing the Astral Body out of the physical body, and this is known as Astral Projection – something I have done a few times over the years with varying results. Many years ago dozens of people visiting sick relatives at Whiston Hospital saw two luminous figures floating over the entrance area to the hospital, and these two 'ghostly men' were throttling one another and throwing punches. One figure was naked and the other wore underpants, and a taxi driver waiting to pick someone up actually recognised one of the apparitions as a well-known local 'hard-knock' named Jimmy. At that moment, Jimmy was under the knife as surgeons operated on his shoulder. The battling ghosts vanished, seconds after they were seen, and weeks later, the cabby met Jimmy and told him about his 'ghost' being seen outside the hospital. Jimmy said he had floated out of his body during his operation and had bumped into an old enemy named Mick who was also floating about. The two adversaries started to fight, and then Jimmy had woken up in bed after the op. Jimmy later discovered that Mick was lying in the next bed after his op. The two men remembered their 'shared dream' and became friends.

This chapter has looked at just a few of the unearthly talents we could all possess if we opened our minds a little and there are many more incredible abilities hiding in the human mind. I will write about them one day in a future book.

THE DEMON IN THE POOL

In the late 1990s a reclusive Liverpool-born man in the Midlands named Stephen who had won millions on the National Lottery passed away, and he left the bulk of his fortune to his 35-year-old nephew in Liverpool, a small-time thief named Dominic, who had recently been kicked out of his home by his father (for burgling the house of a relative) and was now living in his girlfriend Dionne's house in Huyton. The solicitor acting as the executor of the late Uncle Stephen's Last Will and testament faced quite a task getting hold of Dominic, who thought someone was trying to hand him a summons, and when the executor finally caught up with him, Dominic was more than pleasantly surprised to learn that he had inherited almost two million pounds. Dominic tried to open a bank account but was initially refused because of an atrocious credit history, but when he mentioned the fortune he'd inherited, he was eagerly welcomed with open arms by the bank and they tried to give him sound financial advice. The manager advised Dominic to put a million in a certain multinational financial services corporation, and he went into the ins and outs of computerized stock trading, venture capital, PEP investments and mutual funds, and at the end of the unasked-for long-winded consultation, Dominic yawned and said all he wanted to do was go down the pub and have a pint and a pie then book a fortnight's holiday in Lanzarote. Dominic went on the holiday, and when he returned his girlfriend Dionne talked him into buying a huge farmhouse near Tarbock for £500,000. The farmyard was thoroughly transformed by top landscape artists who created a beautiful sprawling garden with wisteria-festooned pergolas, an ornamental pavilion, an outdoor stucco and cement fireplace, a cast iron three-tiered fountain, and at the centre of this Eden there was a swimming pool which measured 50 feet in length and 20 feet in width. This was something Dominic had always wanted as he had won medals for swimming when he was a schoolboy.

Dominic secretly bought Dionne a Steinway grand piano, and the day it was installed at his palatial home, he blindfolded his girlfriend and led her into the lounge, and when she took the blindfold off she cried with joy as she saw the £20,000 piano decked with gladioli. She could only play a bad rendition of *Champagne Supernova* with two fingers but intended to get piano lessons. Every day, Dominic threw a party and invited friends and friends of friends over to his big flashy house, and in the summer the swimming pool parties got out of hand with drugs and drink being freely available to anyone, and a fair-weather friend of Dominic named Jason arranged an orgy – against Dominic's wishes - which went on for days. Jason claimed he was a "Luciferian" who worshipped Satan and started holding Black Masses on the property until Dominic lost his temper and knocked Jason clean out one evening. When Jason came around, he said he'd lay a Satanic curse on Dominic's property and before he left he started to spout words

Dominic found unintelligible. On the following sunny morning, all of Dominic's friends – both male and female - were already drunk and high on drugs, and they gathered in the swimming pool and started to indulge in group sex and all sorts of drunken debauchery. Dominic and Dionne watched in disgust from the poolside, and then the couple noticed something strange. In the middle of the pool, something was bubbling up from the blue-tiled floor of the natatorium – and then it looked as if something was thrashing about in the bubbling white mass. The sixteen hedonistic people participating in the aquatic orgiastic merrymaking all stopped what they were doing and saw something hideous emerge from the bubbling mass in the centre of the pool. It looked like a cross between a gargoyle and something reptilian with shiny scales, and its grotesque horned head had a huge mouth lined with sharp long fangs. A long segmented tail like that of a scorpion rose out of the water, and the "stinger" at the end of it was the size of a steak knife blade and jet black. The tail lashed out and two girls in the pool sustained terrible cuts to their bodies by the stinger. The giant unearthly beast, which rose about ten feet out the waters of the pool, let out a roaring laugh as all of the debauchees tried to get out of the water. Within minutes, naked and half-naked people were running from the farmhouse, and Dominic and Dionne also fled. When the couple returned an hour later, the beast – probably a demon – was nowhere to be seen, but a great grey stain on the floor of the swimming pool which resembled a silhouette of the entity was engrained into the tiles and could not be removed or painted over. Deciding that

Jason really had cursed him, Dominic gave thousands away to charity and turned his back on drugs and crime. He and Dionne moved from the farmhouse, went to live in a humble semi in Prescot, disowned their depraved friends and even started to attend church. The emergence of what seems to have been a demon from the swimming pool has an eerie parallel with a incident which is alleged to have involved the late David Bowie in 1976. That year, Bowie was living at an impressive art deco stuccoed house situated on six acres at 637 North Doheny Drive, Beverly Hills, California. The property was built around an oval-shaped swimming pool which could be accessed on all sides from the many rooms of the residence via sliding plate-glass doors. This was a very dark period in Bowie's life. He had just starred in a well-received film called *The Man Who Fell to Earth* and a burgeoning film career beckoned, and of course, he was also writing some of his legendary hits, but David, who had been fascinated by the occult since his youth, now had a growing interest in black magic, and he was also developing an addiction to drugs, cocaine in particular. One evening at his Hollywood residence, Bowie was curious to see a localised movement in the waters in the middle of the swimming pool which he could not account for. There was no one in the pool, and yet he could see bubbles rising up to the surface of the water in growing quantities until the centre of the pool began to hiss. The pop star was then startled to see an entity he believed to be the Devil emerge from the waters. The grinning being resembled a gargoyle, and Bowie left the cube-shaped room which housed the pool. He told his wife Angie what he'd seen and eventually he sought the services of a witch in New York who told him to buy specific books at a certain occult bookstore which contained banishing rituals and the authentic wording to genuine rites of exorcism. Bowie knew that the previous owner of his Hollywood home had been the famous Gypsy Rose Lee (born Rose Louise Hovick), the witty striptease and burlesque entertainer, and for some reason, she had installed a massive hexagram on the circular floor of one of the rooms at Bowie's residence. Had the striptease artist perhaps been a dabbler in Satanism, and had Bowie's interest in the Black Arts stirred some old evil spirits up at the house? Bowie ended up bravely tackling the demon with the books on the occult piled up on a lectern at the side of the pool. The thing in the pool emerged and began to thrash about as Bowie intoned the part of the exorcism rite which runs: "I adjure you every unclean spirit, every spectre from hell, every satanic power, in the name of Jesus Christ of Nazareth, who was led into the desert after His baptism by John to vanquish you in your citadel, to cease your assaults against the creature whom He has, formed from the slime of the earth for His own honour and glory; to quail before wretched man, seeing in him the image of almighty God, rather than his state of human frailty.'

The exorcism rite went on for over an hour and the entity in the middle of the swimming pool seemed to sink and disintegrate, until all that was left was a dark stain in the shape of something vaguely humanoid. Bowie was so spooked by the experience he left the luxurious house and it is alleged that he later learned from an estate agent that the stain at the bottom of the pool could not be removed.

An old Catholic priest once told me that where there are people with addictions – whether the addiction is to sex, or gambling or to drink or drugs – demons will sometimes move in on their prey, knowing that their victim is weakened by the monomania towards the addiction, and this might have been the case with David Bowie, who was heavily involved with drugs at the time and was also experiencing long periods of sleep-deprivation as a result. The fact that the previous occupant of the house had dabbled with Satanism was probably also a contributory factor, and Bowie did the best thing by moving out of the house. The demon that came out of the pool in Tarbock might have been the one the ancient Mesopotamians called Pazuzu – as he was always described as having a scorpion-like tail with a stinger, and he might have been summoned by Dominic's associate Jason, who was a dabbler in Satanism. That demonic entity also left a stubborn stain at the bottom of the pool, and that is one of the tell-tale signs of demons; they have touched people's backs, even in dreams, and the sleeper has later awakened to find a red handprint on their back which remains for years.

WALTON'S PEEPING LADY

On the Friday evening of 1 October, 2010, a 32-year-old woman named Jacqui was watching the final few minutes of *EastEnders* at her home on Walton's Maria Road, and she had the TV remote in her hand, ready to switch over to Granada to see *Coronation Street* when she was startled to see someone cheekily looking through the gaps in the vertical blinds of her window. It was dark out, but Jacqui thought it was a woman's face peeping in at her. She closed the blinds and in a loud voice she said, 'Nosy bastard!'

Jacqui quickly made herself a coffee and then she settled down to watch "Corrie". By then she'd forgotten all about the nosy parker outside her window. After *Coronation Street* had finished at 9pm, Jacqui looked forward to seeing *Paul O'Grady Live* - the Birkenhead-born presenter was always a scream, Jacqui thought, and she put a few sausage rolls in the microwave. Her mobile then chimed its polyphonic call tone and Jacqui could see it was her friend Lexi, who lived on nearby Buchanan Road.

Jacqui answered the call and said, 'What?'

'I drove past yours about ten minutes ago, and there was this real weird old woman, all in black, peeping through your window.'

'That wasn't ten minutes ago, it was about half an hour ago,' said Jacqui. 'I saw her and I said dead loud, "Nosy bastard!" and I hope she heard me.'

'No, this was about ten minutes ago, probably less, Jacqui, and she looked really weird. Her clothes were old fashioned, and all black. She just struck me as something weird.'

'You're not trying to say she was a ghost are you?' Jacqui asked, and gave a chuckle.

'I don't know – you'd have to have seen her Jacqui,' said Lexi, 'just something about her. I think she had her hair up in a bun and she looked pretty small.'

'What would a ghost be watching me for?' laughed Jacqui, 'I live the most boring uneventful life ever. We'll have to start going the bingo again soon and going out at the weekend Lexi or we're both going to die spinsters.'

Later that evening, Jacqui showered, and then she went downstairs to watch more telly over a glass of wine, and she dimmed the lights in the lounge and watched a sitcom called *The Inbetweeners*, which started at around ten minutes to eleven. As Jacqui watched the programme, she saw something out the corner of her eye which startled her: the silhouette of someone's head and shoulders on the vertical blinds. It was that nosy woman again, and she was trying to peep at Jacqui through a small slit where the blinds hadn't closed properly. Jacqui swore and she got up out of her comfy armchair and switched on the light, then went to the front door and unbolted it. She looked out onto Maria Road. She saw a small woman, perhaps about five feet in height, shuffling along in a black jacket and a dress which went down to her ankles.

'You nosy bastard! Keep away from my window!' Jacqui shouted after her. The woman never looked back or stopped. She disappeared around the corner of Imison Street, and then seconds later, Jacqui watched as she saw the weird little woman's face peep around the corner at her. Nearly three weeks after this, on the night of Saturday 23 October, just before 10pm, Jacqui was watching the end of *The X Factor* when she saw the same silhouette of that woman on her blinds again. Jacqui was absolutely outraged by the bizarre antics of the prying woman, and she threw herself out of her armchair and was at the front door in a second. She opened it and looked out onto a road lit by the full moon – and there wasn't a soul about. There was no sign of that woman in the odd-looking black dress, and there was nowhere she could be hiding, unless she was crouching behind one of the many parked cars in the street, and Jacqui thought this was unlikely. Jacqui went upstairs to her bedroom, stood on the window sill and swung open the top window. She kept watch from this vantage point in her darkened bedroom for about ten minutes, and then she saw the eerie peeping woman's pallid face, protruding from the corner of Trevelyan Street. As Jacqui watched, the woman flitted from Trevelyan Street and silently dashed across Maria Road – towards Jacqui's front ground floor window. Jacqui got down from the window sill and crept down the stairs to the lounge, where she could now see the distinctive silhouette of the woman. She could see her round head with bun on the top, and Jacqui again ran to the door and yanked it open, but when she looked outside she saw no one, and this really unnerved her, as she knew no one could go to ground that fast – unless they were a ghost.

On the following Saturday, Jacqui went out for a drink in town with her friend Lexi, and when the private cab dropped Jacqui off at her home at two in the morning, the driver asked her if she had seen the ghost of the "Peeping Woman".

Jacqui went cold when she heard the question. 'What do you mean?' she asked the driver.

'I've seen her a few times in this area, and people I've picked up and dropped off have told me about her,' said the cabby. 'She's been seen in Buchanan Road and Breeze Lane as well,' the driver continued, 'and I'm told she was someone who got run over years ago in the 1960s, and that she's looking for her kids or something.'

'Oh my God, I've seen her looking through my window,' said Jacqui, and she suddenly felt sober. 'Fancy telling me about all this at this hour in the morning you dickhead.'

'Ha, I'm sorry love,' said the driver, and he grinned and added, 'but my old mum used to say the dead can't hurt you – it's the living you have to watch.'

'Yes, they just scare you to death,' Jacqui replied, paying the driver. She got out the cab and said, 'Can you just hang on there until I get in?'

'Yeah, go on love,' said the driver, and he waited until Jacqui had closed her front door before he drove off.

The Peeping Lady was seen a few more times that month, but in December of that year, when heavy snow covered Walton, Jacqui could see that the woman was indeed a ghost, because her silhouette was seen moving backwards and forwards across the drawn blinds, but when Jacqui had mustered enough courage to go outside, she saw there were no footprints in the fresh layer of virgin snow. Jacqui contacted me and asked if I'd heard of the ghost and I told her I had reports going back to the 1950s. I don't think the little woman in black is the ghost of a person who was knocked down; her attire seems to indicate that she belongs to the Edwardian or Victorian era, and her identity, and her reasons for peeping through people's windows, remains a mystery to me.

THE PINK WITCH

Every now and then I receive accounts of alleged supernatural happenings which seem unbelievable, and yet there are many witnesses to them, and the following story is a good example of this. Being from the area of Grove Street in Edge Hill, I myself had heard a version of the account you are about to read, and I recall my mother telling me about it and mentioning that there was probably a rational explanation behind the alleged levitation of a double-decker bus - and when I mentioned the incident on a local radio programme around 2009, the radio station's telephone switchboard went into meltdown as scores of people called to give their version of the weird incident – or should I say *incidents* because the levitation of a bus is alleged to have happened twice. What follows is an amalgamation of the many calls to the station as well as material from an interview with the bus driver involved in the bizarre case.

One pleasantly warm Saturday afternoon in May 1972, a red-haired girl of about 13 named Lily boarded a double-decker bus on Brownlow Hill. The girl was smartly dressed in a pink blouse and matching skirt, and she paid the fare to Penny Lane then sat at the back of the bus on the bottom deck. Stan Jenkins, the bus driver, thought the girl seemed very shy and softly spoken, and Stan's friend Tony Holland, an off-duty driver who was standing by the cab, saw her sitting with her head bowed, and kept an eye on her because three rowdy lads were already looking at the girl. As the bus travelled along Grove Street, in the Edge Hill district of the city, Tony was gabbing away to Stan about some horses he'd backed at the bookies, and he was standing with his back to the windscreen of the bus. Tony suddenly noticed that two "yobbos" (as he called troublemaking hooligans) were taunting Lily, and one of them tried to stick chewing gum in the timid girl's hair. Tony yelled at the yobs, telling them to 'pack it in' – and he was about to go and tackle them when the bus rocked as if it had careered into something. Stan was thrown forward, almost butting the windscreen, Tony fell to the floor, and the passengers screamed. The bus then *rose about six feet into the air* and glided along at about 20 mph with its wheels turning. Stan was confused and powerless to do anything about the inexplicable levitation of a bus that weighed around 13 imperial tons, but about 10 seconds later the vehicle slowly descended and accelerated along the road as the turning wheels gained traction on the macadam. There was complete pandemonium among the scared and bewildered passengers – but that red-haired girl Lily sat there smiling. A police motorcyclist cut in front of the bus (which had now stopped) and he dismounted the bike and went to talk to Stan. The lawman said 'What in

God's name do you think you're doing?'

'I don't bleedin' know, officer,' Stan fumed at the silly question, 'the bus took off! I had nowt to do with it.'

'Don't talk to me in that tone,' the policeman cautioned, 'it's obvious that you must have hit something in the road.'

'Look, I'm going to see if my passengers are okay!' Stan shouted to the motorcycle cop, and he left the cab to tend to people who had been badly shaken by the strange experience. Everyone, including Tony, was thankfully unharmed. Stan tested the engine and the brakes of the bus and saw that they were in working order, and the vehicle continued on its way with every passenger talking about the extraordinary levitation for the remainder of their journeys. Back at the bus depot, no one believed Stan and Tony's amazing story, and Stan himself told me that he couldn't blame them, as he would not have believed what happened to him if he hadn't been there in person.

A fortnight later, again on a Saturday afternoon, that red-headed girl in the pink outfit got on the bus again, and this time, a lad of about eighteen sat next to Lily and curled his arm around her. Two witnesses said the young man put his hand on Lily's bosom and made some crude remark to her. Seconds later, as the bus was travelling past the Liverpool Girls' College on Grove Street, Edge Hill, the bus suddenly flew up into the air, and this time the front end of the vehicle went up first, and then the back part also rose up. On this occasion the vehicle remained stationary in mid air for a few seconds, about ten feet off the ground, and it moved back and forth for a few moments, throwing the passengers and driver about. The lecherous youth who had groped Lily was thrown to the floor. This time, after the bus came down, a distressed-looking Lily ran to Stan and asked to be let off, and Stan, who intuitively sensed the girl was somehow responsible for the levitation of his bus, asked Lily: 'You did that, didn't you?'

The girl turned her face away and never replied. As soon as Stan opened the doors of the bus, Lily leaped off the vehicle and fled, running up Grove Street and turning the corner to Myrtle Street within seconds. An elderly passenger named Nelly Wright told Stan that she lived in the same neighbourhood as the girl, and she said that her name was Lily, and Nelly claimed that the girl and her mother were said to be witches. This assertion intrigued Stan, who felt that there was indeed something very odd about the red-headed girl. Nelly said that Lily and her mother had originally lived in the Dingle but were driven out the district because neighbours hounded them with accusations of laying curses on people. Stan never saw the girl again, but the two incidents involving the levitation of his bus played on his mind for decades.

I mentioned the story of the gravity-defying bus in my *Liverpool Echo* column "Tales from the Past" and received a lot of feedback from the reading public regarding Lily the alleged witch. The general consensus from the many readers who contacted me about Lily was that she was known as "the Pink Witch" as there were rumours that the girl had supernatural powers and always dressed in pink. The rumours had started as whispered accusations by the neighbours of the girl at her little terraced home on Kedleston Street in the

Dingle. The janglers would stand on their doorsteps fuelling the rumour mills that were churning out slanderous stories about the sinister mother and daughter. The chin-waggers and tattletales claimed that the witches covered their ears when church bells were ringing on Sundays and the daughter had been seen hugging a weeping willow in Princes Park. An eccentric old man in Kedleston Street, upon hearing this, went to fetch a hatchet and declared, 'Then I must destroy the witch's tree, root and branch!'

The unbalanced pensioner was later apprehended by a policeman in Princes Park as he was attacking a weeping willow. The gossipers thought it disgraceful that the young witch Lily did not seem to attend school and one busybody named Mrs Hughes claimed that Lily was a prostitute and that she had seen the girl's mother admitting all sorts of men into the house after dark. After making this outrageous claim, Mrs Hughes suffered a stroke that left her unable to speak, and her sister-in-law also became lame in her left leg. People believed that the women had been struck by malevolent spells cast by the mother and daughter for defaming Lily.

The most interesting information regarding the Pink Witch came from a reader named Tony Marshall Holt. Tony was fourteen at the time of the "witch scare" and lived a few streets away from Lily in the Dingle, and one sunny day in August 1972, he was walking along Kedleston Street with his dog – a huge troublesome Alsatian named Prince – when the animal turned on him and bit at the hand that was holding its leash. Tony withdrew his hand reflexively and the leash slipped from his grasp. Prince ran to the first person he saw – Lily – and Tony, knowing how aggressive the dog was, raced after it bellowing its name. Lily stopped stock-still and the Alsatian jumped up at her, but instead of sinking its fangs into the girl, it began to lick her face, and Lily said something to the dog and it fell down at her feet and rolled over so it was on its back, presenting its belly to her, and a smiling Lily stroked Prince's belly and addressed it with the type of silly babble grown-ups utter when they speak to babies.

Tony was absolutely dumbfounded at the way the huge Alsatian was like putty in the girl's hands. When he tried to grab its leash, Prince growled at him and hid behind Lily.

'He just wants a bit of love and attention,' Lily told Tony, and then she laughed as the dog's head protruded between her knees with the hem of her skirt over its eyes, and she said to it, 'you're just a great big baby aren't you?'

'Watch him, he's vicious,' Tony warned Lily, and close-up he noticed how beautiful the girl was; long deep-red hair, freckles, slightly turned up nose, true-blue eyes, and rose-red lips. He fell for her there and then but felt he'd never have a chance with someone as beautiful as her; she *had* to have a boyfriend.

Prince refused to go back to Tony, who told Lily that the dog belonged to his father – who didn't even know he'd taken the dog out.

'Come on Prince, you've got to go home,' Lily said, and she stooped down and took hold of the dog's leash and she followed Tony home. Tony had to bring Lily into the hallway, where she handed the dog over to him, and then, as she left, the Alsatian barked furiously and almost knocked Tony over as it tried to go after the girl. Lily giggled and closed the door behind her, and Tony hoped he'd see her again. He deliberately walked up and down Kedleston Street each day for a few days until he saw the beautiful redhead. She was wearing a pink outfit like last time and in Tony's teenaged eyes she was a vision of loveliness. She remembered him and asked how Prince was. 'Oh, he still doesn't like me, or my dad;' Tony answered, and then he said, 'where are you going?'

'To the park,' Lily told him, and smiled as she passed Tony.

'Can I come with you?' he found himself asking, and thought she'd she say 'no,' but instead she nodded and answered: 'If you want.'

'Don't go with her Tony, she's a witch!' shouted Joey Conroy, a swaggering boy Tony went to school with. He was on the other side of the road with a bag of sweets in his hand.

Tony ignored Joey and he walked alongside Lily, feeling as if he'd won the pools. 'My name's Tony by the way,' he told Lily.

'My name's Lily,' the girl told him, and she seemed to blush.

The teens went to Princes Park, and Lily said: 'Are you wondering why that boy called me a witch?'

Tony shook his head with a puzzled expression, 'No – Joey Conroy just says stupid things all the time.'

'My mother and I are just different, that's all,' Lily told Tony, who didn't have a clue what she was talking about. He was besotted by Lily, and was trying to think of things to say to her. He hadn't had much experience of talking to girls in this way.

A sparrow startled Tony as it flew to Lily and started

to circle her. The girl held out her hand and the little bird landed on her index finger and chirped loudly. Lily whistled back at the bird, and smiled. Tony could see that she had a lovely way with animals, whether it was with galumphing Prince or this tiny sparrow. The two teens ended up sitting against the thick trunk of tree in the park with a view of the serpentine lake, and they said little, and at one point, Tony reached out and held Lily's hand. She didn't turn to look at him, but looked straight ahead at the lake and gave a low chuckle that was obviously forced. Eventually the skies turned pigeon grey and a chilly wind started to blow. Lily got to her feet and so did Tony, and she wriggled her hand out of his so she could adjust her pink jumper. She reached out for his hand again and they walked out of the park linking with the wind stirring her red hair.

'Do you want to come to our house?' Tony asked.

'Not today, I have things to do,' Lily replied, 'maybe tomorrow?'

'Prince will be chuffed seeing you,' said Tony.

Lily squeezed his hand. 'I promise I'll go round to yours tomorrow; what street do you live in?'

'Chillingham Street, not far from where you live,' said Tony, and then he walked on with Lily a few yards and asked: 'So, are we going together now?'

'Going together?' Lily queried. 'You mean courting?'

'Yeah, like boyfriend and girlfriend,' said Tony, trying to clarify the meaning of his question.

'I suppose so, yes,' Lily told him.

'Come here,' Tony said to her and pulled her into his arms. He was 14 and almost six feet in height already, and she was about 5 foot 3 inches. He stooped to kiss her and closed his eyes, and the wind from the river made her hair stroke the side of his face. It was a moment in time that would live forever in his memory.

They went steady from that day, and as the weeks went on and their love for one another became stronger, Tony heard more and more about Lily and her mother being witches. He had met Lily's mother Mrs Pennythorne, and although she did dress in black and had jet black hair and huge eyes, she did not strike him as anything remotely supernatural – but she did seem a bit eccentric. When he had visited Lily's home, her mother had only allowed him to talk to Lily in the hallway – he was not invited into the living room. Tony had asked Lily where her father was and all the girl told him in reply was that he left home when she was three and never returned.

Then something very odd happened which made Tony realise that Lily had some very intriguing knowledge about supernatural matters. In the middle of January 1973, Tony went down for breakfast one morning to find his father close to tears. 'Your mother's left me, lad,' he told his son, and he showed him the rambling letter he'd found on the mantelpiece. The gist of the letter, written by Mrs Marshall Holt was that she had found a man she loved and she had gone to live with him.

'She's left us? Where's she gone?' Tony asked his father. The boy was a slow reader and he had to read some parts of the "Dear John" letter twice to understand what had happened. His father got a handkerchief out and dabbed his eyes, and in a choked up voice he told his son: 'I don't know why she's gone and left me; I gave her everything she wanted.'

Tony told Lily about his mother leaving home for another man, and the girl said she sensed that there was something 'not quite right' about the sudden departure of Tony's mother. She asked Tony if she could see the note his mother had left, and Tony asked why, but Lily said: 'Tony, please just trust me and get the note. I'll explain later.'

Tony brought the note to Lily's home and in the hallway (the only place where Tony was allowed in the house) Lily read the note, and then she held it in her hands as she closed her eyes.

'What are you doing?' Tony asked.

Lily didn't answer; her long fair eyelashes quivered a little. A minute went past, and then Lily opened her eyes and said, 'Well, your mum hasn't moved that far from home, not even half a mile; she's in – let me see...' the girl pointed to something mid air as she tried to get her bearings. 'She's in a house over that way, by a church – and I know that church – St Michael's. Your mum is in a big house by St Michael's Church, and she was forced to go to that house by a very nasty man.'

'But how can you know this, Lily?' Tony asked, and now he naturally wondered if all those rumours about Lily and her mother were true after all; was the girl he loved more than anything in this world – a witch?

Lily's blue eyes looked deep into Tony's brown eyes and she posed a very unnerving question he was not prepared for: 'Tony, will you still love me if I tell you that I can do things that some would call witchcraft?'

'Witchcraft?' Tony seemed a bit taken aback.

'Yes, that's probably the best word to use,' Lily told him. 'Do you still love me?'

'Yeah I do,' Tony replied, 'so are you saying you're a witch?'

Lily shrugged. 'I suppose so; does it matter? I don't fly around on a broomstick or put frogs in cauldrons and all that.'

'Is your mum one as well?' asked Tony.

Lily nodded, and then she walked into Tony and rested the left side of her head against his chest and his arms enfolded her. He kissed the top of her head.

'I don't care what you are, Lily – I love you,' Tony solemnly affirmed.

'And I love you,' she said, and then she looked up at his face and said, 'so now I know where your mum is, and I think she was made to leave your dad by a male witch – and before you ask he's got nothing to do with me.'

'A male witch?' said Tony, 'What would he want my mum for?'

'Well, she's probably very pretty, and these witches sometimes do this. They see someone they like and they put a spell on them and make the person come to them. It goes against my beliefs and my mum's beliefs, because we believe in free will – that a person should be able to freely choose who they love.'

'Well, if what you say is true, can you break the spell and get my mum back?' Tony asked, and hugged Lily.

'I can't do it on my own,' admitted Lily, 'I'll have to ask my mum to help. Just leave it to us, and we'll see what happens.'

The next morning at seven o'clock, Tony was awakened by someone knocking heavily at the front door of his home. He dragged himself out of bed, but before he left his bedroom he heard his father's heavy footsteps pass the landing outside as he went down to answer the early caller.

The front door was unbolted and yanked open and Tony's mother fell into the house in tears. Her husband caught her and took her into the living room. She cried for what seemed like half an hour, but it must have only been a few minutes, and all the time Tony's father kept handing Mrs Marshall Holt disposable hankies and he would say, 'It's okay love, it's okay,' as he handed her the tissues. Eventually Tony's mum stopped crying and she told a very strange story. She recalled waking up the night before with an urge to get dressed and to get away from the house. She had obeyed her strange impulses and had walked the streets for what seemed like miles in a state of trance. She had almost been run down by a car at one point as she staggered across a road like a sleepwalker. At last she came to a large white detached house, and a bald man with a van dyke type of beard had come out of the house and made a beckoning gesture to her. She had gone into the house and he had guided her to his bedroom. Tony's mum had then found that she was so besotted with the man, she had stayed with him until two women turned up at the house – a *young woman* and an older one – and they had spoken what sounded like Latin to the bald man, and he had collapsed. 'The funny thing is that the young woman looked like our Tony's girlfriend, Lily,' recalled Tony's mum, and she said that the next thing she knew, she was walking the streets, and all of the intense feelings of love for the strange old man had completely gone, but she felt as if he was following her.

Of course, Tony's father believed that his wife had suffered a nervous breakdown, and he called out the family doctor. The doctor said he was no psychiatric expert but he could not see any signs of a mental illness in Mrs Marshall Holt.

Tony immediately called at Lily's house and thanked her for bringing his mother back. She told Tony that the male witch who had tried to take his mother was now contacting his coven, and they would try to take revenge on her and her mother, so they were ready to leave the area.

'Leave?' Tony asked, quite stunned by Lily's words, 'Where are you going?'

'I can't tell you yet, because *he'd* find out, but when I get to my new home, I'll write to you, Tony, I promise.'

But Tony never heard from Lily Pennythorne again, and as the weeks went by, he would hardly sleep and he would lay heartbroken in his bed. Tony's mother and his friends told Tony he'd had a narrow escape from being mixed up with witches, but Tony told them he would never find a girl like Lily again. He eventually found another girlfriend two years later, and ended up marrying her, but Tony still has dreams about Lily even today.

THE CASE OF THE SUAVE ABDUCTOR

Despite 13 million CCTV cameras tracking our every movement, in pubs, shops, schools, football grounds, on the roads and even in churches, a record number of Britons are vanishing. The Missing People charity says that around 270,000 people in the UK vanish each year – the equivalent of almost half the population of Liverpool. A sizeable percentage of these vanishing people are found – eventually - and many will have voluntarily dropped off the grid for a variety of personal reasons, but some 20,000 people each year go missing without a trace and *stay* missing, and I often wonder if some of these absent people have vanished because of paranormal reasons – perhaps through being abducted by someone or something out there. Over the years, I have received many strange accounts that seem to collectively refer to a particular being who seems obsessed with either attempting to snatch females or stealing from them. I'll start at the beginning.

In April 1965, a pretty 20-year-old secretary at a Liverpool solicitor's office named Erica Watts went on her lunch break and decided to call upon her friend Toni, who worked at a shop on School Lane, near to the Bluecoat Chambers. As Erica walked up the lane, she saw something that left her dumbfounded. The head and right shoulder of a man in a black suit appeared out of thin air, as if he was looking out the doorway of a room that made everything inside of it invisible. The man had wild staring eyes, and as Erica tried to rush past him he made a grab at her and the secretary slapped his face and hurried away. Had the man somehow used an arrangement of mirrors to create the illusion of peering out of a hole in space, and was it part of some *Candid Camera TV Show* type of prank? Erica dismissed this possibility; even the most accomplished member of the Magic Circle could not have staged a trick like that. Erica looked back and saw the maniacal man's apparently disembodied head draw back and vanish into the 'invisible' doorway. Erica never told Toni what she had just witnessed because she knew her friend would question her sanity. Erica was at a complete loss to explain just who the weird man was and how he had made part of his body invisible. The secretary avoided School Lane when she returned to work after her break, and went the long way round to the solicitor's office via Church Street. If that weird man had kidnapped Erica and pulled her into that invisible room, would her disappearance have been dismissed as just another unsolved mystery – of which there are so many?

Erica contacted me years later when she heard me mention a very similar case of a man peering at women from what appeared to have been a window into our dimension. The incident in question took place in Liverpool city centre in 1983. In March of that year, a 30-year-old woman named Heidi Williams was looking in the window of a menswear store named Harold Ian on Lime Street when she noticed something quite bizarre. Reflected in the window of the shop, Heidi saw the appearance of a dark rectangle behind her, just to her right, and she reflexively turned to see what it was. Out of the solid black oblong, a man emerged in a black suit, white shirt and a dark tie. He was about six feet in height, had short dark hair and he smiled at Heidi as he reached out towards her. The rectangular area of blackness he was leaning out from was like a doorway that was standing on the pavement of Lime Street with no frame around it nor any supporting walls – in other words, it was an impossible doorway, and the man leaning out from it tried to grab Heidi's wrist, but she drew back with such force, her back hit the window of the Harold Ian store. At this point, a young couple coming out of the cinema next door to the shop saw the man lunging out from the mind-boggling doorway, and the eerie man in the suit looked left at the couple, before backing into the doorway, which suddenly shrunk to a point in an instant. The couple looked at one another, then glanced at Heidi, who said, 'He tried to grab me!'

'What was that?' the young lady asked her partner, 'A ghost?'

'I haven't a clue,' he said, and the couple walked around the spot where the mind-blowing spectacle had taken place, and they walked up Lime Street, joined by Heidi, who kept looking back at the spot. The incident really shook Heidi. She had never been a person who had ever given any thought to ghosts and anything remotely metaphysical, and she often wondered who that man had been and what he had wanted her for.

In 1981, a 23-year-old woman named Claudia left a clothes store called Byzantium on Bold Street when she witnessed something very spooky. The woman walking about twelve feet ahead of her had her handbag snatched by a hand that thrust out of mid air.

That hand was attached to an arm clad in black material with a white cuff. The woman turned around startled, and the supernatural sneak-thief had vanished along with the bag. Claudia told the victim what she had seen and the two women then heard disembodied laughter nearby. Was it from the would-be abductor Erica had encountered 16 years before? Perhaps he was the very same smart-suited man who would try to grab Heidi Williams on Lime Street as she looked into the window of the Harold Ian store two years later in 1983. I have a feeling it *is* the same man and he certainly gets around – in time *and* space. One warm September night around 11.50pm, a man – described as tall and wearing a black suit, a white shirt and a black tie - asked a girl named Izzy McNally if she had a light as she left the White Star pub in Rainford Gardens one night in 2016. The girl rummaged through her handbag and the smooth-talking man said to her, 'Take your time, miss,' and he grinned with what looked like a cheroot between his perfect white teeth. Izzy thought he looked around 35 to 40 years of age, and he was wearing an unusual sweet-smelling cologne. Izzy located the lighter, lifted it to the man's cheroot – and glancing at his striking blue eyes, she found herself unable to move. Izzy could not budge an inch, and she could not even inhale to breathe, which made her panic. The paralysed girl could hear her friends shouting her name somewhere close – as if they couldn't see her. The stranger looked away from Izzy for a moment, and with a look of annoyance at something, he told her: 'You're one of the lucky ones,' and then he vanished, and Izzy seemed to snap out a hypnotic spell. She stumbled backwards against the wall of the pub and started to cry. Her friends gathered about Izzy in a half circle and asked her where she'd been and they also wanted to know why she was crying. When Izzy told them what had happened, one of her friends asked the girl if she'd taken any strange pills off anyone. Izzy shook her head and said, 'No, listen, on my baby brother's life, a weird man stood there and asked me for a light and when I lifted the lighter to him, I couldn't move.'

'I saw him love,' said a man in his sixties, standing by the semi-circle of young people. 'I've seen that fellah before.'

'Oh my God, did you see him?' Izzy asked the man with great relief, and to her friends she said, 'See? It really did happen.'

The man said something chilling. 'Listen kids, I'm not trying to scare you or anything, but that man in the suit's been seen for years, and some think he's the Devil, like. I know that sounds daft in this day and age, but you know what? There have been that many cases of people just vanishing off the face of the earth, and who knows eh?'

'So he's been seen before?' one of Izzy's sceptical male friends asked the mature gentleman. 'And did you see him, like?'

'Yeah, listen son, I know you think you're taking the piss – ' said the man, a little ruffled by the young man's smirking face.

'I'm not taking the mickey, mate,' said the young man.

'Listen, I don't care,' said the middle-aged man, 'but to answer your question: yes I have seen him a few times over the years and I've heard weird stories about him. He's not one of us – not human – because he never changes. He always looks about thirty-odd, and I guarantee when you're all my age, he'll still be knocking about. He's always dressed immaculately, and in my mind I'm inclined to agree that he's evil, like.'

'What stories did you hear about him?' Asked another of Izzy's friends, and she kept stifling a laugh behind her hand.

The man in the last third of his life started walking away, and he said, 'Keep together, and get off the streets this time of night – go to a club or whatever. He might come back.'

The man then walked away and one of Izzy's friends shouted after the man: 'Watch he doesn't get *you* mate!'

Izzy said she wanted to go straight home, and despite being called a party pooper, she convinced two of her friends to go home to her flat with her and she hailed a hackney cab on Stanley Street. Had Izzy's friends not been so jokily sarcastic and bad-mannered to the stranger, he might have told them more about the mysterious suited enigma.

And finally, although the menacing man in the black suit did not put in an appearance in the following strange account, I do find the reference to an unfathomable rectangular opening in space very intriguing. This incident happened in December 2010, about a week before Christmas, and a thick blanket of snow had covered most of the North West, including Liverpool. A 12-year-old Wavertree boy named Adam left his home on Bristol Road at 11am and went to call on his friend Jack, who lived on Colville Street, about a mile away. The journey necessitated a short-cut through "The Mystery" (the local nickname for

Wavertree Playground because the identity of the philanthropist who had donated the park had been a mystery for years) – and upon this wintry morning a very strange mystery was about to unfold. Adam entered the park via the grandiose entrance between the towering black stone gateposts on the eastern side of Wavertree Playground – on Prince Alfred Road, and trudged down the path (which was very hard to see because it lay under a deep ivory blanket of snow). When Adam had covered about 300 yards down this path, he noticed a light to his right which turned out to be a rectangle of blue and green shapes. The light was not some reflection of the sun, as the sun was buried in the grey clouds at this time, and was lying low in the south. The boy's curiosity naturally drew him to the rectangle, which he estimated to be as high as a standard doorway – about six feet and six inches, but twice as wide as a normal doorframe – about four feet and six inches. What Adam saw when he wandered nearer to the rectangle was baffling and almost magical in the child's eyes; through the rectangle, Adam could see the park and the buildings beyond its railings as they'd appear on a sunny summer's day under the canopy of a clear blue sky. He could see the Rose Villas, the elegant stuccoed townhouses of Prince Alfred Road, and the Wavertree Gardens tenements as they'd appear on a hot noon day in July. They looked so bright, Adam had to thin his eyes, and he could feel a warm zephyr coming through the implausible yet manifestly plain rectangular door in the air. He could even detect a sweet fragrance of distant flowers and the stirring aroma of freshly-mown grass. He heard the far-off echoing glockenspiel music of an ice-cream van

– it was the *Match of the Day* theme. He walked a few feet and took another look at the buildings beyond the north-east perimeter of Wavertree Playground – and he could see that outside of the rectangle of summertime, the Rose Villas and those listed buildings on Prince Alfred Road had snow-covered roofs and a bleak leaden greyness to them. Adam gingerly kicked through the snow and came within a few feet of the strange doorway into summer, and his heart jolted, for he saw something he had not noticed before – a size 5 32-panel black and white plastic-skinned football lying in the hot grass, and it looked brand spanking new. The cautious side of his brain warned him not to go through that astonishing doorway, but the childish, devil-may-care part of his psyche urged him to see what it was like – just one step forward and he'd be in summer – an instant hot holiday from this cold and snowy park.

'Don't! Don't go in there, lad!' said a deep adult voice behind Adam.

The boy turned, startled, to see a man as old as his grandfather in a green parka and a brown woollen hat. He had a large black Labrador on a leash, and the animal was looking at that framed summer mirage.

'Get away from it, lad,' said the man, and clouds of ghostly exhalations issued from his mouth as he spoke. 'It'll close up in a minute; step back a bit.'

'What is it?' the boy asked the stranger, and then he looked back at the incomprehensible entrance to what looked like midsummer. 'It's mad isn't it?' Adam mumbled, but then the vivid bright scene within the rectangle shimmered the way the reflected still image of a tree on the surface of a pond does when a ripple from a tossed stone disturbs it. And then the whole rectangle snapped instantly into a point of sparkly golden light which went out in a heartbeat. The old man and Adam looked at the long line of melted snow where the rectangle had touched the ground.

'If you'd gone to get that ball, and that thing would have shut on you, God knows what would have become of you,' said the old man, and his dog sniffed Adam's right shoe.

'What was it, though?' Adam asked, and he found himself too scared to even touch the sleeping blades of grass protruding from that line of melted snow with the toe of his shoe.

'I've seen it before,' said the old man, 'sometimes it shows up over there by the gates. I think it's a trap of some sort.'

'A trap?' Adam felt very fazed by this weird suggestion. 'To trap *me*?'

'To trap anyone who's curious,' said the man, 'curiosity killed the cat, didn't it?'

'Who are they though?' Adam asked, 'How could they make something like that?'

'I don't know,' said the old dog-walker, 'but listen lad, if you ever see that thing again, just keep on walking and stay well away from it.'

Adam told his friend Jack about the strange incident, and Jack called him a fibber at first, then seeing how angry Adam became at this accusation, Jack realised his friend had obviously experienced *something* - and he pleaded with Adam to go to Wavertree Playground to see if the "doorway" had come back, but wary of the old man's warning, Adam refused to go.

The police file is still open on another truly baffling

disappearance. This one took place in the North West on Monday 9 March 1970. That day, 13-year-old Wallasey schoolboy David McCaig kissed his mother Margaret goodbye and set off on a short bicycle ride to his school – but he never arrived and he has not been seen since. His prized blue bicycle was later found in Rake Lane Cemetery and his cycle cape was found lying in a disused hen coop nearby on Thirlmere Street. There was an unsubstantiated claim that children had found the bike at Thirlmere Street and, unaware of the strange fate of its owner, they had ridden it and later dumped it in the cemetery. 'It was as if the ground had opened up and swallowed him,' said one policeman working on the perplexing case, and the missing boy's mum said of the weird disappearance, 'I'm bewildered. It's the sort of thing you read about in the newspapers - but you never think it can happen to you. I just don't know what to think. I'm so dizzy with thinking.'

One of the last things David McCaig said to his mother before he vanished off the face of the earth was, 'Must clean my boots, mum. I'm playing rugby for the school tomorrow.' The lad was also looking forward to a date with his first girlfriend at the cinema at the weekend. When children go missing, there is usually some hint – some indication, however subtle, of what has happened to them, but in the case of David McCaig it's like footprints in the snow that suddenly come to a dead halt. If he had run away from home, he'd have needed money, yet he left behind twelve pounds in his money box. He was seen by a friend pedalling to school in a built-up area yet nobody saw any abduction take place. It was literally a case of now you see him, now you don't. Thirty-five detectives were put on the McCaig case, and there was the usual wide-scale police search, house to house enquiries and police frogmen even searched pits in Moreton, but David McCaig's body was never found and many decades later the disappearance remains unsolved. Superintendent Stanley Fisher, the man who headed the first investigation into the disappearance of David McCaig, admitted that it was the most baffling case in a career that spanned three decades, and the second investigation into the case started in 1973, coordinated by Detective Superintendent Des Green, Detective Inspector Bill Griffiths and Detective Inspector Alan Rimmer, but that investigation also petered out. Was David McCaig the victim of an abductor who was either an opportunist or perhaps a schemer who had meticulously planned the boy's abduction for some time? Or was the Wallasey teenager taken by something supernatural? Hopefully we'll know more one day.

We live in a world of over seven billion people, and a sizeable fraction of humanity goes missing without a trace each year. Some disappearances have even taken place in the vicinity of the ubiquitous CCTV cameras we are now oblivious to. Take the case of Brian Shaffer, a 27-year-old medical student at Ohio State University who vanished into thin air in the early hours of an April morning in 2006 near the entrance of a bar. A CCTV camera recorded him talking to two women shortly before he vanished. The camera recorded Brian entering the Ugly Tuna bar, but the student was never seen leaving the bar on any of the other CCTV cameras which covered every possible exit – and he has not been seen to this day. Of course, we have higher profile disappearances such as the Madeleine McCann case, which, at the time of writing, remains unsolved, as does the bizarre disappearance of 23-year-old Corrie McKeague, an RAF Regiment gunner and medic who went missing after a night out in the early hours of 24 September 2016 at Bury St Edmunds. McKeague entered a cul-de-sac in the town, and it was proven that he could not have left this bounded area without being recorded by one of the many CCTV cameras operating in the immediate vicinity, and yet he has not been seen or heard from since. His mobile phone was tracked travelling north east from the cul-de-sac for 12 miles, but no trace of the RAF man has ever been found. These are just a few of the many baffling disappearances that are taking place around us all the time. Some of these disappearances will undoubtedly be explained one day when new evidence comes to light and certain confessions are made, but some disappearances simply cannot be solved – and even hard-boiled detectives working on those types of cases have described them as odd. Could some higher intelligence in another dimension be taking some human beings, perhaps as specimens for some scientific survey? Or could time travellers with a criminal bent - perhaps just decades ahead of us - be visiting the past to kidnap people for the same sinister reasons kidnappers have today – to torture, kill or sexually assault the victim? That's a chilling possibility, and in the meantime, the mysterious disappearances will continue...

THE CHRISTMAS RING MYSTERY

The strange case of the Christmas Ring started one freezing Wednesday morning in the December of 2014. A 22-year-old Liverpool John Moores University student and part-time busker named Ceri Woodhall was returning to her flat on Bennett's Hill, Oxton, after the daily visit to the local musical instruments shop (where she tortured herself by playing a Rickenbacker she couldn't afford). On her way home, Ceri saw the removal men taking furniture and shelves out of the house next-door-but-one to the Pickfords van, and something small and glittery fell from an upturned leather wing back chair one of the removal men was carrying. It looked like a ring. Ceri made a split-second decision which shocked her – she picked up the ring – and said nothing. She walked into the house where her flat was located up a steep flight of stairs, picked up a bundle of envelopes (all containing bills) from the parcel shelf in the vestibule hall, and then the weird little man who lived downstairs – Mr Stroud – came out of his flat and smiled up at Ceri before he left the house.

Ceri gave a brisk nod of acknowledgement to the old man and went to her door, aching to look at the ring. She went into the flat and was surprised to see her flatmate Danica stretched out on the sofa, looking at something on eBay on her iPad. She was supposed to be at the café, where she worked part-time. It transpired that Danica had been sent home because the café owner had received an anonymous telephone tip-off about an impending visit from a health inspector, so he'd shut the place down for a week to clean the joint up.

Ceri showed Danica the ring she'd more or less stolen. It looked like an old engagement ring of the type Ceri's mum wore – but Danica disagreed, and seemed to know what she was talking about as she screwed her eyes up and had a close look at the ring. She told Ceri: 'That's Art Deco, and it's got a millgrained edge setting, that has.'

'Shurrup,' Ceri grinned, and thought Danica was having her on. 'You don't know the first thing about jewellery and diamonds.'

'Er, my uncle's a jeweller I'll have you know,' replied Danica, handing the ring back to her friend, 'and he used to show me the diamonds in his shop. That's worth a few bob that. Hey hang on, I've got a jeweller's eyepiece somewhere.' Danica threw the iPad on the sofa and went to rummage in her room. Ceri had a fit of laughter when Danica returned with the monocle magnifier wedged in her left eye. She took a look at the Art Deco ring, and immediately noticed something odd – there was a peculiar flaw in the diamond in the form of a shadowy number of facets which created the grey silhouette of a man in a hammer-tail coat. Ceri had a look through the eyepiece and saw him too. 'It's called pareidolia,' said Danica, 'when you see faces or patterns in things like clouds, or the Man in the Moon.'

'He looks like a butler in that coat,' said Ceri, 'wonder how much it's worth?'

'Not much with a flaw like that in it,' opined Danica, 'probably just of sentimental value to someone.'

'Well I like it, ' Ceri slid the ring on her middle finger and it fitted perfectly. The girls went to window-shop in Birkenhead, and when they returned home, Ceri got the shock of her life. Laid out on the sofa was the very Rickenbacker guitar she had been strumming at the musical instruments shop that morning, and it still had its £2,399 price tag on it.

'Who's been in here?' asked Danica, eyeing the costly electric guitar. In a daze, Ceri picked up the Rickenbacker and slowly explained to her roommate how she had dreamt of owning that instrument for over a year. Danica checked the rooms, imagining some thief was lurking about. There was no one hiding anywhere in the place - so who had gained access to the flat to drop off a guitar worth thousands, only to leave again? It didn't make sense.

About an hour after this, the girls decided to go to a café and in the hallway of the house they bumped into the elderly neighbour Mr Stroud, and he said a curious thing to the students.

'The man who left your guitar told me his name was Mr Roby,' said Stroud, and he wiped his glistening blue eye with a handkerchief and sniffled.

'A Mr Who?' Ceri asked, puzzled at the mention of the name.

'Roby,' replied the old man, adding: 'he was a very debonair gentleman, and you know, he reminded me of the old butler my uncle had. My uncle was well-to-do you see – '

'A butler?' queried Danica, recalling that flaw in the diamond of the ring that had looked just like a butler in his claw-hammer tailcoat.

'Yes,' Mr Stroud nodded, smiled, and said: 'so I take

it you weren't expecting him? Some admirer is he? He was rather well-spoken and he walked very quickly and silently up those stairs – almost glided up there he did – very agile and graceful.'

'Oh Roby, yes, er,' Ceri suddenly said, and winked at Danica, 'the music teacher at the uni – of course, yes.'

'I've never heard of a music teacher with that name – ' confessed Danica, and then the penny dropped and she realised that her friend was trying to cover up the strange incident to allay the old man's suspicions. That guitar *was* worth a small fortune, after all.

'You're losing your memory, Danica,' Ceri said to her friend and gave a little false laugh.

'Oh of course, yes, I remember him now,' Danica said, nodding energetically.

When the students got outside, Ceri told her friend: 'You've got a brain like a beanbag. You don't think Mr Stroud will report us to the police do you?'

'No, stop worrying,' said Danica, 'but I wonder who the hell Mr Roby is? Are you sure you don't know anyone with that name?'

'The only Roby I know is a place up by Huyton,' said Ceri. 'I wonder if the guitar was meant for someone else and he dropped it off at the wrong flat?'

'Even so, how the hell did he get into our flat?' Danica wondered.

'True,' said Ceri, maybe we should change the lock to the front door. It's a real baffler this one.'

On the following day Ceri and Danica went to Liverpool to see if they could find a cheap guitar amplifier to plug the Rickenbacker into. Ceri decided she'd be better trawling eBay or Gumtree, and before the girls went home to the flat, Ceri said she wished she could get a vinyl copy of the new album by her favourite singer Tove Lo - *Queen of the Clouds*. The girls got the train home, and when they walked into the flat at 5.40pm, they saw that the mysterious benefactor Mr Roby had visited again. In front of the fireplace stood a 200-watt Marshall guitar amplifier, and resting on the cushion of an armchair was the vinyl album by Tove Lo that Ceri had so desired.

Danica swore and went into the kitchen, then checked the bedroom and even the toilet, but there was no sign of Mr Roby. When she came back into the living room, she saw Ceri gazing at the ring.

'This is wigging me out,' said Danica, but Ceri started to smile at the 'imperfection' in the stone and then she looked at her friend and said, 'He's bringing these things to me. We could have anything. I should have asked for a guitar lead so I can plug the damned Rickenbacker into the amp.'

'Ceri, get rid of it,' advised Danica, and she looked scared. 'This Roby fellah strikes me as well weird – like he might even be the Devil.'

'I'm not throwing my Christmas Ring away,' said Ceri, her eyes alight with greed, 'Every day is like Christmas with this ring. I'm not harming anyone, and he's a harmless ghost; he's not the Devil!'

'How do you know?'Danica challenged her flatmate's assertion, and her throat dried up as she went to speak, so she coughed and said: 'The Devil doesn't give things without expecting to receive something in return, Ceri.'

'Hey, I wonder if he could give me a tattoo,' Ceri mused, and she lifted the ring to her eyes and said, 'Mr Roby, could I have that vagina tattoo Tove Lo has on her upper arm?'

Danica issued an unexpected ultimatum. 'If you don't get shut of that ring, Ceri, I'm leaving.'

'Danica, how selfish of me, girl!' said Ceri, and she threw her arms around her friend, hugged her, and close to her ear she asked: 'Let me get you something, babe – something you've always wanted – but obviously not Nick Drake, that'd be horrific, because like he's been in his grave for forty years.'

Danica wrestled herself from Ceri's embrace and pointing at the diamond ring she said: 'Throw that thing away!'

'No! I won't!' Ceri yelled back at her friend.

'If the police trace all these stolen items to you, you'll do time,' Danica warned her friend.

'I can't get you the vagina tattoo, Miss Woodhall,' said a well-spoken voice behind Ceri. She turned and saw what could only be Mr Roby. He was well over six feet in height, slim, with oiled black hair slicked back with a widow's peak, and he had a very pale clean-shaven face with an aquiline nose and thin lips. His eyes were dark and small, but piercing. He stood there, turned slightly to the right, arms straight down, hands at his sides, and he wore black narrow trousers, a pair of highly-polished black shoes, a white linen shirt with a black tie and a grey buttoned-up waistcoat. He had on a black swallow-tail coat, and Ceri recognised the type of coat from the dark flaw that resembled his outline in the ring she wore. Ceri looked at Danica, and saw that she was not even looking at the apparition of the butler – as if she *couldn't* see him.

Danica read the terror in her friend's eyes and she said: 'What's wrong?'

'Can't you see him standing there?' Ceri asked, and then her eyes travelled back to the eerie manifestation.

'See who?' Danica enquired, and yet she had a good idea who her friend was referring too, but hoped to God in heaven he was not there.

'I think he's Mr Roby,' Ceri gasped, and backed away towards the door.

'Ceri? Are you pulling my leg or is he really here?' Danica followed the line of her friend's sight and estimated the ghost was standing by the window.

'I can see him as plain as day, Danica – I must be psychic – and Mr Stroud too!' Ceri whimpered, then turned, grabbed the door handle, pulled the door open and ran so fast, she almost fell down the stairs, and in a heartbeat, Danica was a few steps behind her. Both girls bounded down the hall and were soon out on the wintry street, where Ceri looked up at her window and saw the shadow of the ethereal butler glide across the curtains and vanish.

A long half hour elapsed before the girls were driven back into the house by a fall of stinging hailstones. Mr Stroud was in the hallway and asked the girls what they'd been doing standing in the street. A small lie about going out to post Christmas cards saved a ton of convoluted explanation.

The ghost did not put in another appearance that evening, but still Ceri continued to receive gifts from the butler – always when she and Danica were out the house.

Expensive diamond necklaces, designer clothes and even a bottle of Boërl & Kroff Brut Rose champagne worth thousands of pound appeared at the flat, and still Ceri wanted more. She even lusted for a Rolls

Royce outside her door, but then on Christmas Eve she had a bath in the morning, then went window shopping at a jeweller's for 'more ideas' – and forgot to bring the ring. When she got home, the flat had been broken into – and all of the spoils of the Christmas Ring – and the ring itself – had been stolen. Ceri never heard from Mr Roby again. I wonder who has the ring and its attendant genie-like butler now?

THE WALTZING MATCHMAKER

One Saturday morning at 3am in 1995, a 22-year-old girl named Melanie came out of a well-known night club in tears with a friend under each arm supporting her in her dangerous size-6 break-neck platforms. Melanie said she had drunk herself "into oblivion" to escape "the horrible reality of today" – no lad was after love, just sex. She'd had enough, and her friends, Jen and Sophie, took Melanie to their tiny flat above a shop on Bold Street, and they placed her in an armchair with a cushion at her head and a pink woollen blanket draped over her. As Melanie rambled and ranted about the unromantic, unfeeling males of today, Jen made some strong coffee and Sophie made them all cheese on toast with grated onion, and Sophie wiped the streaks of mascara from Melanie's tear-flooded cheeks. As Sophie cleaned her up, Melanie started blubbing again.

'Oh come on Melanie you thin-skinned partypooping arsehole,' sassed Sophie, 'welcome to 1995! That's how it is now: wham, bam thankyou m'am!'

'Ah, don't be like that to her, Soph,' Jen appealed from the adjacent kitchenette, 'our Mel deserves a real good fellah – someone like Stephen Dorff.'

By 3.30am, Jen and Sophie had eaten their rounds of toasted cheese and onion – including Melanie's round, as the girl had been too upset to take more than a nibble. Jen stubbed out her cigarette in an ashtray and bent over Melanie to kiss her. 'Try and get some kip, Mel. We love you, and you'll meet Mr Right soon. N'night babe.'

'Use me and throw me away,' Melanie murmured with her eyes closed as her friends retired to their room. The bedroom was that small, Jen and Sophie slept on pine bunk beds – Jen at the top and Sophie underneath (ever since the latter fell off the top one drunk three months ago). Had there been proper beds in the room, one of the girls would have shared her bed with lovelorn Melanie. At 3.40am, Jen leaned over the edge of her bed and looked below into the darkness. To an out of sight Sophie she whispered, 'Aw, listen – Melanie's snoring,' and they both erupted into smothered, snickering laughter.

Melanie had a very strange but soothing dream about being in some Victorian ballroom of long ago. It's almost impossible to recall the specific way a dream begins, but Melanie heard the music of a waltz. The dream was bizarre; a man who looked the spitting image of Brian Cant - a presenter of *Play School* - the children's TV series, appeared in the ballroom and invited Melanie to dance, and she realised she was dressed in a beautiful old-fashioned pink silk dress and feather-light dancing shoes, and she also wore white satin gloves that went up to her elbows.

'We are not imaginals!' her dance partner shouted over the stirring orchestral music. 'We are all long-gone but we still love to dance!'

Melanie became dizzy with the whirling euphoria of it all – how romantic this man was! And eventually the music changed to a slower, sad-sounding waltz – and from Melanie's attempts to play this music to me on a keyboard when I later interviewed her about this intriguing dream, I am positive it was Chopin's *Waltz in C# Minor*. Close to Melanie's ear, her dashing dance partner in that rhapsodic dream whispered: 'I shall light a candle in your heart that will never go out. When you awake, go to this address: [and he gave the number of a shop on Bold Street] and you shall meet David. Remember this!'

And the music ceased, and the room vanished into a wheeling kaleidoscopic jumble of rainbow light, and all Melanie could see was the disappearing grinning face of her lovely partner, like the fading smile of some metaphysical Cheshire Cat. Some humdrum dream involving Melanie counting fishes in a canning factory followed, and the rest of the sleeping hours were filled with amnesia.

Melanie awoke at 11.15am, disturbed by the coughing of smoker Sophie and the theme of *Sweet Valley High* on the telly, and after a scant breakfast of half a bowl of Honey Nut Loops, Melanie showered, washing the icky vestiges of the disastrous night away; she lathered her hair with Organics shampoo and rinsed out the smoke and the traceries of testosterone-infused sweat from those packs of predatory dance-floor beasts, and then, swathed in towels, she stood before the toilet mirror, carefully applying her make-up. On went the foundation, concealer, eye shadow, eyeliner and L'Oreal Lash Out Mascara, and throughout the application of her cosmetics, Melanie intermittently turned over the event about that strange dream in her mind, and as she put on her lip liner and lipstick, she suddenly recalled the address given by the man she had danced with in the dream. The recollection jarred her. She tried to recall other details about the unusual dream but they remained tantalizingly out of her mental reach, but for some peculiar reason she felt that the dream man's name had been William.

Melanie left the flat under the pretence of going to a newsagent for Clorets chewing gum and a magazine, and she nervously went in search of the address she'd received in the dream. It turned out to be a little second-hand bookshop, and the man sitting on a chair in the store was aged about thirty. He was the double of the man she had seen in her dream, only a lot younger – and it transpired that his name was David. Melanie got talking to David about books, and then she plucked up some courage and told him about the weird dream she'd had, and David, who was into the paranormal, seemed a bit stunned, as if Melanie's account of the dream had struck some chord in him. He showed the girl his family album, and there was his great-great Grandfather - William. Melanie saw that it was the matchmaker from the dream; there was no doubt about it. William had been a frequent visitor to the nearby Liverpool Music Hall; the building still stands at Number 52 Bold Street. Melanie believes his ghost waltzed out of the hereafter and into her dreams to save her from a life of being continually preyed upon by men who wanted her for one thing. It soon became glaringly obvious that Melanie and David were soul mates, and within a year they were married.

TALES OF THE FAR OUT

The world of the paranormal is, by its very nature, full of things that we would class as out of the ordinary, be it poltergeist phenomenon, timeslips and so on, but every now and then I come across stories that even strike my seasoned mind as particularly bizarre, and you'll find just a few of these far out tales in this section. I'll start with possibly the most outlandish of these accounts, concerning two young offenders on the run from the law.

The story unfolded in the Spring of 1967. Two 17-year-olds – Davy, who hailed from Birkenhead, and Mick, a lad from the Dovecot area of Liverpool – escaped from a borstal in Lancashire by taking turns to saw through the bars of a bathroom. Davy had been in borstal for a year after being found guilty of breaking into a house and stealing money and property valued at £136 1 shilling and 3d (three pence). He'd also pleaded Guilty to being in possession of housebreaking implements and an antique dagger. Mick had been sentenced to six months' for loitering with intent to steal contrary to section 4 of the Vagrancy Act 1824, and also for attempting to steal cash from a telephone call box. After the escape from borstal, Davy broke into a gleaming crimson MG Magnette outside a house in Rainhill and quickly hot-wired the vehicle, and while police with dogs were scouring the surrounding countryside, the youths were on their way to the Widnes-Runcorn Bridge, headed for Wirral. Davy unrealistically had plans to steal tents from a Millets store and camp in the "wilds of Capenhurst" whereas Mick said the Delamere Forest was a safer bet – but Davy didn't know how to get there. The fugitives crossed the bridge and made it through Runcorn without encountering any police and they continued on to Frodsham.

'Do you think we'll stay free or will they catch us?' Mick asked his friend with a despondent expression.

'Mick, we are going to be alright,' Davy replied, bombing the Magnette along a country lane, 'we've got a tiger in our tank and the coppers are miles away now.'

Mick switched the car radio on, and turned quickly to another station when he heard the news about Home Secretary Roy Jenkins considering the use of military camps for civil prisoners. A DJ – possibly Radio Caroline's Emperor Rosko – introduced a song by Georgie Fame and the Blue Flames that made Davy laugh; the aptly-titled *Get Away*.

Sixteen miles and twenty-five minutes later, the juvenile escapees were singing to *All or Nothing* by the Small Faces when they happened to pass a Morris Minor in police livery parked off a lane on Parkgate Road. Davy kept as cool as a cucumber and decelerated, then took a quick turn down what seemed to be a dirt track and he kept going. The teens looked in the rear view and wing mirrors of the Magnette, expecting the police car to follow, but it didn't, and the getaway car emerged near a wood. 'We're lost aren't we?' Mick asked, and Davy said nothing for a moment, then he nodded to the wood and told his friend: 'That shouldn't be there – Shotwick should be there; the whole village has gone; it's barmy this.'

Mick laughed and said, 'You got lost, Davy – we might be in Wales.'

'We're *not* in Wales,' he said, and parked the car in the shade of a massive thick-trunked oak. The two teens wandered into the wood, and Davy expected to see the village of Shotwick, but instead, he saw a quaint old thatched cottage – with cotton wool puffs of smoke coming from its chimney. The cottage had a little red single-arch door and two windows, and the walls of the single-story dwelling were made of rubblestones with turf gables. The escaped borstal inmates thought there might be food and money to be had in that cottage and made their way towards it through long grass. They passed a fallen weathered sign that read: 'Bear Cottage' in flaking black letters. 'I bet a couple of old people live here,' said Davy in a low voice, and then he knocked at the door. Davy and Mick heard the patter of feet on a hard floor, and then a little blonde girl in a sky-blue dress with white polka dots answered. She looked as if she was about ten, and had a huge pair of cornflower blue eyes. She recoiled in shock when she saw the teenagers, and almost fell back into the cottage.

'Where's your mam and dad, love?' Mick asked, scanning the room as he barged into the place. There was a spinning wheel and a big old table and a little chair and three huge chairs. A fire was burning cheerily in the grate, and Davy's nose detected the aroma of something sweet hanging in the warm air; it was coming from about a dozen Eccles cakes laid out on a large white oval plate with a pale blue pattern around the rim. The plate was set on a table covered with a pink gingham tablecloth and Mick noticed a large brown glass jug bottle about two feet in height, standing in the corner, and imagined it would contain cider. He intended to find out soon, but first he and Davy had to check the bedroom to see if the girl was alone. The bedroom had one small bed and three enormous ones. 'You living with giants?' Davy asked the girl, who remained in the living room, the fear in her face now replaced with anger.

'They'll be back soon,' she said, and her accent had a tinge of Welsh. 'You'd better run.'

'I bags the drink in that bottle,' declared Mick walking to the big brown glass jug bottle.

The front door burst open, and in came a bear, walking upright. Davy swore out of shock and as soon as the six-foot-tall beast lunged at him, he was out of there. He heard Mick scream as he ran out the cottage behind him – and there, coming down the path to the cottage, were two even bigger bears – they looked seven feet tall at least!

Mick and Davy took immediate evasive action by running across the long grass but when they reached the car, they saw that a tyre had been slashed and the roof was crumpled to the tops of the buckled doors. All the windows were shattered. The terrified teenagers ran down the long dirt track, pushing and elbowing as they tried to overtake one another in the flight from those three fierce-looking animals – and when the teens ran around the corner at the end of the lane, they both hit the oncoming bonnet of that police car they'd passed earlier. Davy fell, doubled up, holding his stomach from the impact, and Mick landed on the verge, dazed and completely detached from reality. As he got up, he realised he had two deep scratches across his buttocks, and the blood from these scores through his skin had soaked his jeans. He could feel the blood trickling down his legs. Mick thought he had felt something strike his behind as he fled from the cottage, but had felt no pain.

'Davy and Mick, I presume?' said one of the policemen, getting out the car.

When Mick told the policeman what had just happened, the constable said, 'You must be on some powerful drugs lad – bears in a cottage with a little blonde girl? Have you been taking purple hearts or prellies?'

'Was the little girl's name Goldilocks by any chance?' asked the other laughing policeman.

Only then did Davy realise what the policeman was referring to – Goldilocks and the Three Bears – that ancient children's story – and now he felt more confused than scared. 'Officers,' Davy told the bemused policemen as they led him into their car, 'I swear on my mother's life – there *is* a cottage down that lane in a wood, and there are three bears and a little girl. Why would I make it up?'

'I need to go to hospital,' groaned Mick, unable to sit with his injured buttocks on the back seat of the police car, 'it won't stop bleeding.'

'Oh shut up you scouse fairy,' one of the coppers laughed at Mick, 'it's just a scratch; you're not going to get gangrene or anything!'

'Ganger-reen?' yelped Mick with a very distressed expression, 'Get me to the ozzy now!'

The police drove down the lane leading to the alleged cottage where Goldilocks and the Three Bears lived, and Mick kept screaming, 'Don't! They'll get us!'

There was no wood and no cottage – only the peripheries of Shotwick, and this fact knocked hard against the head of Davy, who gasped, 'But it was there! We went in the place! The wood was there and the cottage was just there.'

Maybe some higher intelligence – some Cosmic Joker – was playing with the minds of those teenagers that day, putting imaginary nursery characters in their minds, perhaps for amusement or just to see how the teenage runaways from justice would react. Something unearthly seems to have taken place that day in 1967, for how can we explain the serious claw-like wound sustained by Mick and the wrecked car? Many years after the strange incident, in 1975, Davy, who was now a 25-year-old carpenter, was house-hunting in Wirral, and decided to have a look around the area where he and Mick had visited the ethereal cottage. Davy had told his girlfriend Prue about the incident many times over the years, and she rolled her eyes when he drove down the little road that led to the spot where the cottage had allegedly stood. There was a beautiful little old cottage with a To Let sign outside. Prue said, 'Ah, Davy, isn't that a beautiful little house? Can we live there pretty please?'

Davy smiled and parked outside the dwelling, and then he saw the wooden plaque on the white picket gate. Upon it was the word: 'Goldilocks'. Straight away, the name conjured up the terror of that surreal trauma of eight years ago, and he tried to draw Prue's attention to the name of the cottage and its significance but she pushed the gate open and went and knocked on the door.

'Prue, I don't want to live here, let's go!' shouted

Davy but his girlfriend stood her ground and the door of the cottage opened. A tiny old woman, not even five feet in height, answered and smiled. Prue said something to her and then Davy's girlfriend went into the cottage. Davy reluctantly followed. A sweet smell reminiscent of honey greeted his nostrils immediately. The ceiling was so low, Davy had to stoop so he didn't knock his head on the crossbeams. All of the furniture was like something out of a infants' school, with little chairs and a low table. Prue asked about the price of the house and the woman, who never gave her name, said she wasn't sure, as Mr Green – presumably the estate agent – took care of all that.

'My name's Prue, by the way,' Davy's girlfriend said as she carefully sat on a tiny two-seater sofa which looked as if it couldn't take her weight, and she was only eight stone. 'And this is my fiancé Davy,' Prue nodded at Davy and still the woman did not say what her name was. She made tea and gave Davy and Prue a little saucer with something resembling a bakewell tart.

Davy came right out with the question that was burning a hole in his mind. 'Why is the cottage named Goldilocks?'

The old woman raised her eyebrows and told Davy: 'Well, it was named that before I was born, you see, they say that the story of the Three Bears and Goldilocks was based on a real cottage that used to stand here. I think they were three circus bears – my husband knew the story, and he's dead now.' The elderly lady then turned to Prue and continued: 'A little girl lived with them – the bears.'

'You're kidding,' said Prue, finding the old woman's claim hard to believe.

The woman nodded, 'That's what they said; she lived with them and they never harmed her. This would be a long time ago, back in early eighteen-hundreds, like.'

After the tea and cakes, Davy and Prue left the cottage, and in the car, Davy said: 'I am not living there! That old lady gave me the creeps.'

'Don't worry, love, she put me off the place too. There was something eerie about her, and did you notice she never told us her name?'

'Yeah, as if she was hiding something,' Davy decided. 'Let's just get away from here. Heswall's supposed to be nice.'

The mystery of what took place that day in 1967 will probably remain a mystery. Did three people dress up in bear costumes to scare the two young borstal escapees? It's possible but not likely in my opinion. I interviewed Davy and Mick and they were absolutely sure that the bears were real animals. There were around 14,000 bears in Britain in the Stone Age before humans hunted them to extinction. Bears have not roamed England since 1000AD, and even three 'trained' circus bears living in a small cottage would be a very unlikely scenario. Bears are mostly solitary omnivores with a voracious appetite and a tendency to sleep through the winter. Whatever those three animals were in Bear Cottage, they couldn't have been normal bears. I personally believe they were a product of a hypothetical entity I call the MMM (the Mystery Mind Manipulator) – a sinister intelligence which fabricates certain types of UFO sightings and conjures up holograms of things like Bigfoot, Mothman, religious visions and perhaps even prehistoric creatures similar to the Loch Ness Monster. The MMM – if it exists – is probably immortal and was active aeons before the emergence of the human race. As well as producing realistic-looking tactile beings and objects, I think the MMM also toys with human perception by tampering with the circuitry of the brain's neurons. Why the conjectural MMM populates our reality with these outlandish beings is anybody's guess; perhaps it simply makes the entity's endless life more bearable when it fabricates its ephemeral spoofs – or then again, we might all be the equivalent of lab rats in some grand test that's gone on for millennia. I wonder if our theoretical MMM is responsible for the following 'far out' incident?

In August 1982, Frank Johnson, a widowed Huyton businessman, was drinking in the Stanley Arms pub on Roby Road one Saturday afternoon, and despite the warmness of the afternoon and the summer sun sparkling through the pub windows, he felt so down in the dumps. Frank sat there on a bar stool, gazing with out-of-focus eyes into the slowly vanishing froth of his newly-pulled pint as he thought of his late wife Marguerite. He had tried to drive the memories of her away, but it was no use. It was coming up to that awful anniversary of her death; three years ago she had been having an affair with Frank's closest friend Roy, when the car they were in skidded in a downpour one night and crashed, instantly killing the two of them. Marguerite had walked out on him without a word of explanation a week before, and he'd had the job of identifying her body. He hadn't dated anyone since then because he had a habit of comparing every woman to Marguerite; she'd been beautiful and intelligent and Frank believed he'd never meet anyone like her again.

Someone patted Frank's shaven head, startling him.

'Sitting there with your mouth open like a frog in a brown study!' came a familiar voice from behind Frank. It was Jimmy, Frank's friend from his school days. He tried to pull Frank out of his depression and pointless reminiscences, and suggested going on a long holiday to Florida. Frank said Florida had been Marguerite's favourite holiday destination so he couldn't bring himself to go there. Frank resorted to his usual attack on God "for letting Marguerite die" – it was his usual rant about life not being fair and the Creator standing by letting it all happen.

'That's why I'm an atheist now,' seethed Frank, and some in the pub cast nervous glances at the stocky shaven-headed six-footer.

'Oh don't start all that, Frank,' sighed Jimmy, and he gave what looked like a peace sign to the barman, signalling for two pints of the usual for him and his self-tortured friend.

'It's true though, Jimmy,' said Frank, 'the atheists are right; the guy upstairs does nothing to help anyone.'

'You don't disbelieve in God, Frank, you just personally dislike Him!' retorted Jimmy, sick of his friend's wallowing in the loss of his wife three years ago. 'A true atheist just doesn't believe in a deity and that's that, but you blame this God you supposedly don't believe in for everything – and that contradicts your claim to be an atheist.'

'Anyway, I don't want to talk about all that theological nonsense,' said Frank, waving his hand dismissively at Jimmy. You were talking about holidays – well, I think you might be right – maybe I should head off for the sun and sand.'

'Now you're making headway, Frank,' said Jimmy, and the barman brought over the two pints.

'Yeah, probably a right step in the wrong direction,' said Frank with a smirk. He decided to fly down to Altea on the Costa Blanca for a fortnight, and Jimmy was very impressed and relieved at his overworked and emotionally distraught friend actually taking time out to relax.

Two days after Frank had arrived at Altea he decided to go and have a drink on the veranda. Through binoculars Frank had a look at the sparkling bay of the coastal resort and its picturesque labyrinth of streets, all of whitewashed houses and the odd chapel – when two people caught his eye on the veranda of a hotel some 120 yards away. Frank doubted his senses for a moment and thought he was dreaming, but the woman he could see was, without a shadow of a doubt, his late wife Marguerite – and the man with her – although he wore shades - was Roy! But how? They'd been killed in that car crash three years back. Frank took the binoculars from his eyes and started to worry about his sanity. He took a deep breath then took another look, and he saw it really was Marguerite and Roy. Had they somehow faked their deaths to start a new life in Spain? Frank watched them for about fifteen minutes – until they left the veranda and went into their hotel room. The temperature was in the seventies and yet Frank went cold inside. He walked in a daze to his room telephone and asked the receptionist to place a call to Liverpool. The phone in Jimmy's Huyton home rang and he answered it. When he heard what Frank had to say, he said: 'Frank, you identified your wife at the morgue. She's dead. You've just seen someone who looks like her.'

'Jimmy I'd bet my life savings on you being wrong;' said Frank, 'I was married to Marguerite for twelve years and it's her, and it's Roy, and I don't know how they did it, but they're alive and well, and I don't know whether to tell the police or a solicitor or the damned Spanish Interior Ministry, but I'm going over to their hotel to get some answers.'

'Frank, unless you believe in ghosts, and ghosts that take holidays at that, I'd drop this now,' advised a concerned-sounding Jimmy, 'or it's going to get you into a heap of trouble.'

But Frank couldn't drop it. He started hanging round outside the hotel where his resurrected wife and best friend were staying, watching through sunglasses from under a trilby, and days after he had first spotted them through his binoculars, they walked out the hotel and passed within six feet of him – two supposedly dead people who looked very tanned and healthy. Frank tried to follow them but they jumped in a cab. He went to their hotel and offered the receptionist ten thousand pesetas to tell him who the couple were who had just left, and Frank described them. He discovered they were booked in under the names Roy Ortiz and Marguerite Appleton. According to the receptionist, they were both English and had been staying at the hotel for a week.

Frank returned to his hotel and grabbed his Kodak Pocket Instamatic camera, and then he went back to the hotel were his 'reanimated' wife and her lover were staying. Frank sipped numerous Martinis in the lounge as he waited for the planned confrontation, and the couple came in two hours later. Frank shouted to them: 'Say cheese!' and took a flash photograph.

They acted as if they didn't know who he was; all puzzled expressions and up and down glances cast at him.

'For two people who have been pushing up the daisies for three years, I must say you're both looking remarkably well!' yelled a tipsy Frank. 'Now, let's get your best side Marguerite!' He took another flash photograph.

When the couple walked on past him, Frank swung his fist at Roy, but missed, and fell through a glass coffee table. He was lucky he didn't sustain any serious injuries. Within minutes the hotel manager called the police and Frank was taken away, charged with being drunk and disorderly, and he had his belongings – including the camera – deposited in the police safe. They jailed him for nearly twelve hours, and Frank threatened a police sergeant with legal action for 'wrongful arrest' and when he tried to tell the story of his wife and her lover coming back from the dead in Spanish he was mocked by the personnel at the station. Frank made his way back to his hotel the next day after drying out in the police cells. His skull-pounding hangover was so bad, he drew the blinds in his room and crawled into his bed, but two figures appeared in his hotel room some ten minutes later. It was Marguerite and Roy – at least that's what Frank thought from their voices, as they were more silhouette than anything against the sun-filtering blinds. In an unearthly weird voice, "Roy" said he was not human, and that he and 'this other one' (as he referred to the lookalike of Frank's late wife) had been using the identities of two people who had died some years back for 'certain reasons' – reasons that were not explained to Frank.

'You must tell no one about us or we'll kill you,' said the man, speaking in an emotionless monotone voice, and then the figures vanished. They were there one moment and gone the next, and Frank got off the bed, switched on the bedside lamp and saw he was definitely alone.

The Kodak Pocket Instamatic camera Frank had used to take snaps of the eerie impostors in the foyer of their hotel was never found. The bogus couple was never seen again. Were they aliens in disguise? Beings from some other dimensional realm? All we can do is speculate, and Frank remains perplexed by the incident to this day.

From Spain we return home to Liverpool – to the skies of the city to be exact – the backdrop to another mystery of the far our kind.

Sound can play some very strange tricks at night when the constant background noises of the day are absent. There were two dockers years ago in the 1960s named Tommy and Billy, who lived in Birkenhead and Everton respectively, and both had voices like foghorns as well as perfect hearing. Billy could stand on the Pier Head landing stage at night and shout to Tommy at the Wallasey Landing Stage across the eleven hundred yards of Mersey. When the river is calm at night, it can reportedly carry sound so perfectly on its reflective surface, people on New Brighton promenade have heard late-night revellers singing up in Bootle, but some nocturnal sounds reported to me over the years defy a logical explanation and some are downright spooky. Every few years I get reports of female screams being heard in the night-skies over Merseyside. I originally assumed that the reported screams were merely the sounds of clubbers reflecting off layers of air of different temperatures like a mirror in the sky, but in recent years people have reported figures in the sky accompanying the shrieks from above – and the remarkably consistent descriptions of these figures simply cannot be explained. In February 2012, Steve, a cabby, was parked on Copperas Hill at three in the morning and he clearly heard echoing female screams, and he assumed it was a clubgoer 'having a barney' with someone – but then a young lady tapped on the cab's window and Steve let her in. 'Where to?' he asked his fare, and the girl seemed all flustered and kept glancing upwards through the door window.

'Belle Vale! Just get a move on!' she shouted, then said something strange. The girl pointed to the roof of the cab and said, 'There're two things flying about up there, fighting with one another, and they've got wings! Honest!'

There was a pause, and with a faint smile Steve asked, 'What *have* you been drinking tonight, eh?'

The girl swore and said, 'Have a look yourself, then – and get me home!'

'God, there's a full moon tonight – that's got to be it,' Steve remarked, eyeing the lunar orb over the end of Renshaw Street, and he wound down the offside window to look up – and by the light of the moon he saw two humanoid figures with huge wings flying round one another, high above the roof of the Adelphi Hotel. Steve tried to capture the weird spectacle on his phone, but the passenger screamed for him to get a move on, and the footage Steve got was useless – all blurred and dark. Security guards, a policeman and God knows how many more saw the winged creatures that morning, and one student had a look at them through binoculars from his Chinatown flat. He described them as looking just like women with bat-like wings as they fought one another – and they vanished after a few minutes when clouds temporarily hid the moon. Could the figures have been kites or even balloons used by a hoaxer? All the witnesses said the entities looked too lifelike – so what on earth are they? From all of the descriptions of the airborne creatures I have (especially the descriptions of the winged women having long flowing hair), they remind me of the 'lovely-haired' Harpy of Greek and Roman mythology – half human, half bird creatures, usually depicted in myths – and on Roman and Byzantine pottery – as beautiful yet sinister-looking women – and sometimes as ugly females who flew about with great rapidity. Their name means 'swift robber' and they were said to snatch food, and even lone people travelling at night, and were classed as spirits of the wind. The only difference between the Harpy and the things seen flying over Liverpool is the lack of feathers in the latter. The Harpies had feathered wings like the birds but the unholy things shrieking in the skies over the city are consistently described as looking like the wings of bats. I have given these bizarre creature a lot of consideration over the years and I must admit defeat – I simply am unable to explain them, but at least I'm not explaining them away. Nor can I dismiss the following example of a far out tale which seems to concern something evil masquerading as a character out of a nursery rhyme.

In the late 1960s a bin lorry trundled into Ilchester Square in Birkenhead, and a refuse collector – still known colloquially as a "binnie" - emptied dustbins and the contents of the tenement rubbish chute into the lorry when something unusual caught his eye. Among the tin cans and their hazardous rotary-saw lids, fish skeletons, the sludgey mire of used tealeaves and the usual mass of heterogeneous waste, the binman – whose name was Roger – spotted a doll of what could only be Humpty Dumpty; it was egg-shaped and had a greenish velvety finish to it, and it had two little arms, and legs with tiny black boots – but the face looked positively sinister. Roger grabbed the doll, which looked about three or four inches taller than a football – about 12 inches in height.

'Hey, I wouldn't mind that for my girl,' said a fellow binnie named Alf, but Roger swore at him and said, 'Finders keepers, mate!'

Roger was a 40-year-old bachelor, and as he walked home after his job had ended at around 5.30pm, Sharon, an attractive woman in her thirties who lived a few doors away from him, smiled at Roger. He wanted to ask her out but he just couldn't get the words out. He felt inferior. He had heard that she was a manageress in a factory, and with her looks, she surely had someone.

The binman put Humpty on the kitchen table, and after gently wiping the little amount of grime from him with a tea-towel, Roger located a small lever on a hinge that came out of the doll's lower back. He turned this lever and listened to the whirring sound inside the doll.

After a dozen windings, the lever wouldn't budge so Roger folded it back into the niche in the clockwork doll's back and sat it up on the table, waiting for it to react. The binman's cat Orangey appeared on the kitchen window ledge, so Roger let it in, but when the feline saw Humpty it hissed and ran out into the yard.

'What's your name?' asked the doll, and its voice did not sound tinny like the ones produced by the little plastic records found in some dolls; it sounded very realistic.

'Ha! My name's Roger, what's yours?' the smiling binman answered, stooping slightly to look at the doll.

'Hello Roger, my name's Mumpicker, but just call me Mump,' said the doll, and it grinned, and showed two rows of badly misaligned teeth. The eyeballs seemed to be faintly glowing, and the irises were black buttons.

'That's amazing – the way you can answer back and speak my name,' said Roger, and he found himself slightly scared of Mump; it looked *alive* and not a clockwork contraption at all.

'Roger, don't take this the wrong way, but you stink,' said Mump, and gave a slight, mocking chuckle and shook as he narrowed his eyes.

'That's not very nice, Mump,' said Roger, hurt – and shocked.

'They all think you're an oddball round here, especially the women,' said Mump, and he stood up now as he spoke, and Roger backed away. 'The women think you're a weird loner and they know you're always peeping at them from behind your curtains.'

'Eh? I-I don't peep at them,' Roger stammered, and felt sweat break out on his brow. In fact he was a bit of a Peeping Tom, and he *was* always taking sly peeks at the opposite sex through gaps in the curtains whenever they walked past his house. Roger was a shy chap regarding females and was fascinated by them but too self-conscious to approach them. But how did this "Mump" know about his snooping behaviour?

Mump raised his tiny hand and pointed a finger upwards to make a point. 'But if you start getting a wash, start buying some clothes and stop wearing that cap to hide your perfectly normal bald patch, you might get your rocks off.'

Roger's eyes travelled across the kitchen to the red metal toolbox in the corner where he kept a lump hammer. He felt as if this clockwork creep could attack him – and those teeth could obviously inflict quite a bite.

'Don't you dare, smelly!' the doll growled, and its eyes burned yellow for a moment. 'I'll bite through your jugular in a jiffy!' And Mump snapped his metal jaws together to underline his deadly threat. 'I'm trying to help you here, Roger, you dead loss!'

'What *are* you?' Roger asked, feeling his heart pounding and skipping beats. He considered running out the house via the kitchen door.

The doll ran to the edge of the table and warned: 'If you even try to run, you foul-smelling failure, I'll jump on you and after I pull your eyes out I'll bite through your windpipe! I've done it before. Do you remember that unsolved murder – '

The kitchen door opened and in barged Ted from the back yard. Ted was the window cleaner Roger hadn't paid for over a month. 'Hello Rog, glad you're in at last, chummy,' said an annoyed-looking Ted.

Mump remained stock-still on the table as Roger dashed to the toolbox in the corner. He opened it, took out the lump hammer, and a startled Ted watched as the binman pointed at the ovoid doll and cried: 'That thing's alive! It's going to kill me!'

'Eh? What are you talking about?' asked Ted, looking at the doll.

'That horrible bastard! Bastard! Bastard!' Roger smashed the hammer down on Mump with each exclamation and the doll exploded into cogs, teeth and reddish brown liquid which sprayed the walls of the kitchen – and Ted. There was a brief screech from the doll, and then more frantic hammer blows and innards resembling minced meat and gelatinous white liquid flew out of the egg-shaped doll. Ted wrestled the hammer from Roger's hand and slapped him hard across the face. Through his tears, the sobbing, trembling binman saw bubbles of some red liquid form in the flattened doll on the floor. The police and a doctor took Roger away, and before he was committed to what they then called a lunatic asylum, the traumatised binman told his sister everything. She tells me Roger later died from a heart attack at the psychiatric hospital. I don't believe Mump was a figment of Roger's imagination, and I still wonder just what that thing was. The universe is a big place and this earth is wide open to so many strange beings that could easily infiltrate our world disguised as anything – even a harmless-looking Humpty Dumpty doll. Some of these beings could be among us now, disguised as a pet, or a toy in a nursery – or even hiding in an ancient piece of amber – and this latter possibility leads us to our next tale of the far out.

In July 1998, Desmond Clarke, a 45-year-old history teacher at a secondary school in Huyton, decided to go to Porth Padrig Beach on the north coast of Anglesey with an old school friend named Clifford March to try out a new metal detector he had bought. Desmond found an old long-defunct silver coin called a groat, which dated back to the 12th century, and he also found a small piece of amber on the Welsh beach. The groat coin was a bit eroded but worth around £100 and Desmond said he'd split the money he got for it with Clifford. He returned to Liverpool and found himself feeling increasingly depressed, which was not like Desmond; he occasionally did feel down in the dumps but he had always pulled himself out of his despondency with his self-deprecating humour and eternally optimistic outlook on life, but this was different; the teacher literally felt as if a shadow was hanging over him.

Desmond showed the groat coin and the amber to his pupils, and later that day, during the lunch-break in the school staffroom he became so ill the headmaster strongly advised him to go home to recover. Desmond reluctantly went home, and he experienced an icy cold sensation at the back of his head and the feeling that there was something attached to his back. He feared he had some neurological condition, and went into his back garden to get a little sun. It was here that he suddenly felt as if something was embracing him from behind with what felt like several arms. He knew it was a silly thought, but it felt as if an octopus was on his back with its tentacles wrapped about him. Eventually the strange sensation of being cuddled by the invisible octopus faded, and Desmond felt a little better that sunny afternoon, so he had some soup, then set out for a stroll up Blue Bell lane. Whilst Desmond was walking up the leafy lane, he saw a very attractive raven-haired woman in her thirties named Laura Deakin who lived near him, and said hello to her, but Laura looked at him with an expression of shock.

'What's wrong?' Desmond asked, and Laura backed away and seemed to be looking at something in the air behind him. The teacher turned and saw a very faint outline of what looked like some creature resembling an octopus, hovering a few feet behind him as if it was some helium-filled inflatable. It had huge pale featureless eyes the size of grapefruits and over a dozen writhing tentacles which reached out from a quivering pinkish body. The thing faded away, and Desmond said, 'What the devil was that?'

Laura had an interest in the supernatural and had always professed to be psychic, and she said that she felt as if the entity wanted something Desmond had. He gave a baffled look at first, and then he mentioned the groat he'd found on the Welsh beach; it was still in his inside coat pocket with the piece of amber. Laura invited him to her home, and she seemed fascinated by the entity. She sketched it, and it became apparent that she had seen more details in the weird creature, perhaps because of her alleged psychic sense. She handled the groat coin and said she'd try psychometry – an ability of hers where she could pick up the history of an object just by holding it. She said she could see a sinking ship, but said that the entity was not connected to that item. She asked the intrigued teacher: 'Desmond, did you find anything else on that beach?'

'Yes I did – just this,' Desmond showed her the

piece of amber – and Laura inspected it. She noticed something that Desmond had mistaken as some ancient flower. There, trapped in the centre of the ancient golden resin, there was a very bizarre-looking creature, about an inch across; it looked exactly like that tentacled airborne being that had floated behind Desmond. Laura held the amber, closed her eyes for a while, then told Desmond something which sounded very 'out there' to him. Laura said that the thing that had been encased in the amber for millions of years was the deceased son of that entity they'd both seen, and she told Desmond to return it in its amber 'coffin' to the beach, or the 'mother' (as she called that unearthly life form) would make him so ill, he'd die. Desmond recalled the strange impression he'd had when he was ill – of something akin to an octopus on his back, hugging him with its tentacles, and he went stone cold.

Desmond and Laura travelled to the Anglesey beach that very day, and the teacher placed the amber in the sand at the very spot where he had found it, and the depression and mysterious illness departed from Desmond Clarke and never returned. The teacher asked Laura what the hideous thing had been and how it would be able to survive aeons as it grieved over its long dead son.

'I don't know, Desmond, but I felt that intense grief the mother had for her son, and perhaps time for her – whatever species she belongs to – is different to her kind. I suppose it could be like comparing the length of our lives to the lives of a bacterium or a housefly.'

This weird experience was a turning point in the life of Desmond Clarke. Laura had opened his mind, and in the months following the 'conversion' the history teacher fell in love with Laura and later married her.

Of course, these are not the only far out tales you'll read in this book; these ones have just had a touch of the surreal to them. The story in the following chapter is a little far out but seems to at least have some sort of fuzzy logic behind it.

THE MYSTERY OF TOY FARM

There was an amazing case of a woman coming back from the dead at Wallasey's Victoria Central Hospital in April 1972. Mrs Ruth Young, a 36-year-old mother-of-two from Tudor Avenue, Wallasey, had fallen off the platform of a bus as she had tried to save her two-year-old son Craig, after he had fallen down the steps of the double-decker. Craig escaped with grazes and minor bruising but Ruth sustained a broken skull when she landed in the road and after she was rushed to hospital she was soon declared dead. All the same, Ruth was hooked up to a heart-beat monitor known as a cardiorate which was left on for a while – just in case it picked up any heart activity. A whole day went by, and still there was no cardiac activity, and then, out of the blue, minutes before the machine was due to be unplugged, the cardiorate's sensor picked up very faint electrical signals coming from the heart. Doctors immediately leapt into action and Ruth Young was resuscitated – literally brought back from the dead. She eventually made a full recovery.

In late September 1973, another woman – Jasmine Jones, a pretty 22-year-old Liverpool college teacher, collapsed at her doctor's one afternoon after complaining of a strange lethargy that kept overtaking her. Her heart stopped for fifteen minutes, and the doctor and a nurse carried out cardiopulmonary resuscitation procedures on Jasmine and then her heart restarted. Jasmine was diagnosed with anaemia and chronic brucellosis – when she was in fact suffering from a condition that had not yet been recognised by the medical establishment – ME (myalgic encephalomyelitis), which would later be known as Yuppie Flu and Chronic Fatigue Syndrome in the 1980s. Jasmine was given a bright red raspberry-flavoured tonic (containing sodium bicarbonate, potassium bromide and tincture of nux vomica) and, scribbling on his prescription pad, the doctor then quipped, 'I'm also going to prescribe 4 fluid ounces of glue, 3 fluid ounces of ink, and 12 ounces of paper!'

Jasmine returned a puzzled look.

'A book!' the doctor clamoured, 'Curl up in bed with a good book and relax for a couple of weeks Miss Jones. You've been overdoing it. Rest!'

Jasmine was given a fortnight's leave from her teaching job at college, and her Aunt Barbara in Thurstaston persuaded her to recuperate at her cottage. On the first night at the cottage, something very strange took place. Jasmine lay in bed, and she had been slogging her way through the second volume of Proust's *In Search of Lost Time* when she had felt her eyelids become as heavy as bags of lead. Jasmine always launched herself optimistically into this thick paperback, and always she ended up paying for it in the coin of fatigue. On this evening she dozed off for a moment but awoke in the semidarkness to a vision! It was as if she were looking through a porthole in mid-air at a beautiful sunny rural scene, and in the centre of this hallucination stood a towering windmill, its sails turning slowly, and the gentle rotation was hypnotic to

Jasmine, for she felt her consciousness was being drawn out of the darkened bedroom and into the mirage of what seemed to be farmland. She knew this opening to summer's day was not some nonsensical phantasm of the hypnagogic because she could see that the sunlight streaming through the portal was shining upon the bedclothes and the brass bed-knobs were casting shadows on the wallpaper. And then in one swift moment she was lifted up bodily and sucked through the hole to elsewhere, and her mind felt as if it was travelling ahead of her physical body. Jasmine drifted like a soap bubble across golden fields of wheat and mosaics of Mikado-yellow barley and vast tracts of chartreuse corn, and all the time the great windmill turned, and then Jasmine found herself walking thigh-deep through a meadow of lucerne – and she felt the sun's savage solar rays filter through her centre part and its infernal pitiless radiation seared her face. She thought she was still wearing her nightie but she was in fact wearing some antiquated dress and a blouse, and she had boots on her feet.

Jasmine was met by a tall broad-shouldered hunk of a man with shoulder-length black hair and a very angular masculine jaw; facially he reminded Jasmine of the actor Oliver Tobias. He wore a white shirt of the kind Jasmine had seen on the men adorning the covers of her many copies of Regency era novels; a thick brown leather belt with a round golden buckle, a pair of ochre knee breeches and a pair of black calf-length riding boots. Even from a distance of about twenty-five feet she noticed his ice-blue eyes, and he smiled at Jasmine and said, 'Oh my love, you came! We hoped you would!' And he threw his muscular arms around her, kissed her hard on the lips, and took her by the hand. His hands felt rough, probably from manual labour.

Jasmine somehow knew his name was Jack, and that he was a ploughman. He led Jasmine to the grey stone farmhouse, and they passed a scarecrow with a tattered topper on what seemed to be a grey-brown turnip head, and the figure had a red umbrella hanging from its left arm.

'Hello Mr Gillray,' Jack shouted to an old man in a flat grey cap and dark blue bib and brace as he pushed an empty green wheelbarrow down a path. The couple passed a pink pig and a black one, a large sandy dog in a kennel guarding an outhouse, grazing Hereford cattle with velvet-brown hides, and a smiling woman of about seventy with large dreamy grey eyes and a stoop who was leading a huge old muscular shire horse across a yard.

'Afternoon Mrs Somerset,' said Jack, and he gripped Jasmine's hand hard as he greeted the passing woman who only nodded to him. The couple from different existences walked on hand in hand down the dusty path which eventually led to a grand-looking residence. Jasmine's knowledge of history and architecture was a piecemeal affair, but to her eyes this building looked like some Georgian country house. What year was this? She wanted to know but she thought that this lovely dream would end if she pried too much.

Jack knocked gently at the door of this impressive manor house, and a snooty-looking servant answered, nodded to Jack, then left him at the doorstep and returned with the ploughman's boss. Jack introduced Jasmine to Farmer Green, a stout, middle-aged rosy-cheeked man in a crimson waistcoat, gamboge breeches, calf-length boots and a squat coachman's hat. In a gravelly yet warm voice he congratulated Jack and Jasmine on their 'forthcoming marriage' – and then Jasmine heard a bang – and she woke up with a start in a pitch-black bedroom. She turned on the bedside lamp and saw that the Proust paperback had fallen on the floor. That had been the accursed bang she'd heard that had shattered that beautiful dream – but it had all been *too real* to be a dream. Jasmine lay there on the bed for some time, trying to make sense of her visit through that strange circular opening to that farm somewhere in the past and those realistic characters. She had felt so close to Jack, and now in the land of wakefulness she felt like crying. How strange, she thought, to miss someone from a dream who didn't even exist. Eventually Jasmine fell asleep and hoped she'd visit Jack again but she just had a succession of the usual absurd and surreal dreams.

However, on the following night at around 10.30pm, Jasmine sat up in bed, going through the mechanics of reading her Proust book by the orange-yellow light of the bedside lamp, but every few lines she would look up and hope to see that windmill turning in the gateway to some other exciting existence. Jasmine felt that something had happened to her when she had clinically died in the doctor's surgery for that quarter of an hour – and she felt as if she had returned *altered* somehow from that place of blackness where there were no references of existence; no up or down, no past, present or future; no yesterday, today or tomorrow – just some void of nothingness. She hardly remembered her time outside life, but she now believed something had happened to her when she had left this sphere of mundanity.

By 11pm, Jasmine thought that perhaps her journey to the farm *had* perhaps been some mere border-of-sleep will-o'-the-wisp illusion after all, and she felt a little sad dismissing her romantic suspicions as the result of tiredness. She'd broken up with her boyfriend Giles almost two years ago and had not dated since. Her friends said she was picky regarding men, but Jasmine found most of the men who came her way to be shallow and after one thing only – her body. Jasmine was tall, and according to her old art teacher Mr Jones, she possessed the perfectly proportioned body; Jones had strongly advised her to try the world of fashion modelling. Jasmine had large olive green eyes fringed with black, and a huge glossy mane of long black hair. Her girlfriends were forever telling her how they envied her looks and how their boyfriends always remarked upon her beauty.

Jasmine sighed, slapped her hand down in the pages of the paperback, and relaxed back into the feather-filled pillows propping her up. She was just about to wallow in a quagmire of introspection when she decided to switch on the little transistor radio she'd brought with her for the 'holiday'. Surely upbeat modern pop songs would dispel her melancholic mood. *Amoureuse* by Kiki Dee, was playing on the radio, and Jasmine loved this song, which was all about a young girl making love in her first romance. As the song ended some four minutes later, Jasmine closed her eyes, and the DJ on the radio began the usual inane banter, when the teacher suddenly felt warmth from somewhere, followed by strong light which shone through the lids of her eyes. For a moment, Jasmine felt as if she was lying on her back in the park of a daytime with the sunlight filtering through her eyelids, because she perceived that distinct type of translucent tenné glow in her closed eyes. Those eyelids flew open and her eyes saw that mystical windmill with its turning sails, and this time it seemed nearer. Surrounding the towering mill was that impossible circular opening in the air above the bed, and sunlight was pouring through the large aperture into the room. The voice of the DJ on the little bedside radio echoed and faded away and Jasmine smiled as she was pulled in head-first through the opening, and she glided down, light as a feather to the picturesque farmstead below. This time she found herself in a tiny cottage where she cooked Jack's dinner, and he came home from the fields and told her how lovely her cooking was, and in her normal life, Jasmine could hardly boil an egg, and was bordering on becoming a vegetarian, yet in this pastoral life she plucked chickens, cured meat, baked venison and mushroom pie, cooked shoulders of pork, made tasty terrines and delicious casseroles, as well as rustling up rice puddings from the raw ingredients and she could even make her own cheese, butter and jam. Honey came straight from the hive, and Jack made his own scrumpy cider. This day in Jasmine's other life ended with Jack making love to her. During the lovemaking, Jasmine felt intensities of pleasure she had never experienced before, and afterwards she snuggled into Jack and for a moment she wanted to ask him what was going on, and what year this was and why she was being brought here, but she decided to just accept the strange situation. She fell asleep as he stroked her hair, and when she awoke she was in her bed at Aunt Barbara's cottage. She got up, was immediately filled with choking sadness, but she bravely forced a smile and left the bedroom to go to the toilet. When she looked in the mirror, she saw a reddish purple love-bite on her neck. This proved she was not dreaming up the visits to that farmstead; Jack was real. How on earth was she journeying back to that time and place which was now regarded as a paradise to Jasmine? Had she returned from that fifteen minutes of death with some unearthly talent? How long would this go on?

Her aunt's rapping on the toilet door brought these profound questions to a halt.

'Jasmine? Do you feel like a little breakfast dear?' Aunt Barbara asked.

'Oh yes please, auntie,' Jasmine replied, her hand on the doorknob, 'I'm feeling a lot better.'

Down at breakfast, Jasmine had to pretend that the love-bite was some skin eruption brought on by stress. Her aunt smiled and said, 'It looks just like a hickey. Been a long time since *I* had one of those things.'

Every night, Jasmine would doze off in bed and see the windmill appear, and she began to enjoy her life married to farm-labourer Jack. At the end of the two weeks at Aunt Barbara's cottage, a tearful Jack told Jasmine she'd have to leave soon. He dropped this bombshell after riding with Jasmine to a glade in a quiet wooded area a mile from the farm.

'Leave?' Jasmine thought he was pulling her leg for a moment, but then she saw the sorrow in those bright blue eyes, and the way he looked as if he was going to cry.

In a broken voice he said: 'They let you come here because you were changed that time when you came over. And I can't say any more like, because it's not allowed, but the thing is my love, you have to go back.'

'But I can't go back,' a stunned Jasmine told him, and a tear fell from her eye, 'I can't leave you.'

'There's nothing we can do about it,' he said, and he wiped the tears from his eyes with the cuff of his shirtsleeve then gritted his teeth, trying to hold back the heartbreaking thoughts that were no doubt flooding his mind. 'But I shall never love another, that I promise you.'

A golden light suddenly infiltrated the trees and in a flash, the wood – and Jack – had gone.

'I'll come back to you!' Jasmine cried out, and she thought she heard a faint voice, possibly Jack's, say something that sounded like: 'I'll be dust, my love. Goodbye.'

There was a roaring sound like that of a rushing wind in Jasmine's ears, and a sensation of travelling backwards, and then the teacher lost consciousness. She woke up in her bed at the Thurstaston cottage, and as soon as she fully realised what had just taken place, Jasmine burst into tears. Her crying was so loud, her aunt came into the room and asked her repeatedly what the matter was, but Jasmine was so utterly broken with sorrow, she couldn't get her words out for some time. When she had partly recovered from the harrowing shock of the separation from Jack, she told Aunt Barbara the whole story, and Jasmine's aunt predictably said the whole thing had been down to her chronically fatigued condition.

Jasmine never had any more dreams at the cottage,

and almost had a breakdown when she realised she'd never see her dream husband again. Just before she departed for Liverpool, 7-year-old Beth, the daughter of Aunt Barbara's neighbour came to visit, and she brought Jasmine a huge bouquet of roses and some chocolates to cheer her up. They'd been bought by Beth's mum in the hope that they'd cheer up Barbara's niece somewhat. On that final day at the cottage, as Jasmine was packing her belongings away, Beth cheekily went into the loft of the cottage and found an old tin chest that Barbara knew nothing of. In that chest, Beth found a toy farm building and painted lead figures of people and animals which included a pink and black pig, a scarecrow with an umbrella, a dog in a kennel, an old woman leading a shire horse by its reins, six brown and white Hereford cows, an old man pushing a green wheelbarrow, a rotund rosy-cheeked farmer that looked like Farmer Green, and a farm labourer that looked just like Jack.

When Jasmine saw that these little toy figures looked exactly like the people and animals she had seen in her dream, she felt so unsteady on her feet with the shock, she had to sit down. She reached out and picked up the little figure that looked like Jack, and she could see it resembled him in every detail – even the tiny pale blue points in the eyes of the model. Jasmine looked up at Aunt Barbara, and she could see that she too was dumbfounded by the people and animals of the toy farm. Beth brought the big manor house down from the loft and as the child wiped the cobwebs off the painted wooden building, Jasmine could see that it was the exact replica of Farmer Green's country house.

Aunt Barbara said that the previous owner of the

cottage had been a man named Arthur Dolley, and she knew hardly anything about him beyond what a neighbour had told her – that he was a toymaker and had died in his eighties a years or so before Barbara and her late husband had bought the cottage in the early 1950s.

Jasmine eventually met a visiting French student three years later, and she married him and went to live in Paris, where she taught English. She is still haunted by the mystery of the toy farm even today, and I suspect the strange matter will never be explained.

I DREAM OF OLGA

Night after night in early November 1939, John Stewart, a 35-year-old policeman living in the Kensington area of Liverpool, had the same dream about a beautiful blonde girl named Olga. In these recurring dreams which went on for twelve consecutive nights, Olga cried and John tried to comfort her but then something black and cloudlike would engulf the blonde girl and she'd let out a shriek as the shapeless billowing mass made off with her, taking her kicking and screaming into a grey swirling mist until only her cries could be heard. And then John would see the number 13 slowly appear in the mist in black nebulous numerals. John would always wake up at that point gasping for air and without fail his wife Jean would threaten to sleep in the spare room because she was sick of him crying out Olga's name when he had these nightmares. John reassured his wife that he had no idea who Olga was, and that he was not seeing any young blonde behind her back, but on the following Saturday morning of 11 November 1939 - as PC John Stewart walked up Renshaw Street on his beat at 8.50am, he almost collided with Olga as she walked up Ranelagh Street from the direction of Central Station. It was definitely the girl from his dreams, and he found himself following her into Lewis's – the original department store that was later destroyed in the Blitz. John established that the girl worked as a waitress at the store restaurant, and he ached to go up to her and tell her about the disturbing dreams he'd been having about her each night, but he thought he might scare her if he mentioned the weird nightmares of her getting carried away by some cloudy monster, so he turned around and left the building, continuing on his beat. Ten minutes later on the corner of Lime Street and London Road, PC Stewart bumped into his colleague PC Billy Brown, a wiry and very worldly-wise man in his forties, and also something of a ladies' man. Billy was chatting to a well-known platinum-blonde prostitute nicknamed Snowdrop, and PC Stewart overheard him say to her, 'That's two you owe me now, got that? I'll see you at the Grafton tonight, half-eight sharp. Got that?'

Snowdrop smiled and walked away up London Road.

'She's a case her, you know,' said Billy, watching the prostitute walk away. 'Heart of gold, but all her fingers are the same length, you know? Can't help herself; real tealeaf she is.'

'Billy listen to this,' said John Stewart, struggling to find the words to describe the dreams he'd been having about the blonde girl, and how he had just discovered that she was a real person.

'I don't follow you,' admitted PC Brown, looking a young passing lady up and down. 'You had dreams of a girl and now you've seen her?'

'Yes, she works in Lewis's, as a waitress in the restaurant,' said PC Stewart, 'but how did I see her in my dreams?'

PC Brown closed his eyes as he walked along, smiled and nodded slowly as he opined: 'What it is John, is this: you probably *have* seen her before but it hasn't registered. You've probably seen her pass you on your beat, and she's gone in to the back of your mind and then it's all come out in dreams. Dreams are bloody funny. The other night I dreamt I was on the top deck of a tram pissing out the window. Dreams don't make sense half the time.'

'I don't think I have seen her before,' said PC Stewart, 'I think it's something, well – supernatural.'

'Rubbish,' laughed Billy, 'it's just your brain, mate. You've got sex on it you see. What's she like, this girl?'

'She only looks about twenty – too young for me,' said John, 'and I'm not even thinking of her in that way.'

'I'd be up her like a ferret, lad,' said Billy, 'get in there before someone else does. I love the old slithery with blondes – real blondes like. I might call into that restaurant in Lewis's myself.'

John's eyes widened. 'Don't you dare, Billy, all you think about is hanky-panky.'

Billy nodded. 'I love sex. Beauty's skin deep, and that's about as far as I want to go; don't want all that true love rubbish and starry eyed promises in the moonlight. Just use them and move on; shallow but less bother. I get me French letters at the chemist off a nice girl, and then straight to the dance halls. It was chock-a-block at the Grafton last Saturday and you should have seen the figure on this woman John, but when she turned round she looked like Ernie Roderick, but I was that pissed, I didn't care because I just wanted a bit –'

'I don't wish to know what you wanted, thankyou, Billy!' John interjected, 'Now, if you're just going to be coarse, let's change the subject.'

'You're like an old woman sometimes, John,' said an

annoyed Billy, 'all you need is your hair up in a bun and an old pinny. Well, this blonde you were talking about – what was her name again in these dreams of yours?'

'Olga,' said John, and he blushed slightly.

'Isn't that Norwegian?' Billy asked, then continued: 'Well I would ask Olga out and I'd have an affair with the young lady.'

'But I'm a married man, Billy,' laughed John, 'Jean would kill me if I did that.'

Billy stopped walking, and he grabbed his friend's forearm hard. 'John, life's short mate, you never know what's around that corner. If this war they've just declared take's off, God knows what's going to happen to us. And only the other day, you told me that your wife's always arguing with you and criticising you; you told me yourself. You only get one shot at life lad, so ask this Olga out.'

On Monday morning, John was on his beat again when he saw the blonde girl approach, and he felt butterflies in his stomach at the sight of her. She halted for a moment, looked at him *as if she knew him*, and the policeman saw immense sadness in her eyes. He wanted to ask her out but he froze. She seemed to halt for a moment, and then she went into Lewis's.

'Maybe next time then,' John Stewart sighed under his breath, and continued on his beat.

The next time PC Stewart came down Renshaw Street around a quarter to one in the afternoon, he turned the corner onto Ranelagh Street and as he was about to cross the backstreet that runs behind Lewis's – Fairclough Street – he was startled by the piercing screams of female shoppers, and a middle-aged man some thirty feet in front of the policeman cried, 'Jesus!' and looked upwards – to the upper windows of the store. PC Stewart followed his gaze, and there was Olga, falling from a height of about eighty feet. The fifth floor window behind her was open. Before John could even react, Olgla's body slammed into the cobblestoned road of Fairclough Street, and her blood sprayed all over him.

'No- no, Olga – no,' John staggered to the body, which was twitching with nerves, but the eyes of the blonde girl were lifeless, and looking at the sky. Blood came out of the girl's nostrils and her left ear and from somewhere beneath her, and John stooped near to the body. He held the dead girl's hand and he felt the warmth of her palm slowly fade away.

He heard the sound of running boots, and he glanced back and saw PC Billy Brown turn the corner and come running to the awful scene.

'It's her, Billy – Olga,' John told his friend, 'the girl I told you about.'

'She looks – ' Billy said, and couldn't finish the sentence.

'Why, Billy?' the tears cascaded from John's eyes now. 'I should have asked her out. You were right! I would have saved her.'

Billy unbuttoned his police jacket and delved into an inside pocket. He produced a crumpled box with a couple of cigarettes and found a small box of matches. He lit the cigarette, puffed on it, then knelt down beside his friend and placed the fag in his mouth.

John took a drag and coughed as he cried, then again he asked Billy, 'Why did I see her in all those dreams – just for this to happen?'

'I don't know mate,' said Billy with an air of resignation in his voice. 'I'd better call an ambulance.' He stood up, took his jacket off, and gently laid it over the body of the girl, and then he started to push his way through the crowd that was gathering in Fairclough Street.

A gaggle of sobbing girls came out the wide back doors of Lewis's where the goods of the store were brought in and one very petite girl told PC Stewart: 'Her name's Olga - Olga Liljernberg – she was my friend,' and then she burst into tears.

This mention of the dead girl's name shook John Stewart to the core, for it confirmed that those recurring dreams must have been supernatural in their nature, for he had somehow known the girl's name in them.

'Is she alive?' asked one of the girls who had come out the back of the store. She seemed in shock and was watching the strange movements of the body under the coat.

'No, that's just nerves,' said John, and he saw the twitching of the body suddenly stop.

An ambulance beeped its horn and the crowd slowly parted to let the vehicle through. The body was taken to the Royal Infirmary where a sombre surgeon shook his head and said, 'It looks as if death was instantaneous.'

On the following day, PC John Stewart read about the sad events which had led to the suicide of Olga in the *Daily Mirror* and *Liverpool Echo*. Olga Agnes Liljernberg, aged 22, of Southport Road, Litherland, had been depressed because her boyfriend had told her that their forthcoming marriage was off. They'd had a tiff, and on her last morning alive, Olga had put on her wedding dress and veil, and her mother had caught her looking at herself in the mirror in her bedroom. The wedding should have taken place on the previous Thursday. The wedding cake had been made and the wedding banns were still up in the church. That morning Olga had taken a last look at the trousseau laid out on her bed before setting off for work at the restaurant in Lewis's. At noon that day she had written a goodbye note and handed it to her friends. Olga then went into the cloakroom and heaven knows what psychological state she was in when she opened the window and jumped to her death.

How or why John had dreams about a girl he didn't know remains a mystery. Was some Cupid up there in the great unknown trying to pair John with Olga out of sheer desperation? Had Olga seen John in *her* dreams perhaps? John said she had looked at him in their brief meeting as if she had recognised him from somewhere. The whole affair is tragic but also an unfathomable mystery.

THE ODD COUPLE

Over ten years ago a retired police superintendent told me a very intriguing story of what must have been a timeslip incident. I was supposed to feature his story on a radio programme but the producer deemed it too controversial because of its subject matter – homosexuality. The producer thought the listeners would either be somehow offended by the story or think the account was condoning gay marriage. I therefore had to file the story away till more enlightened times arrived. I've changed a few names for reasons of confidentiality, but beyond that the story is exactly as it was related to me by a very down-to-earth hard-boiled police official who had spent almost forty years in the force. It all began on the warm Monday evening of 8 August 1960 at a certain police station on Wirral. Chief Inspector Len Mills was sitting in his office at 9.25pm when a detective named Jack Marshall brought in two men, described by the desk sergeant (who also came into the office with him) as "a couple of queens" – 1960s slang for two gay people.

'Gross indecency, sir,' said a young constable who had accompanied the sergeant into the chief inspector's office, 'kissing they were.'

'And,' the sergeant butted in, then handed Mills an open box with some unfamiliar things in it, 'they had this paraphernalia on them.'

At this time in history, the Sexual Offences Act had not yet received royal assent, and would not be passed until 1967. That act would state that two gay people acting in private would not be committing an offence provided they consented to what they were doing and were both 21 years or over. In 1960 you could go to jail, lose your job and even face 'chemical correction' if you were gay and caught in the act with another gay person, so when two outlandishly dressed men speaking in what were regarded as 'effeminate' voices were brought into the station that humid August night in 1960, some of the detectives sneered, some sniggered, but Chief Inspector Mills immediately sensed there was something different about the couple, who looked as if they were in their early to mid thirties. Their hairstyles and clothes looked odd, Mills thought, and when the sergeant ushered them into their seats facing Mills at his desk, the usual lines of interrogation commenced.

'Name?' Mills asked the man to his left, a smiling chap with collar-length sandy-brown hair and a prominent aquiline nose. He wore a green coat with a hood and orange-coloured jeans.

'Mick – ' he started, then paused and said, 'Mikhail Ivanov.' His accent sounded Liverpudlian.

'That doesn't sound very English,' said Mills suspiciously, 'sounds Russian. You taking the piss?'

'No, honest, I was born in Moscow,' said Mikhail, and he had a glazed look in his eyes and a faint smile which convinced Mills that he was either drunk or drugged.

'And your date of birth, comrade,' said Mills, glancing at his sergeant before he looked into the box containing the men's belongings.

'August 12, 2014,' Mikhail replied, and his friend

next to him giggled. This friend of Mikhail was a very handsome blond with large blue eyes and an almost elfin, boyish face, Mills recalled. He wore a smart dark maroon suit and matching waistcoat, a satin pink shirt and red tie.

Mills tapped the point of the pen on the sheet and said, 'You look as if you're drugged up to the eyeballs – love.'

'Psyke,' sighed Mikhail, 'it's legal, don't worry.'

'So, you're admitting you've taken a drug – a narcotic?' said the Chief Inspector, angling his head slightly to the right with a quizzical expression.

Mikhail nodded and casually replied: 'Yes, it's just Psyke though, it's not cancer like.'

'Can you spell the name of that drug?' Mills asked, his pen poised to record the reply on a form.

'Er, yes, it's P-S-Y-K-E,' said Mikhail.

'And what was that you said about cancer?' Mills asked.

'Eh?' Mikhail seemed puzzled, then realised the misunderstanding. 'No, when I said it's not cancer I meant it's not serious. It's just old slang isn't it?'

The sergeant grunted behind the two men and slapped his hand hard on Mikhail's shoulder. 'Don't give cheek to the Chief Inspector you nancy boy!' he growled.

Mills looked up at the sergeant and shook his head, and the policeman took his hand off Mikhail's shoulder and stepped back, saying, 'Sorry sir but I can't abide them.'

'What a nasty quim *he* is!' said Mikhail with a chuckle, referring to the desk sergeant.

Chief Inspector Mills then turned his attention to

Mikhail's friend. He asked: 'And your name and D.O.B sir?'

'Charlie Ivanov, officer, and this makes me feel so old but I was born on September 30 2012.'

'So, you're brothers eh?' said Mills with a painful smile, 'the brothers Ivanov? Sounds like a Dostoyevsky novel.'

'No, we're married,' Mikhail replied, all matter-of-factly.

'Watch it!' the sergeant seethed behind Charlie, and to his superior he pleaded, 'just leave them with me sir and I'll soon get some sense out of them.'

'It's okay sergeant,' Mills raised his palm, and then he turned his attention back to the odd duo seated before him. They were like some theatrical double-act in his eyes. 'So both of you haven't even been born yet, then?' Mills tapped the top of his pen against his smiling lips and leaned back into his chair. 'And where do you live, Mikhail? The Kremlin by any chance?'

'Landican Glades,' came the reply.

'And before you ask, I live by him in Storeton Gardens,' said Charlie.

'I thought you two were both married to one another?' said Mills, quick as a flash. 'Get your story straight!'

'We *are* married,' retorted Mikhail with a succession of nods, 'just separated for now, that's all.'

Chief Inspector Len Mills opened a desk drawer and produced a large fold-out map. 'I've never heard of any Landican Glades and Storeton Gardens, so come and show me where they are,' he said, and the two men rose from their seats, and, accompanied by the sergeant and the constable, they stooped to look at the fold-out Bartholomew map.

'Landican Glades is just facing The Brothel pub there,' Mikhail pointed to a trapezoid of blank farmland next to Storeton Village.

'That's just farmland,' said the Chief Inspector, 'and I know of no pub in England called The Brothel. So, sunny Jim, you are going to sit down there and you and Charlie Drake are going to tell me your real names and where you live; got that, mush?'

'I wouldn't be surprised if we're tripping all this,' Mikhail said to his friend. He sat down with Charlie at the desk and waited for the questions as Mills went through the belongings of the men in the box.

'What's this?' Mills picked up what looked like a shiny black card.

'A phone, isn't it?' Mikhail answered.

'And this? A lighter?' the police official picked up something which looked like a white cigarette lighter to his eyes. It was about five inches in length, rectangular in shape, and had small flat buttons that lit up in red, blue and white when touched.

'Don't aim that towards me!' Mikhail recoiled at the sight of the object being handled and the legs of the chair he was in screeched across the tiles. The sergeant seized Mikhail with a hand on each shoulder and snarled, 'Oi!'

'That's a stunner!' Mikhail told Mills, 'It knocks people out. Don't press any of the buttons.'

Mills put the object down and looked at a small blue plastic box with a white button. He accidentally pressed the button and a small white pill came out of it.

'That's a drugbox,' said Mikhail, and he told the

Chief Inspector the drugs in the box made him clever, gave him weeks without sleep, and even enabled him to perform like an Olympic athlete. 'Sex with them is peak if you want to try. Where are you in the continuum anyway?'

'You are asking for a hiding you bent – ' the sergeant started but Mills stood up and said, 'Right, I think it's time we got down to business,' and to the sergeant he said, 'take them into the interrogation room sergeant.'

'Wait, I know the law,' said Mikhail, as the sergeant twisted his hand up his back. 'I'm allowed to make a call to a lawyer!'

'A solicitor, yes, but – ' Mills said, exhaling cigarette smoke.

'Phone!' Mikhail shouted.

The black shiny card in the box lit up and displayed a beautiful swirling geometric pattern on its screen. 'Yes, Mikhail,' said a woman's voice, and it came from that card.

Chief Inspector Mills, the sergeant and the young constable stood behind Charlie Ivanov all looked at the speaking card in wide-eyed amazement.

'Get me a lawyer!' shouted Mikhail, and he struggled to free his arm from the sergeant's hold.

'I can't Mikhail, there's no network,' said the female voice emanating from the card.

When Mills saw that the card-thin phone was indeed some communications device, he thought about the Russian surnames of the detainees and had them put in a cell while he contacted Special Branch. He told them about the incredibly thin telephonic device and the "stunner" and he was told that two officers from Special Branch would visit the police station in the morning.

'Are they spies, then?' Mills asked the Special Branch official.

'I'd say so, Chief Inspector,' came the reply. 'We've been intercepting quite a few Hungarian and Soviet agents posing as stowaways at the Liverpool landing stage. We recently arrested two of them on the Cunard liner *Carinthia* at Liverpool. Strip them and search them again Chief Inspector, and keep them under armed guard till we get there in the morning.'

'Yes sir,' said Mills, and as he continued to speak on the phone, the sergeant and the fledgeling constable pushed the two suspected spies out of the Chief Inspector's office and into a corridor.

'Don't strip them till I join you in a few minutes!' Mills shouted after the police officers. He hung up, put the belongings of the 'agents' into a safe, then got on the telephone to his superior to report the matter of suspected espionage.

Ten minutes later, the sergeant and the young constable burst into the office of Chief Inspector Mills and told him that the two prisoners were gone. They had somehow escaped from a locked cell.

'That's impossible – how could they – how could they get out of there?' a stunned Mills stammered. 'I can't trust you idiots to do anything!' he stormed out of his office and saw that the holding cell was indeed empty. He went to the only two exits and asked two police constables if anyone had passed them. 'No sir,' said one of the policemen, 'not a soul.'

'I am going to be a bloody laughing stock over this!' Chief Inspector Mills growled, and he rushed out of the police station and looked up and down the main road as other policemen filed out after him. The policemen could see no one remotely resembling Mikhail and Charlie. The desk sergeant grabbed a passing Teddy boy and he asked him, 'have you just come from down there?'

'Down where?' the startled ted asked.

'That road down there!' bawled the sergeant.

'Yeah, just now, why? I haven't done anything!' the Ted was naturally scared at the way the policeman held him by the scruff of his astrakhan coat.

'Did you see two odd-looking fellahs pass you?' the sergeant asked through clenched teeth.

'No, I saw nobody officer,' said the Teddy boy.

'They can't have gone far, Chief Inspector,' reasoned the young constable, looking about.

'Well they've gone you idiot!' Chief Inspector Mills roared at the young policeman. 'And all because you didn't keep an eye on them!'

'I only looked away for a minute – ' the constable said, and seemed near to tears. 'I'm sorry, sir.'

'Oh it's okay, constable, I shouldn't blame you,' Mills said, calming down, 'those two were obviously experts. Come on.' Mills walked back into the station. He went straight to the wall safe in his office and opened it. The belongings of the men; the drugbox, the stunner and the impossibly thin communications device – had all vanished without a trace.

Mills believed the men were ghosts; not the usual chain-clanking ghosts people saw haunting castles and graveyards – but ghosts from the future. He eventually came to the conclusion that those two men had somehow walked from some future age – an age where same-sex marriages were allowed, drugs had evolved, and technology had produced wafer-thin telephones, but it was the year 1960, and the Chief Inspector knew he could not voice his theory or he'd be instantly dismissed and declared mentally unstable. And so, fearing dismissal he had to pretend that he and his officers had been hoaxed by two mischievous students.

TIMEWALKER

In the year 2000, a 22-year-old girl named Hayley was drinking with her friend Liz in the Beehive pub on Paradise Street, when she suddenly started to cry. Today would have been the birthday of Hayley's beloved Nan, Rosie. Hayley said the happiest days of her life were the ones she spent visiting town with her Nan from the age of three till she was six, when her Nan suddenly passed away after suffering a severe stroke. Hayley had never forgotten her Nan, and on this day she told Liz she wished she could see her grandmother just one more time, just to tell her how much she loved her.

'You can't go back, Hayl,' said Liz, hugging her sentimental friend, 'you've got to look forward. Your Nan will know you love her; she'll be looking down now.'

When Liz went to the pub toilet, a man of about seventy approached Hayley. He had wild grey hair, a snow-white 'horseshoe' moustache, and a pair of very sympathetic eyes. He was dressed casually in dark blue jeans, a brown suede jacket, and possibly a black polo shirt. In a well-spoken voice devoid of any regional accent, this man said to Hayley: 'I overheard you talking about your Nan then, and from what I heard you obviously loved her. If you could pick a year you could go back to - and a place - what would they be?'

'That's a strange question to ask,' Hayley replied with suspicion in her eyes, but she told the stranger: 'I suppose if I could go back in time, it'd be to the year 1981, and I could even tell you the very day – my birthday, the 30th of June, and the place would be Woolworths, just round the corner.'

The old man slowly shook his head and seemed deep in thought for a few moments, and then he said, 'Come on, before your friend comes back,' and he took hold of Hayley's hand with a firm grip, and tried to pull her up out of her seat, but she resisted and said: 'What are you doing?' She naturally thought he was mentally unstable or just some old geezer who fancied his chances with a girl young enough to be his daughter.

'Just trust me, please,' the old man replied in a reassuring voice which gave a great impression of sincerity, and he placed his other hand on top of the hand that was already clasped around Hayley's hand, and in a soft, solemn-sounding voice he said: 'I can take you back – back to see your Nan!'

Hayley didn't know if she was doing the right thing believing in the unknown man's claim, but she found herself slowly getting to her feet, and she walked out the pub and the pushy old man led her to "Holy Corner" – where Whitechapel, Lord, Church and Paradise Streets converge in a cross.

The quirky senior citizen stood in the middle of Church Street and with great urgency in his voice he told Hayley: 'Close your eyes, and think of your Nan – nothing else but her; think of your beautiful Nan, and I promise we shall meet her.'

'This is silly,' Hayley said, but she closed her eyes and thought of the best friend she ever had – and then she became dizzy as Church Street tilted. She really did think that the street had pitched to the right and with a start she opened her eyes and fell sideways but the old man caught her and said, 'We're back, but not for long I'm afraid.'

The hairstyles and fashions were vaguely familiar – late 1970s early 1980 by the looks of them, and there stood old shops that had closed their doors years ago. Hayley noticed a structure she hadn't seen since she was a little girl: the Church Street "Plant Pots" – these were three cylindrical interlocking structures made of blue bricks which contained plants.

Coming towards Hayley was her Nan! She wore her usual glasses and had on her headscarf and that raincoat she always seemed to wear – and those funny fur-lined boots to her shins. Hayley ran to her but the old woman didn't recognise her grown-up granddaughter and thought she was being mugged. Her Nan froze and her magnified eyes behind her glasses seemed full of fear for a moment. Hayley hugged her and cried, 'Oh Nan, it's me, Hayley, I love you and miss you so much.'

The fear in her Nan Rosie immediately subsided when she heard these words, and the woman seemed to vaguely understand that this emotional adult was somehow a grown-up version of little Hayley. Rosie kept saying, 'But how? How? I don't understand how it can be you!'

That beautiful scent of something like lavender that her Nan had always wore – a scent that Hayley had forgotten about – seemed intoxicating to the girl now, and she just wanted to cling on to her grandmother and never let her slip away ever again.

The mysterious old man pulled Hayley away from her Nan, and Rosie said to him, 'Aye aye, who are you and where are you taking her?'

Hayley struggled to break away from the old man's grip and she came close to belting him, but he was incredibly strong, and he walked back to Paradise Street pulling Hayley along with him as if she was a rag doll. And then suddenly it was 2000 again. The Church Street Plant Pots structure had vanished, along with so many of the old shops – and of course, Hayley's dearly loved and much-missed Nan was also gone now. She had been swallowed up in the days of a bygone decade.

'Why did you do that – and then take her away again?' a sobbing Hayley cried to the old man, who stood there looking into her eyes with a penetrating sorrowful stare.

He looked down at the pavement, and fixing his coat, which had been disarranged by Hayley as she struggled to get away from him, the mystifying man said: 'You're right, I shouldn't have done that. I – I just thought – well – never mind.'

'Take me back again – please!' Hayley pleaded with him, and people, noticing her tears, halted and a crowd started to form.

The old man shook his head, and said, 'I'm sorry, it's wrong to do what I did before. I'm my own worst enemy. Bye.' He then walked off up Lord Street, and Hayley ran after him, but somehow she lost sight of him. It didn't seem to be a case of him vanishing into the crowds; it was as if he had vanished into thin air. I mentioned this case on the *Billy Butler Show* during my weekly afternoon slot talking about local mysteries on BBC Radio Merseyside in 2004 and I received some intriguing feedback from listeners concerning the old 'timewalker' (as I referred to him on the programme).

A few recalled an old man with the white shock of

hair and moustache who seemed a bit cranky, and most said that he frequented the Beehive public house, but one particular listener provided me with some tantalizingly fascinating but scant information. He was an estate agent named Martin who contacted me after the broadcast to tell me how, in the late summer of 1998, he had been spending his lunch break in the Beehive pub on Paradise Street five days a week and had often seen a very noticeable man, aged between seventy and seventy-five, with a wild head of snow-white hair and a moustache. This man often sat talking and sipping whisky in a corner of the premises with a Scottish-sounding man of about fifty, and Martin recalled that the conversation between the men was about "some fascinating but heavy stuff" that seemed to range from talk of early civilizations and Stonehenge and Atlantis to convoluted discussions about quantum physics – a subject Martin had a superficial understanding of because his son was studying physics at college and often talked about the topsy-turvy mind-bending nature of quantum theory. Martin asked a barmaid at the pub about the men and was told that the Scotsman was Jim - some lecturer at a local college - and the older man was said to be a rich eccentric the way he threw his money around, but she did not know his name or where he was from. He always gave generous tips and he'd been seen to lend money out to various people at the pub. As far as Martin could remember, Jim and the old eccentric did not talk directly about time travel, but they did sometimes talk about the nature of time, but he cannot recall what was discussed in any detail.

So, the identity of that cryptic man Hayley met in the

Beehive pub that day remains unknown. Hayley believes he actually took her back in time nineteen years to 1981, whereas her friend Liz thinks the man was a charlatan who used hypnosis to make Hayley *think* she had gone back in time to meet her Nan. Hayley told me, 'However he did it, I would dearly love to meet that man again, just so I could hold by lovely Nan once more.'

THE TICKLER

I've had to change a few names in this strange story for legal reasons, but the rest is, to the best of my knowledge, true – and very eerie. One gloriously sunny Saturday morning in the late summer of 1990, a pretty 20-year-old lady in the Claughton area of Wirral named Jane Maple was about to set off to the church to marry her childhood sweetheart, 21-year-old Robin Newstead, when the vicar who was due to marry Jane telephoned her with some dire news. She couldn't take it in at first. 'Jane my dear,' said the Reverend Richard Wickham, 'I've had to call the wedding off as there's been mistake regarding the banns.'

'The what?' asked a shocked and puzzled Jane.

'The banns dear,' the clergyman replied. 'The banns are a required legal notice of any wedding that's due to take place, and I read them out on three Sundays in a row at the church. If anyone knows of any reason why the marriage shouldn't be taking place, it gives them time to object. It's the law.'

'Well, didn't you read these banns out Reverend?' asked Jane, with sorrow welling up in her throat.

'Yes *I* did,' said the clergyman, 'but the Reverend Blackburn didn't, and by law he should have done because the banns also have to be read in the parish where the husband-to-be lives. I checked with the Registrar and I'm afraid Blackburn didn't do his job.'

'So, will you marry me and Robin as soon as this

matter has been sorted out?' asked Jane, and began to sniffle. She thought of the wedding cake her father had bought, of the pre-booked honeymoon holiday in the south of France, and all that food and drink that had been bought for the wedding reception.

'I've already pencilled you in for a Saturday next month,' said the Reverend. 'I didn't know about the banns not being read until I received a telephone call from a woman about an hour ago. She threatened to inform an archbishop if the wedding wasn't stopped.'

'Who *was* this busybody?' Jane asked, her sorrow turning to anger.

The vicar said he didn't know who she was; she'd hung up when he asked her for her name. Jane asked Robin if the anonymous caller had been some old flame of his, but he said, 'Don't be daft – I've only been going with you since we were at school. I never went out with anyone else. That woman has just been some nosy parker putting her oar in.'

The wedding went ahead in September, and after the honeymoon in France, the couple moved into their new home – a beautiful semi on Prenton's Lorne Road. Robin landed a job at a building society, and while Jane looked for work she enjoyed the role of a housewife. She was in the kitchen one dull afternoon, baking an apple pie when she happened to look out the window. She saw someone in a strange mask who wore what looked like a wedding veil, peeping over the fence at the far end of the back garden. The weird snooper naturally startled Jane, and she saw the person duck down. She waited to see if the strange peeping tom would look over the fence again, but he didn't.

Jane later told Robin about the incident when he

came home from work and he said it had probably just been one of the neighbour's children playing a prank. Around this time, Robin became obsessed with fitness and he bought two bicycles and convinced Jane to go cycling with him on weekends. Despite constant drizzle on the following Saturday, the couple cycled half a mile to Birkenhead Park, and when they had a brief rest near the park lake, Robin drew his wife's attention to something bizarre. 'Look at that,' he pointed to two garments hanging from the branch of a tree. The couple cycled to the abandoned dresses – and saw that they were an expensive-looking ivory wedding gown and a pale blue bridesmaid's dress.

'Who on earth would leave a perfect wedding gown and a dress on a branch?' Robin asked, and Jane, who now had the feeling she and her husband were being watched, said, 'Let's go home; I've got a bad feeling about this.'

'About what?' a bemused Robin asked.

Jane looked about furtively and replied: 'I've just got this weird feeling – I dunno – just a creepy feeling that someone put that gown and the dress there to see how we react.'

'That's ridiculous Jane,' her husband told her, 'some poor girl who was supposed to get married has probably been jilted or found out her fiancé is a rat and she's dumped the gown and that bridesmaid dress.'

'Let's just go, Robin, please.' Jane pushed her sole on the pedal and set the bicycle in motion.

On the following day around three in the afternoon, the sun was out, so Jane put out her washing in the back garden. It was a Sunday and Robin was due back from the pub in about half an hour, and Jane wished he'd be back a bit earlier, because once again she had the unsettling feeling she was being watched. She thought about the ghastly face of the peeping tom with the wedding veil on, and she looked to the end of the garden – to the fence where she had seem him looking at her. As she looked, the terrifying figure of a tall thin man dressed in some short-skirted version of a wedding outfit, embellished with striped orange and black tights and workmen's boots, climbed over the garden fence. It was *him*. His face was covered in thick white make up and his nose was red, giving the impression of being a clown, and he wore that transparent veil he'd worn last time. He picked up a pair of garden shears and in a high-pitched voice that sounded feminine, he shouted: 'If you run I'll cut your head off with these! I mean it now!'

Jane wanted to run but her legs felt as if they were about to give away under her, and she froze and screamed, but the weirdly-attired trespasser threw down the shears and in a flash he was upon her. He slapped her across the face with a hand clad in some white glove, and then he seized her shoulders and spun her around so she faced away from him. He pushed her onto the lawn, and tied her wrists together with a length of lace behind her back. He started chuckling, and now his voice sounded more masculine and rough as he said, 'I am going to tickle you till you die! Horrible bitch!' He dug the fingers of his left hand into the left side of her torso first, prodding the ribs, and then he placed the fingers of his right hand so they touched the right side of her torso, and he began to tickle her ribs. Jane laughed and cried in terror at the same time, and begged him to stop but he just laughed, and he pinned her down by placing her bottom between his legs, but he did not try anything sexual. He tickled Jane for what seemed like ten minutes - until she threw up, she recalled trying to breathe but being unable to draw her breath, and just when she thought she'd die. She heard her neighbour – a retired man in his sixties – shout something from his garden next door. The neighbour – a Mr Stride – had seen the strange scene after hearing the commotion coming from Jane's garden. Mr Stride climbed over the fence and chased the bizarre and obviously unbalanced man, but the sinister assaulter laughed hysterically and vaulted over the garden fence and got clean away. The neighbour said it had almost been supernatural the way the weirdo had vanished after running behind the shed of a neighbouring garden. When Robin came home and heard what had happened, he said he was going to call the police, but Jane said they'd never believe her because the account would sound so outlandish; a man dressed like a clown in a wedding gown. Robin insisted, and Jane begged him not to call the police, so Robin bought a shotgun from a friend and sat at his bedroom window for several nights after dark, hoping to see the cross-dressing oddball so he could blast him to kingdom come.

Jane was so terrified of encountering the outlandish figure again, she got her sister Elsa to stay over with her each day while Robin was at work. About a week after the weird attack, Elsa went to the bottom of the garden with Jane and looked over the fence the creepy man had come over to perpetrate his cowardly attack.

All she could see was a small garden and another

garden beyond that. There was plainly no one about or the women would have seen them. But someone threw a plucked rose over the fence as soon as Elsa and Jane turned their backs. Jane panicked and ran away, but Elsa shouted to whoever had thrown the rose: 'You're obviously a shithouse, picking on a defenceless woman. Try me yellow-belly and I'll put a knife in you!'

'No!' Jane shrieked to her sister, 'Don't say that! You'll have him attacking me again!'

'I'm not scared of the big girl's blouse!' Elsa shouted, looking towards the fence, expecting the weird man to appear, but he didn't.

Jane bawled at her sister: 'Elsa, it's alright for you – you can go home later, but I've got to live here! Now come here!'

Thankfully, Jane never saw the maniac again. She wondered if her attacker had been the one who had called the church to have her wedding cancelled; the assailant had sounded female, even though he was obviously a man, so perhaps he'd put on a woman's voice when he spoke to the Reverend Wickham. And had the clown in the gown been the person who had left the wedding gowns at Birkenhead Park? Jane read further reports of even more wedding gowns being left at the park over the next three years. On Boxing Day of that year, Robin received an anonymous telephone call at his home. A woman who sounded well-to-do told him: 'Hello. I would like to throw a little light on why your wife was attacked in her back garden some months back.'

'Who *is* this?' Robin asked, recoiling in shock.

'Never mind who I am,' said the woman, talking

over him, 'my son was the one who did it and he hanged himself last night. Hanged himself!' The woman yelled the last two words, was heard to start sobbing, and then she hung up.

When Robin told Jane about the call she started to tremble, and refused to stay at the house alone whenever Robin was at work.

On a hot July afternoon in 1996, almost six years after the attack on Jane Newstead, her sister Elsa Gill was sunbathing in the back garden of her Wavertree home on Heathfield Road. All she wore was a bikini, and she was reclining on a sun lounger, talking to her friend Joanne on a cordless telephone – when a shadow fell across her, making her jump with fright. It was a man, well over six feet in height, and he wore a white satin wedding gown with huge puffy 'mutton chop' styled upper sleeves, and a short knee-length skirt, together with orange and black striped stockings and scuffed-looking steel toe-capped boots. The face behind the diaphanous wedding veil was a nightmare; plastered with white make up with two black holes of mascara for eyes, blue grinning lips, and a red aquiline nose. In a flash of horror Elsa recalled that sinister attacker who had assaulted her sister over on the Wirral, and she tried to get up off the sun lounger, but the intruder placed the sole of his heavy boot on her bosom and pushed down hard. He then stooped and he lunged at Elsa and his gloved hands seized her curly black permed hair and he began to shake her head violently as he screamed something unintelligible. The sun lounger tipped over, and Elsa screamed into the cordless phone: 'I'm being attacked! Help!'

The unearthly assailant grabbed the phone and threw

it over the fence into a neighbouring garden, and then he pinned Elsa down so she was between his legs facing upwards, and he clamped his huge white gloved hand over her mouth and growled, 'I am *not* a yellow-belly! I am not a coward! You don't know half of it!'

He then started to tickle her, and on this occasion, Elsa heard a clicking noise. It was the claws of her Alsatian dog, Bruno as he trotted across the patio. He was not allowed in the back garden because he had a habit of jumping over the hedge to try and mate with a neighbour's poodle, but somehow, he had managed to open the kitchen door, perhaps by pressing down on the handle with his huge paws. Bruno went for the freakish-looking trespasser and managed to tear off the veil and the back of the wedding gown. On the exposed back of the unknown assailant, Elsa saw multiple red lines criss-crossing his skin, as if he had been whipped or cut by a razor, and some of the marks looked deep red and freshly made. The terrifying attacker ran away down the garden with the Alsatian at his heels, and he managed to get over a fence. Whoever he was, he would have had to cross the back garden of the house behind Elsa's on Sinclair Drive. Elsa asked the old widowed man who lived there if he'd seen anyone in his back garden, and the man said he hadn't. Elsa could not believe that the fiend who had attacked her sister six years ago had travelled all the way to Liverpool to attack her, and when she told her husband about the attack, he said it might have been some oddly-dressed burglar, even though Elsa said he had complained about the names she had called him over in Wirral all those years back.

If it was the same person who had attacked Jane

Newstead in 1990, had the Boxing Day call to her husband by a 'woman' saying her son had hanged himself at Christmas been the attacker himself putting on a woman's voice again? There is some matrimonial theme to this mystery – the anonymous caller preventing Jane and Robin's wedding, the strange wedding gowns and bridesmaid's dresses found in Birkenhead Park, and the outlandish wedding gown the attacker had worn. There is something in all of that which could probably be unravelled by a psychiatrist, but to me, the "tickler" remains an enigma.

THE WOMEN OF THE WOOD

I've had to change a few names in this story for legal reasons but the rest is alleged to have really happened, and, like many of the stories that come my way, it's hard to explain. In the summer of 1981, a 25-year-old petty thief and drug addict named Martin Guyse was accused of stealing £33,000 in untraceable cash from the Huyton house of a small-time crook named Jason Roud. Martin told everyone he was innocent, and that Jason was putting the blame on him because Jason himself had either appropriated the money or someone he knew had taken it. Martin confronted Jason at his home and told him he was not being a fall guy for anyone, but Jason gave him an ultimatum: 'It's dead simple; return the money in three days or you'll be done in – end of.'

Martin had been trying to turn over a new leaf in his life at this time. There were two million unemployed and jobs were very hard to come by but he'd started a voluntary job at a charity shop and he'd been plucking up courage to ask out a woman named Jacqueline who worked at this shop. The three days came and went, and Martin panicked and did a runner, knowing that Jason Roud was not a man who made idle threats. Martin hid out on farmland off Fox's Bank Lane,

Whiston, having snatches of a kip in the open in a sleeping bag, but a Land Rover arrived there one afternoon, and out of it got Jason and a lackey of his nicknamed Stab, who, unseen by Martin, ran in a curve to the other end of the field. Jason chased Martin across fields of barley, almost into the arms of Stab – a former amateur rugby player - who performed a spear tackle of the kind he had often executed for his old rugby team. The tackle involved intercepting the rehabilitating heroin addict, lifting his bony 8 stone frame into the air and then slamming him down into the ground. And this not only winded Martin – it also knocked him into a state of near senselessness for a few minutes. When Martin sat up and complained of double vision, Stab delivered an upper cut that almost knocked the alleged thief out. Jason approached with a hunting knife and told the stunned young man, 'Now, you either hand over my money or tell me where it is – or I'll stick you with this,' Jason seethed, and glanced at the knife. 'I am sick to death of people taking liberties with me!'

'I haven't got your money and you know it,' groaned Martin. He got to his feet and walked to Jason, pleading for mercy. 'Jay, don't kill me! Get your mind in gear mate! If I had thirty-three grand do you think I'd be wearing no-name trabs and clobber like the stuff I've got on? You know the lumber I had with the smack, Jay, and you know I'd be on it right now if I had your readies mate.'

'Bastard!' Jason swung his fist forward and Martin thought he'd punched him in the solar plexus, as he did not feel the blade go in the first time. 'Robbing, dirty, smelly smack head bastard!' shrieked Jason, and with each of those six words the knife was launched into the abdomen of Martin, and now the victim could see the blood blossoming through his pale blue Army & Navy Store tee shirt. And then in shock, as the pain made him double up, he began to urinate with fear.

'Ha! He's pissing himself!' observed Stab, who was standing behind Martin as the latter fell to his knees.

'I told you I meant business! Taking liberties with me!' Jason screamed at the dying 25-year-old, and then he looked about, wiped the sweat from his face with his palm, then ran off, back to the Land Rover with Stab, who shouted: 'Straight to Hell, Martin!' as he fled.

'It's a nightmare,' Martin gasped to himself as he fell face-down in the field, 'I'll wake up now. It's just a dream. Just a dream.'

He felt cold, and the pain was leaving him, but so was all feeling in his body and although the numbness was wiping out the abdominal agony, it scared Martin. A strange darkness dimmed the glaring sun above, and then he passed out.

The next thing Martin remembered was the feeling of something large and warm and pneumatic pressing against his face. For all the world it felt like a huge rubber ball full of warm water, and then he realised he was sucking at something in this thing pressing against him – something sweet and creamy and *milky* - and then a strange possibility came into his disoriented mind: that he was being breast-fed. At this point he recalled how he'd been stabbed and wondered if he'd been reincarnated and was now at the bosom of his new mother. He opened his eyes and saw the glare of sunlight filtering through the upper branches of trees, and that sunlight was also shining through wavy brown hair. At this point, Martin realised he was being held against a woman's bosom, and he tried to ask what was going on but whoever *she* was, she pushed his face into the mamilla. Her hand on his back felt huge, as if the ball of the hand was at his bottom and the top of her middle finger was touching his head. The sensations really threw Martin, and he decided to keep suckling, as he felt weak, and yet he could not work out just why he was still alive. In those terrible recollections, he counted the number of times the knife went into him; seven times. Seven times the eight-inch blade of the hunting knife had gone in. He trembled at the thought of the damage he must have sustained but the giantess comforted him by patting his back reassuringly, and then she started to rub his back. He felt so warm and safe again now, he drifted off into a dreamless sleep, and when he awoke again, he saw a crescent moon peering through the silhouettes of tree branches. His face was snuggling into some soft velvety garment which seemed to be white. He slowly looked up and saw the flawless chin and face of a woman as if he was far below her. He could see up her nostrils and her top lip seemed prominent at this vantage point. He could make out dark eyebrows and the eyes were looking straight ahead. The irises looked dark and so did the long eyelashes.

'Who are you?' Martin asked, and he still felt so weak, it took some effort to get the words out.

Without looking down, the mysterious woman pushed him into the folds of the white fabric that clothed her, and again, Martin dozed off. When he opened his eyes again, Martin felt the nipple in his mouth, and he heard birds chirping. There was a golden-red sky visible through the trees, and he sensed it was sunrise. He thought he heard the beautiful female saviour humming a tune and she started to gently pat his back. He stayed awake a little longer this time, and was alarmed to see there was another gigantic woman there. She peered over the shoulder of the woman holding Martin, and she wore a white head-dress similar to a turban, and although she looked beautiful, her eyes looked black and penetrating. Her enormous finger and thumb came into his view, and now he realised how small he was to these colossal women. There was something between the finger and thumb, and the second woman almost pushed it into his face. Martin opened his mouth and nibbled on whatever it was. It had a taste of mushroom to it, and it was hard to chew, and yet he enjoyed the unknown food. This second woman fed him more of the brown foodstuff, and then she went away, and he could hear the heavy slow padding of her feet becoming fainter. He suckled again, then looked up at the beautiful titan and was about ask her who she was when he felt himself defecate. He felt so embarrassed at this; it was as if he had no control of his bowels. He felt the woman clean him with some cloth. He felt his abdomen, and expected to feel mutilated skin, but instead he felt only the bumps of his six-pack – the rectus abdominis muscle it was officially called, and he could not detect a trace of any scarring – but it felt a little sore down there. He turned his head away from the gigantic prominence of the woman's left breast and saw that they were in a wood, but her huge hand cupped around him and pushed him back to the nipple. 'I'm sorry,' he found himself saying to this strange lifegiver – and he started to suckle again. Time seemed to run at a different rate than the clock time Martin had been accustomed to before this peculiar episode of his life. Minutes sometimes seemed like a quarter of an hour, and at other times the whole day flew by and night was soon upon him, and always, this mysterious 'mother' doted on him with the other woman, feeding him, cleaning him, and allowing him those snuggling sleeps that seemed to be rejuvenating him. A bizarre thing happened during this latter time in the wood; Martin started to recall a time when he must have been in the womb of his natural mother – a lady who had sadly passed away a few years ago. He recalled the feeling of weightlessness when he would have been suspended upside-down in the amniotic sac, and he shuddered at the appearance of what seemed like a tunnel of light as he left the womb, bound for the light of day and the glare of neon in the maternity ward at Walton Hospital. The separation from the first woman he had loved – had always loved. He thought it had been a crime when the midwife had cruelly sliced through that umbilical cord. He found himself weeping, and this present mother wiped away his tears and gently stroked his back, and he heard her strange lullaby, hummed in a low voice that resonated through his body and soothed him asleep. 'It all goes wrong when we leave mother,' Martin recalled himself muttering as he dozed off.

'I want me mam,' he said, and those childish words startled him from his sleep, and he immediately noticed the absence of the breasts. He was lying there, cold and naked in the middle of a wood, and those beautiful behemoths were nowhere to be seen. Twelve feet away, a fox was looking at Martin, poised to run off, as he sat up and tried to get his bearings. He looked at his abdomen, and he could see the faint seven scars of the knife, and he gently ran the tip of his pointer finger over them. How had they healed? He lifted his hand to his face to rub his eyes, and his fingers brushed against a beard. He got to his feet, and the fox ran away. There, lying in a pile at the bottom of a tree trunk were his clothes and trainers. The pale blue tee shirt had dried black and scarlet bloodstains upon it. He dressed, and reluctantly put on the bloodstained tee shirt last, and then he walked out of the wood and surveyed the field where he had been stabbed and left to die. He saw a solitary red Royal Mail van travelling along Fox's Bank Lane, and he left the wood – known as Fox Clump – and he made his way across farmland till he found a way to the lane. He reached his home and his sister Bonnie asked him where he had been and when she saw his tee shirt she said, 'You've been fighting again I see.'

'How long have I been away?' Martin asked her, and he went to the kitchen, turned on the cold water tap, and put his mouth to it.

'That's disgusting, Martin, use a cup!' Bonnie grimaced at the site of her bearded brother drinking in that way.

'How long was I gone?' he asked her again.

'I don't know,' she said, 'about three weeks. Where have you been dossing?'

'Weren't you concerned about me? Didn't you go to

the police or anything?' Martin asked her, wiping the droplets of water from his beard.

'Oh we know what you're like, gallivanting and doing the smack and that,' Bonnie told him in a condescending manner, 'but that woman out the charity shop came round a few times and asked where you were. I had to say you'd gone to London to look for work. She's too good for you, mate.'

'Jacqueline,' said Martin, and a tear came to his eye. 'She was concerned eh?'

'While you were gone, Stab Thompson died,' said Bonnie with a lopsided grin.

'Did he now? What happened?' Martin recalled him shouting 'Straight to Hell' as he collapsed from those stab wounds.

'Yeah,' said Bonnie, all matter-of-factly as she opened the fridge door to grab a can of Coke. 'He erm, over-dosed on smack. He robbed around thirty grand off Jay Roud and he was doing all these drugs and he ballsed up and they found him reaching for the telephone; he must have been trying to phone an ambulance. No great loss though.'

That night, Martin knocked on the door of Jason Roud, the man who had plunged a knife blade into him seven times. Jason must have been expecting someone because he opened the door immediately and did not even look through the wide-angle door viewer. He didn't seem to recognise the bearded Martin for a moment, and then he looked to the left of the door, where he kept a loaded shotgun resting upright next to a hat stand.

Martin threw a punch so hard at Jason, he fractured the man's jaw. Jason fell on his back and writhed as if he was having a fit. He could not open his mouth and when he saw Martin pick up the shotgun, he made a subdued howling sound and held his palms out towards him. 'I told you I didn't take your money and you stabbed me!' Martin bellowed.

The decision to kill Jason or to spare him rested on the edge of a razor blade. The double barrel was already pointing at Jason's head, and Martin intended to pull the trigger for a moment, but the memory of those women in the wood and the way they had somehow saved him from death filled his mind, and Martin turned around and took the shotgun outside. He tried to open it to take out the cartridges, but Martin knew nothing about firearms and somehow the shotgun went off and blasted the back left tyre of Jason's Land Rover. The blast set every dog in the area barking and people flew to windows and opened doors to see what was going on. Martin threw the shotgun into the shadows of a hedge and walked all the way to Jacqueline's home in the Clock Face area. He laid his cards on the table and he told her all about the attempt on his life by 'bad people' he had fallen in with, and he also told her about the extraordinary women in the wood who had literally brought him back from the dead and nursed him to health. He showed Jacqueline the seven scars and swore that everything he had told her was true. Jacqueline knew that Martin simply didn't possess the imagination to make up such a tale, and she told him that those women might have been some sort of deities from ancient times. She told Martin he should leave the area with her and move in with her sister who lived in Taunton in Somerset; otherwise it would only be a matter of time before Jason tried to kill him again. Martin agreed to the plan and he managed to stay clean. He and Jacqueline married down in Somerset, and he took her surname just in case Jason tried to trace him. Jason Roud was a heavy cigar smoker and he died three years later in a car crash when he suffered a massive heart attack at the wheel of his Land Rover. Martin wrote to me, as he had naturally been haunted by the memory of the women of the wood for years. I told him that according to many folklorists and occultists, the two women of superhuman stature were known as Hevera and Devera, and they had allegedly rescued other people over the years. They had been encountered at various places in the North West, and those they had saved often left flowers of thanks in the woods where they had been rescued from certain death. The flowers were always left bound to a tree by white ribbon on or around the first day of Spring (the Vernal Equinox). And who are Hevera and Devera? They are two ancient pre-Christian deities of motherhood, and as the centuries went on, their names for some obscure reason became associated with the numbers eight and nine. The shepherds of old used to cite these names in the nursery rhyme we know today as "Hickory Dickory Dock". Originally the first line of the rhyme ran as: "Hevera, Devera Dock, the mouse ran up the clock."

Yet another example about the hidden occult history of nursery rhymes.

THE DWELLERS IN THE VOID

In the summer of 1962, a 25-year-old Huyton man named John Garnet-Chaffins met a beautiful 19-year-old girl at a party in Whiston named Jo Ann Carlson. John and Jo Ann fell madly in love with one another, but the only obstacle to their burgeoning romance was a distance of nearly sixty miles, because Jo Ann lived in the little picturesque town of Holmfirth in West Yorkshire, so John borrowed some money from his father and bought a second-hand Morris Minor to make the twice-weekly journey to see his girlfriend. One night in September 1962, at around 11.30pm, John was taking Jo Ann home via the A635 – a lonely road which crosses some of the most bleak and barren moorlands of the Peak District, and on this night, as the car was passing through Saddleworth Moor (aptly lying in the Dark Peak area), the low oppressive opalescent moonlit clouds started to billow and change shape as if a whirlwind-like atmospheric disturbance was stirring them up. The effect reminded John of the blossoming shapes drops of milk make when they disperse into a tumbler of clear water. Jo Ann had a phobia of storms after being struck by lightning as a child, and gazing at the turbulent heavens beyond the windscreen, she clung onto John's left arm as he drove along the road. A strange grey ground mist rolled along the moors and covered the road ahead, and as the clouds continued to billow into strange, unnatural forms, Jo Ann let out a yelp and asked, 'What's that over there?'

'What?' said John, startled by his girlfriend's outburst. At that same moment, the car stalled and its electrics failed. Jo Ann pointed to something shadowy and towering which was loping across the moorland to the left of the road. It looked vaguely human in shape but it was gigantic – about fifty feet in height perhaps – and it had a faint orange glow around its greyish body. This giant entity was leaning heavily in the direction it was walking, at an angle of about 25 degrees, seemingly about to topple forwards, yet it remained upright. Jo Ann wound the window down and now she and John could hear the slow rhythmic thuds of the oversized humanoid as it moved across the moor. At one point the head of the creature turned to face the car and the young couple saw its eyes flare up into two bright points of white light. The face looked flat with a prominent protruding bottom jaw. About five hundred yards distant in the gathering mist, John and Jo Ann noticed a second gigantic figure, only it was in silhouette, but it looked as if it was coming towards them. Jo Ann began to scream, and John attempted to restart the car. When the nearer giant stepped over the road ahead with one gargantuan stride, the resulting ground tremor shook the car and its engine started for some inexplicable reason. John reversed the vehicle, travelling blindly backwards in the mist until he managed to turn the car around. He was about to drive all the way back to Liverpool when he saw a group of figures walk out of the fog. They walked abreast of one another as they came down the road towards the vehicle. They all had on black hooded robes that were identical to the habits worn by monks. John beeped his horn and flashed his headlamps but the crowd of about a dozen men continued to bar the way. John tried to call their bluff by revving the vehicle and accelerating forwards for about twelve feet before he slowed and braked. One of the hooded strangers broke away from the group and ran around the Morris Minor to the driver's window and with some urgency John told Jo Ann to wind up her window. The tall hooded man had wild staring eyes as he looked through the driver's side window and in a Scottish accent he said, 'Get out of the car! Come on! Get out of the car now or we'll drag you out!'

John remained seated in the vehicle and revved the car. The weirdly-dressed Scotsman then produced a dagger and looked as if he was going to try and smash the window with its handle. John floored the accelerator and the Morris Minor shot down the road. The other hooded figures dived out of the way and Jo Ann screamed. In ever-worsening fog, John raced down the road and in his rear view mirror he could see the weird group of robed men standing there as grey silhouettes as they fell into the distance and were swallowed up by the mist.

Jo Ann then yelled, 'Look!' and to his right, John saw a massive deformed bare foot at least ten feet in length land with a thump then lift up again as another one of those unearthly giants strode along the moors running parallel to the road. Thankfully, the thing was going in the opposite direction to the car, and John and Jo Ann saw that the foot and lower leg of the grey-skinned goliath had an orange aura with a tinge of violet around it like St Elmo's Fire. The couple talked about the terrifying events of the night for the remainder of the journey and John's parents did not believe the account of the glowing giants of the moors and the hooded men.

A few years after this weird event, John saw a picture of the Moors murderer Ian Brady in the newspapers and his blood ran cold, because he was fairly certain that he had been the very same Scottish weirdo in the monk's habit with the dagger who had told him to leave the car that foggy night on the moors. He showed the picture of Brady to Jo Ann and said, 'Does he remind you of anyone?' and Jo Ann said he looked like the man with the dagger who had ordered him to get out of the car that night on the moors.

One night in November 1970, John and Jo Ann, who were now married, took the same route to visit Jo Ann's parents – down the A635 – this time in a Morris Minor Traveller. The time was midnight as they passed Saddleworth Moor, and the couple could not believe their eyes because once again they saw two giant figures with orange auras striding across the foggy desolate landscape. This time John sped along the road and got out of the area in record time. Jo Ann's mother said she had heard of some very strange goings-on around Saddleworth Moor over the years, but the girl's father said the so-called giants had just been the enlarged shadows of walkers out on the moors.

I was told by occultists a long time ago that there are ancient extremely evil beings that roam this land of ours – and the places these entities frequent include places ranging from Bidston Hill, certain rural expanses of Knowsley and Lancashire and especially the area around Saddleworth Moor. The beings I am referring to are called the Yovar, and they are said to even predate the Devil and are far more evil than him. Occultists say the Yovar – called by some arcanists as "The Dwellers in the Void" - were once part of an ancient race of gigantic people who reached a cultural and technological pinnacle just after the sudden death of the dinosaurs – about 65 million years ago – and then the Yovar became depraved immoral beings who turned to absolute evil. They legalised murder, incorporated torture into their twisted creed, experimented with all sorts of unheard-of sexual practices, slaughtered their own offspring for kicks, and even plotted to murder the god they had lovingly worshipped for millennia. It is said that it took thousands of years for their god to contain them, and they were all put into a type of comatose state of stasis in the glowing core of the planet because the nickel and iron there are the only two elements that can weaken the power of the Yovar. Some occultists say that a weakened group of the banished entities have since escaped from the core and are now living beneath the Earth's lithosphere, and they amuse themselves by meddling in human affairs, causing great wars and even earthquakes. They periodically demand human sacrifices and on a whim they can unleash plagues, cause great fires to break out and turn people's minds so they become mass murderers. Given the tragic history of the North West's moors, the ancient legends of a class of unimaginably evil beings have a chilling ring to them.

THE FAMILIAR GIRL

The following strange story unfolded at a supermarket on Seaview Road, Wallasey, in August 1966. Jon Woodford can't remember now if the supermarket was named Lennons or Gateway – probably the former, he thinks, but he does recall that he went into the supermarket on his lunch-break from a second hand bookshop where he worked part-time. The bookshop was owned by his oldest uncle – Larry, and today, being Wednesday – pay day – skinflint Larry paid his nephew the royal sum of one guinea – 21 shillings. It was an infernally hot noon on the last day of August and 17-year-old Jon went into the supermarket to get a bottle of Corona cream soda, a Fry's Five Centres bar, and then he'd pop into a newsagent and get a copy of the *Hotspur* comic (price 5d). Uncle Larry was always telling him he was too old to read comics like the *Hotspur* and the *Lion* and how he should be swatting up for his apprentice as a pharmacy assistant next year by reading books on medicine, but when Jon was immersed in the comic's thrilling tales of Wilson the Wonder Athlete and Richard Starr – the Blazing Ace of Space – the teenager didn't have to concern himself with mundane worries like finding a well-paid job and a serious girlfriend. As Jon entered the supermarket that day, he had the feeling someone was watching him

– and he also experienced that intriguing, almost magical feeling we all experience from time to time – déjà vu – the impression that a certain situation has occurred before in every detail, even though it apparently hasn't. You somehow know what's coming next, as if it's all happened before – like you're reliving some part of your life, and you know what's around the corner so to speak. Psychologists have tried in vain to explain the déjà vu phenomenon for years, but as of yet, no one has come up with a hypothesis that fits the facts. Just as weird as the déjà vu was the acute sensation of feeling watched; Jon turned and saw that a pretty girl who looked around his age was staring at him. She was petite, about 5ft 3, fashionably dressed with a bob of black shiny hair, and as soon as Jon set eyes on her, she swiftly turned away, but Jon thought she looked very familiar, and he felt as if he had done all this before; gone into the supermarket and seen this girl standing in that exact same spot. He'd had déjà vu before but never as intense as this. He found himself following the beguiling girl around the supermarket, and he noticed she was not carrying a basket, and without buying anything, she left and vanished into the milling crowds of Seaview Road. Jon returned to the second-hand bookshop and his best friend Spencer Brown called in on his lunch-break to see him. Spencer was an apprentice TV repair man and straight away he could see Jon looked distracted and worried. Jon told him about the girl and the déjà vu. 'You've probably just seen her before somewhere, that's all,' said Spencer.

Jon shook his head, 'No Spence, it's something else. I just can't put my finger on what it is, and there's something about her; she's not even stunning – just pretty – but she seemed to be waiting for me in the supermarket.'

'Maybe all this has happened before!' said Uncle Larry, peeping round a bookcase and giving the two lads a start. He adjusted his wireframe bifocals, opened a green book of poems and said to the teens: 'Lend me your Philistine ears. Listen to this old poem: "I have been here before, but when or how I cannot tell. I know the grass beyond the door, the sweet keen smell, the sighing sound, the lights around the shore." Written by a Victorian poet named Dante Gabriel Rossetti. Deep, isn't it?'

'So you think we've all been here before, then?' Spencer asked Uncle Larry with a toothy grin.

'We might all be in some never-ending film that goes round and round in a big loop – who knows?' Uncle Larry replied, before walking away. He vanished into the back room of the shop and shouted: 'By the way, Jon, your lunch break is over now! I've got four big boxes of books for you to sort here!'

Jon Woodford started to have recurring dreams about the familiar girl each night, and they always ended with him being knocked down by a Number 31 bus on Wallasey Road and he'd awake with a start at that dramatic point. Sometimes the same dream would play in his mind twice a night. He told his mother about them and she told her son they were just caused by his constant worrying about his future and would soon go when he met a girlfriend and knuckled down to study for his Pharmaceutical Chemist's Diploma next year when he was eighteen.

'That barmy uncle of his is filling his mind with all

sorts of rubbish,' Jon's father told his wife, 'philosophizing and all that airy fairy nonsense. Jon should be in a proper job – engineering or something.'

'My brother is *not* barmy,' protested Mrs Woodford, 'eccentric yes, but he's got Jon interested in books and that's a good thing.'

Jon started noticing the girl more and more as the days went by, and one morning as he walked to work, he saw her coming his way and he plucked up the courage to confront her. 'Who are you?' he asked, and he saw tears well in her eyes. She tried to get past him but he surprised himself by grabbing her forearm. 'No, tell me who you are!' he insisted.

She grinned – and then sniffled, seemingly ready to cry, then smiled again, and he heard her gulp.

'Make your mind up whether you want to cry or laugh,' he said, confused by the alternating emotions in her.

'You'd never believe me if I told you – ' she was saying when she suddenly became all choked up.

'Come on,' said Jon, 'tell this story over a coffee.' He led her to a café, and surprisingly she went very willingly. She had a Pepsi and he had a coffee and she told him a very outlandish story. As she fought back tears she said: 'You were mine once – don't ask me how – but you were, and I lost you – the first time around. We were just about to be engaged when it happened. My love for you was so great, I asked someone – you'd call her a witch - to give me another chance. She turned everything back too far though, so now you don't know me.'

'When you said you *lost* me – what happened?' Jon asked, intrigued.

'So you believe me then?' she said, excitedly.

Jon glanced out the window for a moment, unsure of what he believed. 'I – I don't know, but can you answer my question? What happened to me? How did you lose me?'

She dabbed her eyes with a paper napkin and told him. 'We had a tiff and you ran off – and you were knocked down by a bus.'

'That explains the nightmares,' muttered Jon. He grasped her hand over the table. 'So now we have to start all over again?' he asked, and the girl nodded, her face streaked with tears. 'My name is Tara,' she said, and Jon just knew everything she had said was true.

Jon only told Spencer about the strange situation at first, and then he told his Uncle Larry, who met Tara at the second hand bookshop. Larry quizzed Tara about her extraordinary claim, and she answered every question, but when she was asked to name the "witch" who had allegedly turned back time to give her a new start, all she would say was that the woman in question lived in Liverpool but that she could never name her because she had promised to keep her identity a secret.

The recurring dreams of death stopped that day when Jon and Tara became a courting couple, and eventually they became engaged. They married three years later, when a Liverpool woman in her forties named Helen attended the wedding, Tara said she was an auntie, but Jon had the feeling that Helen was the witch who had allegedly turned back the wheels of time somehow, but he never said anything to Tara. Jon and Tara are still together today and have many grandchildren, and rarely talk about that strange episode in their history. Love is a power that must never be underestimated – it has caused wars and conquered more than any army, so who knows? Perhaps through the unstoppable love of a girl and the power of a witch, even time and tide *were* turned back.

X THE UNKNOWN

Give me a ghost, poltergeist, even a witch, any day – but X is the bane of many an investigator of the paranormal. X is the variable I assign to those things that are truly unknown; entities that swan into our mundane sphere and vex us. They are weird beings that are as inexplicable as the origin of the universe and they make a mockery of our common sense view of reality. The following story is just one example of X among us. There are many more in my files. I've changed a few details for reasons of legality and confidentiality.

In the late 1960s, Sir John Waldron, Commissioner of the Metropolitan Police, ordered a full investigation into the activities of self-proclaimed private detection agencies in London, because there had been so many complaints about them using illegal wiretaps on GPO telephones and all manner of bugging devices, as well as some private investigators resorting to violence to obtain information. Silver Eye Investigations, run by Des Abbatt of Birkenhead and Terry Ryecroft of Liverpool (both aged 32), were duly probed, and so they abandoned the capital and moved to Birkenhead, where they set themselves up above a shop on Grange Road, and the Abbatt & Ryecroft Detective agency was formed. A highly-efficient 50-year-old secretary named Hazel was recruited at £23 per week, and then the agency was advertised in the local papers and cards were stuck in every shop window. There were calls and visits from clients concerning lost pets, the tracing of old flames, and then in walked big money one October afternoon in the form of a well-heeled client named Rose Latimer, the wife of prominent businessman Stephen Latimer. Rose said that her husband was being blackmailed by the pimp of two prostitutes who claimed they'd been attacked and seriously assaulted by her husband. Rose assured Des Abbatt that on the night of the first alleged attack on the streetwalker - in a shop doorway on the corner of Chester Street and Duncan Street at 1.30am three days back - Stephen had been sound asleep in bed with her.

'And there was a second incident?' Des asked, prompting her for the rest of the details.

Rose fidgeted with a cigarette packet and nodded. 'This morning at three, but Stephen was with his mistress at her flat in Poulton.'

'A mistress?' Des queried, and Rose lowered her heavy eyelids and nodded. She said her husband had told her the truth after the latest allegation. The second alleged attack had been on a prostitute on her patch in Hamilton Square.

'And you believe it wasn't him?' Des asked the lady, and she said that on this occasion the pimp had seen Stephen throttling the woman of the night, and he had run off after punching the pimp. 'The procurer recognised Stephen from his photograph in the newspapers. He's always in the business pages.'

Des said it was really a matter for the police but Rose begged him to help her. 'Stephen might be unfaithful but he hasn't got a violent bone in his body,' she said. Des said he'd look into the matter and was paid a deposit. Des and Terry confronted the pimp and the latter told him that blackmail was a very serious offence and the ponce abreacted and yelled, 'And so is attempted rape!' and pulled a switchblade knife on the private investigators. 'So get the hell out of here! Got that?' warned the pimp. Des and Terry reluctantly backed away and considered other approaches to this case.

In the meantime there were more attacks on prostitutes and women out late by a man who (according to many witnesses) looked and sounded identical to Stephen Latimer, and all of the attacks were near Hamilton Square. To make matters worse, a thick fog invaded Wirral, and after dark, Des patrolled the areas of the attacks in his Jaguar and Terry roamed the surrounding areas in his Mini, and they kept in contact with one another via walkie-talkies. One morning at 3am, Terry was driving through Hamilton Square when he actually witnessed an assault on a prostitute, and he radioed Des before going to the woman's aid. What he saw was terrifying. The prostitute screamed and fainted, and the attacker – who wore a smart, well-tailored pin-striped suit - threw her to the ground. Terry shouted to him – and when the assailant turned, Terry saw that he had no facial features at all. The face was as smooth as an eggshell. Seconds later, Des arrived in the square in his Jag and he tried to confront the attacker, but he not only saw that the culprit was faceless, he saw that face open up from its centre as five flaps of skin peeled back. The thing made a hissing sound, then the face closed and the features of Stephen Latimer appeared. The unearthly thing masquerading as a man then ran off into the fog and quickly vanished from sight. It was established that the real Stephen Latimer had been in bed with his wife at the time of the latest attack. The pimp backed off when Des threatened he'd have him investigated for procuring and pandering, as well as attempted blackmail, but the whole remarkable and downright uncanny case was never satisfactorily solved, and a year later, something chilling took place which left Stephen and Rose Latimer shaken to their marrow. The couple was sitting in the window seats of a restaurant in Liverpool on a Saturday evening when the weird 'doppelganger' of Stephen walked by, dressed even in the same clothes. It turned to look at the stunned couple, before vanishing into the busy weekend crowds. This was not some lookalike but the exact double of Stephen Latimer, and it even wore the very same clothes he was wearing that evening. Mr Latimer and his wife have thankfully not seen the sinister double since. Why the thing had chosen to copy the face and body of a Wirral businessman is a mystery that will probably never be solved. In the aforementioned case, the unknown X was something that was possibly alien or an intelligent organism from one of the many other dimensional realms of the kind that quantum physicists and superstring theorists allude to in their surreal disciplines. The X in the following strange story is harder to pin down, and I find myself leaning towards a figure of superstition, religion and folklore to find a suspect. The incident in question took place on a beautiful hot August noon in Liverpool in 1968, back in the days when the sun blew bubbles in the road tar and the resulting odour of toasted asphalt blended with the Mersey mist to produce an agreeable summery incense. On Castle

Street a radio in the newsagents piped out a sleepy commentary on the Glamorgan-Lancs cricket match, and beneath a tobacconist's awning stood a tall busker dressed in a black Spanish sombrero cordobés hat which kept his face in shadow. Despite the tropical heat of that day, the busker also wore a bizarre black ankle-length frock coat as he played a lively rendition of Bach's *Badinerie* on a flute. Peggy and Jimmy Bligh, both aged seventy, walked along holding hands on their 50th wedding anniversary, and ahead of them strolled Penny, a very pretty and petite lady in a pink dress who held the hand of her 4-year-old son, Tim. A 40-year-old policeman named Terry came walking towards Penny, smiling, when Tim suddenly said, 'Mummy what's that?' and he pointed at something about twenty feet away on the pavement. It was a mound of paper which proved, on closer inspection, to be bundles of fivers, tenners, pound notes and 10-shilling notes, lying across three flags of the pavement, and some of the notes had been blown by a summer zephyr onto the kerbstone and into the gutter. Traffic on Castle Street slowed as eagle-eyed motorists noticed the pile of unguarded banknotes, and Jimmy Bligh, noticing the money, shook his wife's hand from his and ran to the heap of green, orange and blue notes of currency. Penny also closed in on the heap of cash, dragging her little boy Timmy so hard he almost fell over.

'Finders keepers, isn't it?' septuagenarian Jimmy said to Terry the copper as he bent down and grabbed bundles of tenners and fivers.

'No, sir, it isn't, put it back!' Terry advised.

'I work for a solicitor, officer,' Penny informed the

policeman, 'and I know the law! There's no legal requirement to turn over money you find on the street!'

'It's someone's money, though, and it's wrong to take it!' protested Peggy, amazed at the money-grubbing antics of her husband of 50 years who was now on all fours filling his jacket. 'Come on love,' she said to her husband on the floor, 'leave it, or you might get into trouble.'

Terry blew his police whistle and warned people encircling an approximate million pounds to stay back. One motorist was so mesmerised by the little mountain of moolah he tripped over the kerbstone and fell into the money mound and Terry dragged him away from the cash and dropped him on his back in the gutter. His glasses came off and he cried, 'Police brutality! Greedy plod wants the money for himself!'

'Come on you dozy mare, pick some up!' Jimmy Bligh yelled at Peggy, and she started to cry. Only a few minutes ago, Jimmy was telling her how he treasured their love more than all the gold in the world, and he had even mentioned renewing his wedding vows. Now this money had turned him into a ghastly money-grabbing maniac.

'Now put that back miss!' Terry warned Penny, who had thousands in her arms.

'Get lost!' she yelled at Terry, 'Why aren't you catching criminals instead of trying to prevent honest people from benefitting from a windfall?'

'This is *not* a windfall, love,' answered the infuriated copper, 'it belongs to someone and I will not stand here and let you pilfer it!'

'I am not a pilferer!' shouted Penny, snatching a

bundle of fivers bound together with a green elastic band. She turned – and suddenly noticed her son Timmy had wandered off, and she didn't know whether to look for him or grab another few grand. She was a little disturbed by her own behaviour, and she walked away from the pile of money in a daze, looking for her son.

Peggy belted Jimmy with her handbag and he cried, 'What are you getting all aeriated about? Silly cow!'

She whacked him again with the handbag as she ranted: 'You unfaithful, greedy, selfish money-mad deceiver!'.

'Aye, aye love – stop that!' Terry told Peggy holding his palm out to her.

There were rear-end collisions on the street as more drivers were distracted by the free-for-all around the welcoming pile of dough, and Terry was pushed to the ground as a scrum formed on the pavement. The lure of so much money seemed to have an intense entrancing effect on all who saw it, and Terry really did think he'd be trampled by the avaricious mob – but then he heard voices crying, 'It's gone!' and 'Where did it go?'

Terry got to his feet and saw some thirty-odd people looking at the ground and at one another. It transpired that the money had suddenly vanished; every single note. No one was any richer; it had all been some illusion. At this point, the policeman noticed that the busking flautist was laughing, and then, in a flash he was nowhere to be seen. Terry was a simple policeman – a man who functioned on facts and common sense; a person who was not prone to believing in ghosts or seeing things, and yet he was left with the unsettling impression that the flute-playing stranger in black had been the Devil himself, mocking the victims of a cruel joke of his: the promise of thousands of pounds of free money, just for the taking. The greed had dented a couple's fiftieth anniversary and a mother who usually doted on her four-year-old son had almost lost him as she became obsessed with an insatiable desire to grab as much of that pavement money as she could. That money had removed the thin veneer of civilized behaviour from its victims to reveal their true ruthless nature, and it had not been a pretty sight at all. I remember mentioning this case on a programme about strange local stories on BBC Radio Merseyside and the station's switchboard operator took many calls from people who were either present when the vast amount of cash appeared on the sidewalk or knew of someone who had been there. Some thought it was just an urban myth, but the accounts of the people I interviewed who said they had been present dovetailed together nicely. Something undoubtedly happened that day which, in my opinion, lies beyond human understanding. The X in this unknown is the eerie flautist in black who seems to have been connected with the transient presence of that stockpile of banknotes. Was he actually the Devil, perhaps proving that he can bring out the worst in people by conjuring up a hallucinatory pile of money? It really is a strange case.

I have another case of X the unknown in my files, and this X is a variable I am assigning to a group of unknown entities which I term "the mockers" for reasons that will soon become clear.

In 2005, Faye, a 24-year-old West Derby psychology

student studying at a local university, decided to dabble with the Ganzfeld Effect - a state of altered consciousness which arises in the mind of a person once the outside world is shut off. The person wishing to experience this effect wears a sleep mask, blindfold, or anything to block off any visual stimuli, and the subject then listens to the gentle hiss of uniform white noise through a pair of headphones. White noise can be obtained from many YouTube videos, or even from an FM radio tuned to a 'dead spot' between stations. In the resulting absence of normal sensory stimuli – where you see nothing and hear nothing but white noise - strange things appear in the mind of the subject which most psychologists dismiss as hallucinations. A common one is a crowd of people laughing at something – described as sounding like the canned laughter we often hear on old TV comedy programmes. The psychology student Faye heard this eerie laughter as she lay on her bed during a Ganzfeld experiment one evening. She wore a blindfold made from a scarf and listened to white noise via her iPad earphones. The girl's mother disturbed the experiment by entering the room and shaking her before she asked Faye if she wanted some pizza for supper.

A week after this, Faye was in her back garden when the neighbour mowing the lawn next door literally dropped dead of heart failure – and up went a crescendo of laughter and applause. No one else heard the phantom laughter, only Faye. This really unnerved her, and she wondered if she had some neurological disorder. She did not use marijuana or any psychoactive drugs (which can cause auditory hallucinations with long-term use) so she began to blame lack of sleep – even though she had been having around seven hours' sleep each night. Weeks after the phantom laughter incident, Faye fell over her cat as she hurried from her bedroom to answer the door to the postman, and she tumbled down a flight of stairs, breaking her wrist. As she lay there in agony, she heard the unseen audience roaring with laughter again. Faye eventually reasoned that the Ganzfeld voices she had heard had somehow intruded into her everyday life and her waking beta-wave level of consciousness, and this possibility scared her. What *were* those voices and why were they invading her waking state of consciousness?

Faye became visibly stressed as she worried about the bizarre voices, and her father Allen, noticing his daughter seemed on edge, decided to take her for a day out in Wales in his new car. During the outing to Wales, the brakes of Allen's car unaccountably failed as the vehicle hurtled down a lane in Betws-y-Coed. Faye and her father heard weird echoing laughter fill the car, and this time, an array of ghostly laughing faces, all with shaven heads, materialised in front of the windshield, completely blocking the view of the road. Faye's father downshifted to a lower gear, but still the car flew along, and so the emergency brake was applied. The car swung 180 degrees and almost turned over as it hit an embankment. The eerie laughter continued for about thirty seconds, and then stopped abruptly. Faye's dad thought ghosts had somehow caused the accident and Faye never told him about the previous occasions when the 'mockers' had manifested. Thankfully, the laughter from beyond was not heard after that accident, and just what the jeering heads were that materialised in the windscreen is hard to say. If Faye alone had heard them we could comfortably explain the entities away as a figment of her imagination or a symptom of some mental illness, but Faye's father heard the laughter too – and he also saw the faces of the derisive intruders from elsewhere in the windscreen – so they were not a construct of Faye's mind. People are still hearing the menacing laughter during Ganzfeld experiments today – but no one can say what is producing the ghostly laughter; the mockers remain an excellent example of the unnameable and unknowable variable X. The following story is another excellent example of an inexplicable incident which cannot be satisfactorily explained by the disciplines of science. A psychologist would probably opt for 'suggestibility' to explain how a group of dolls were seen to move about and talk many years ago. The witness involved in the story told me she was not under some hypnotic spell, but saw the dolls move and speak while she was wide awake, and moreover, the family of the witness allegedly knew about the animated dolls before she did. If the incident I am about to describe had taken place in a church, with moving statues and holy visions – it would be explained away as religious mania. Incidentally, such an incident *is* documented as having taken place at Limpias in Spain in 1919 when many people – including "scientifically educated persons" – saw images of various saints step out of their paintings and make certain holy gestures to the spellbound churchgoers. Religious mania or hypnotic suggestion cannot be offered as explanations in the following weird story, though.

On the Wednesday afternoon of 11 July 1973, 7-year-old Liverpool girl Michelle Meredith arrived at the semidetached home of her scatty Aunt Bridget on Tranmere's Albany Road, and with her was Bluebell, an old vintage doll that bore some resemblance to the child actress Shirley Temple with its mohair head of golden curls and large twinkling hazel eyes. Bluebell was an unusually large doll, and stood at almost four feet in height. Michelle's bin-man father had found it 'looking all lonely in an entry off Scotland Road', but Michelle's mother thought her husband had found it before it had been lost (i.e. stolen). Bluebell wore a short-sleeved powder-blue dress with a belt at the waist and a pair of white Mary Jane style shoes with press studs to fasten the straps.

For some reason, Aunt Bridget took an instant dislike to Bluebell; Michelle could plainly see this, and she said to her aunt: 'Don't you like her? Her name's Bluebell.'

'Yeah, she's nice,' said Bridget, 'but she's a bit big isn't she? She's almost as tall as you, Michelle.'

Michelle hugged the doll. 'We go everywhere together, Auntie, and I know this sounds silly but I feel as if she's a real girl sometimes – like she's alive.'

'Oh,' said Aunt Bridget, with a suspicious look in her eyes, and she asked her niece: 'Has your mum said anything about *my* dolls?'

Michelle's cherubic face immediately went red. On many occasions her mother had indeed mentioned her sister-in-law's claims that her dolls were alive – and she hadn't been a kid when she made the assertion – she had been saying it back in her thirties.

'You've got guilt written all over your face, Michelle,'

said Bridget, and then she stooped down and brought her face close to the face of her blushing niece and added, 'and I'll bet your mum's told you I'm loopy because I still collect dolls.'

'No,' murmured Michelle, 'no, honest.'

'Some dolls are very special – some of them have spirits in them, and they're just like you, little one. See, when you were made in your mum's belly, a spirit got into you – breathed life into the tiny baby that was that big,' and Bridget pinched an inch of air. 'Did your mum mention how many dolls I have?'

'I just think she said you had a lot, Auntie Bridget,' replied Michelle, and she looked at her auntie's ankle-length boots, and her red stockings and pleated blue dress; she dressed oddly.

'Well they're all locked up in the shed in the back garden,' said Bridget, 'and if I pop my clogs I might leave them all to you!' she said, and laughed.

Already, Michelle was regretting coming to her aunt's; her older sister had warned her against it, saying she was nuts, and her mum had tried to talk her out of staying for a week, but Michelle's dad – Bridget's brother, had a row with his wife and said there was nothing wrong with his sister.

Bridget took Michelle – and Bluebell – out to the shops and when the returned the girl was treated to fish and chips, followed by apple pie and ice cream, and a big glass of Tizer. That night, at around 10pm, Michelle retired to the spare bedroom which had a view of the back garden and the shed where the dolls were stockpiled. Bluebell slept next to Michelle, and while it was still dark, the girl was awakened by what sounded like excited voices. For a moment, Michelle thought she was back in her home – which faced a primary school – for that's what the voices sounded like – excited children at playtime. Those unruly voices were coming from the garden. When Michelle went to the bedroom window, she looked out – and saw a dim light in the garden shed, and lots of silhouetted heads milling about. The dolls! The girl ran back to the bed and hid under the covers. The bedroom door opened, and Aunt Bridget came in dressed in an old long white nightie. 'Listen precious,' she said, 'is it okay if I put Bluebell in the wardrobe? I think she's making the dolls jealous.'

Michelle trembled in the bed, and she clung to Bluebell, then said, 'I'm going home tomorrow – I'm scared of those dolls.'

Bridget sat on the bed. 'Just put her in the wardrobe, love, and then go to sleep, and they won't bother you. It's *her* that's bothering them.'

'I want to go home; I want my mum,' said Michelle, and she started to cry.

Bridget swore, and she seized Bluebell, threw her in the wardrobe, and then she locked it and returned to her bedroom shouting, 'You ungrateful mare!'

As Michelle lay there, softly crying, she heard a bang downstairs, followed by the tumultuous sound of many childlike voices. Then footfalls! They were coming up the stairs. Michelle hid under the blankets, gasping for breath as the door burst open and it sounded as if the room was being invaded by dozens of kids. Somehow they opened the wardrobe, and left, swearing like dockers. Michelle saw her doll was gone, and she went down into the back garden and found a gate open. In the moonlight she saw about thirty dolls pouring into Victoria Park, and she watched them lynch Bluebell with a clothes line – and then they went back to the house. Michelle pulled down the line leading to the hanged doll, and saw her face had been smashed in. She wandered the streets with Bluebell until a policeman spotted her, and eventually she went home to Liverpool. She never visited Aunt Bridget again.

On this side of the Mersey, we come to our final tale of the unexplained in this chapter, and believe me, I have so many cases of this kind I could easily fill a book with them. This one concerns an unknown entity named Smiler.

On the Saturday morning of 1 September 1984 at 5am, 21-year-old Mandy Sullivan awoke in the attic of her friend Jo Holland's house on Bold Place – just behind St Luke's (the "bombed out church") in the city centre. Mandy was staying with her friend till she could get back on her feet financially. It had been a terrible year so far for Mandy. Her 25-year-old boyfriend Terry had left her in May for a girl of seventeen, and then through some unidentified stress-related illness that had lasted for well over a month, Mandy had lost her job at the Victoria Wine off licence through absenteeism. Now she had a job at a café on Victoria Street but the hours were painfully early. On this dark morning she was out the door after a round of toast and a speedy make-up session. The eastern predawn sky was fiery with an imminent angry sunrise and some of the shops were lit-up but still closed as Mandy hurried down a deserted Church Street. This was her third day at the café and she hoped she'd get into this early-morning routine. The only problem was the late nights; she had a habit of gabbing the head off her friend Jo till two in the morning, and the topic of conversation was usually her ex, Terry. Mandy told herself she really should just forget about him and move on.

As Mandy passed C&A she noticed the silhouette of what looked like a little boy of about ten, straight ahead facing WH Smith, and he was standing with his back to her, facing Lord Street. What on earth was a child doing out at this hour? Mandy wondered – was he lost? Her maternal instinct kicked in and she just had to go to the lad's aid.

'Oi!' she shouted, and without turning to look at her, the little figure suddenly ran off towards Whitechapel. Mandy trotted after him and when she reached the corner near the Greenwood's store, she looked down Whitechapel and saw no one about. Yesterday at this time there were a few delivery trucks about, but this morning, all was as quiet as the grave. Mandy decided to go to the nearest public telephone box – on Lord Street – and she called the police to report what seemed to be a lost minor. She gave her name and address after giving a hopeless description of the child, as she had only seen him in silhouette, but she believed he had black short hair, and was about three feet and five inches in height. He seemed to have a black blazer on, dark trousers and shoes.

When Mandy told her boss at the café about the boy she'd seen on Church Street, he returned a peculiar wide-eyed expression as if the mention of the child struck some chord; it was as if he'd heard about the boy before, and in an uncharacteristically awkward manner he changed the subject and said one of the girls at the café was not cleaning the table surfaces properly.

That evening around 11pm, Mandy asked Jo to read her tealeaves as her friend seemed to have a talent for tasseomancy – the official name for the of divination by tea leaves. Jo reluctantly agreed, as in the past she had seen disturbing things in the leaves, and knowing what a dreadful year Mandy had been through so far, she was scared she'd see some bad sign in her cup. Jo decided that if she saw the littlest indication of anything ominous in the leaves, she'd say nothing to her friend.

As Jo studied the leaves, peering into the cup as she slowly turned it, Mandy enquired: 'Can you see Terry in them at all?'

Jo shook her head and replied, 'I can see a little boy. How old is your brother Kevin now?'

'Our Kevin's fifteen now and he's taller than me!' said Mandy and gave a faint suspiring laugh through her nose – but then she recalled the little boy she had seen on Church Street as she went to work. Before Mandy could tell Jo about him, her friend said, 'It's weird because this little boy looks as if he's taken a shine to you – he's looking at you. It's an odd one this.'

'Jo, I saw a little boy this morning on Church Street,' said Mandy, 'I thought he was lost and he ran off when I shouted to him.'

'Really?' Jo turned to look at Mandy then turned her gaze back to the interior of the cup. 'It looks as if this boy is in a street as well, but what can it mean?' she said in an almost whispering voice.

'Maybe it's a man of small stature you've seen,'

Mandy suggested, 'a midget or something. Maybe I have some secret admirer who's a little man or something.'

'No, I don't get a grown man from this, Mandy,' said Jo, thinning her eyes and angling her head as she looked at the leaves. 'It's definitely a child – a child with a prominent grin. Boys can get crushes on grown women but this isn't that – I'm getting a different vibe altogether. I hate it when this happens – when the leaves start being mysterious.'

On Monday morning, Mandy arose at 4.40am, and Jo's husband Patrick was already up because he had a bout of insomnia. He asked Mandy if she fancied a full English breakfast but she said she'd prefer some porridge if there was any. Patrick found a box of Quaker's Oats in the cupboard and quickly made some delicious porridge to which he added cream and honey. After the porridge, Mandy had a mug of black coffee to keep her awake, and by 5am she was out the door. She crossed Berry Street and went down Bold Street, and she thought about Terry; he'd probably be snuggled up with his young girlfriend in bed at this unsocial hour. Around ten minutes later, Mandy was hurrying past C&A on her way to work when she recalled that it was here where she had seen the boy, and she received quite a jolt when she saw him again, standing in the very same spot on Church Street, and she thought this was somewhat eerie. The 'boy' turned to face her, and she saw he had a pale sinister grinning adult face. His eyes were like two dark crescents on their sides, and his bushy eyebrows met in the middle. He opened his mouth to laugh and Mandy could see his fearsome pointed teeth. Mandy turned and ran and that creepy little man ran after her, and he moved at quite a speed. He shouted something unintelligible and laughed and he chased Mandy as far as Parker Street, where he seemed to vanish into the shadows. Mandy was that scared, she went to work via a long-winded route that took in Lime Street, William Brown Street, and the Old Haymarket, until she arrived at the café on Victoria Street, ten minutes late. When she told her boss what had happened, he returned that same telling expression which clearly indicated that he knew something about the 'boy' and Mandy said to him, 'You know something about him don't you? Is he a ghost? What is it?'

Her boss took her into his tiny office off the kitchen and he told Mandy about "Smiler" – the nickname of that little man who'd been seen for years on Church Street, and he told his employee that Smiler was always an omen of bad luck.

Mandy seemed to go weak at the knees when she heard this, and she fell into a chair and gasped, 'You're kidding.'

Her boss shook his head. 'Look, Mandy that's what they say anyway. It might be a load of rubbish for all I know; this city is full of these stories. Look, if you're worried, you could always go and see a priest and get blessed or something. You'll be okay love. In fact, when you think of it, the little man you were chased by was probably just some cheeky kid.'

Mandy shook her head. 'No, it wasn't some cheeky kid at all – it was a man, and his face was horrible and pale, and his eyes – they looked evil. Oh my God I can't go through any more bad luck – I've had enough already.'

Days later, Mandy had a succession of illnesses, including jaundice and glandular fever, and in the space of two months she had three bereavements in her family, and then in the New Year she almost died in a car crash. Mandy gave up the job in the café and vowed to never go anywhere near Church Street after dark or early in the morning. She later moved to Chester and then her luck started to pick up again. She met a decent man named Dean and later married him.

"Smiler" – that little grinning harbinger of doom – has been seen since the 1970s but no one knows just what he is; he seems like a ghost, but whose ghost remains a mystery, and he was seen as recently as August 2018.

NOSY PARKER

One night in the autumn of 1965, the emergency services telephone operator for Lancashire received a strange call from a lady who sounded quite well-to-do.

'I am protesting at the nurses at the Mossley Hill Hospital wearing trousers! It is most unladylike and the police must arrest whoever is responsible!'

The bemused operator said the introduction of trousered suits for female nurses at the hospital was perfectly legal and in a huff the caller hung up at the telephone box – logged by the operator as being near Sefton Park. The same woman with the distinctive refined voice called the operator on many further occasions to report various crimes in places ranging from Allerton, Wavertree, Mossley Hill and Calderstones, and often gave her name as Hilda Parker. She was not only a voice on the telephone line – people started noticing the elegantly-dressed silver-haired lady on the streets of south Liverpool. PC Derek Wrigley was on his beat on Penny Lane one Saturday afternoon in October 1966 when a smartly-dressed woman of about sixty years of age in a pink outfit came up to him and said a man with a knife was threatening a vendor in his ice cream van on nearby Crawford Avenue. PC Wrigley rushed to the scene and apprehended the knifeman – who was making off with the ice cream vendor's takings. A policeman on an adjoining beat came to PC Wrigley's aid and the armed attacker was taken into custody.

On another occasion PC Wrigley and a colleague were on the Menlove Avenue beat one afternoon when the same woman in pink came running towards them. 'There's a flasher on the loose by Allerton Library!' she cried, and this time PC Wrigley asked the lady what her name was as a matter of routine.

'Miss Parker, Ballantrae Road,' was her reply, and she described the exhibitionist. Wrigley and his associate hurried to the library, caught the man in the act as he flashed at two women, and he was arrested on the spot for indecent exposure. The police station was literally just across the road from where the flasher was exposing himself, and Wrigley thought the pervert might have enjoyed some thrilling element of danger of being caught by being so close to the station.

At the police station, the desk sergeant asked Wrigley if the woman who had reported the flasher looked like some Avon lady, and Wrigley nodded and asked, 'Yes, why?'

'She's got curly white hair, and she wears a pink jacket, matching pencil skirt and dark elbow length gloves – right?' said the sergeant, and he gave a smug grin.

'Yes – have you seen her as well?' Wrigley asked.

'Yeah, about ten years ago. She's a ghost, mate,' said the sergeant, 'they call her Nosy Parker. She's always reporting things and phoning us up.'

There was a pause as PC Wrigley waited for the punch line, because he thought the sergeant was telling some elaborate joke.

'I'm serious,' the sergeant said, with a lopsided grin.

'Oh come off it mate,' laughed Wrigley, 'she was a

real person. She's a bit eccentric, and probably thinks she's Miss Marple, but she's a decent citizen and I wish there were more like her.'

'Derek, she's a bloody ghost!' insisted the desk sergeant, 'Go and ask Chief Inspector – '

'And a cow went and laid a big brown egg!' PC Wrigley interrupted and went to the canteen for a cup of tea.

About three weeks later, Miss Parker again appeared on the scene as PC Wrigley and another constable named Evans were on Smithdown Road, this time to alert them to a man who was carrying a gun with intent to hold up a betting shop. On this occasion Wrigley recalled the claims of the desk sergeant about the old lady being a ghost, and just to prove that sergeant wrong, Derek Wrigley held out his hand to the woman and said, 'Thanks for your help Miss Parker' – and the woman almost jumped backwards– as if she didn't want to be touched. This overreaction to the offering of his hand struck Wrigley as more than odd; it made him wonder if Miss Parker *was* some rather solid-looking ghost. The elegant informer in pink then gave a strange knowing look with her huge pale blue eyes which gave the streetwise hard-boiled copper the creeps. She looked at him as if she knew what he was thinking – that she was not a member of the living. The policeman then went off to the betting shop and the gunman was duly arrested on the premises, and it was subsequently established that the gun had not even been loaded.

Back at the police station, PC Wrigley had a word with the desk sergeant about Miss Hilda Parker. He told the sergeant the way she had backed away in such a dramatic fashion when he had offered to shake her hand.

'Yeah, that's because she's a piece of toast, mate,' said the sergeant.

'A what?' asked Wrigley, too discomfited to understand the rhyming slang for 'ghost'.

The sergeant stopped smiling, sensing that Wrigley seemed a bit afraid. 'She's been seen in Wavertree, over in Calderstones, down in Mossley Hill, and one of the cleaners in here – Madge – saw her one morning walking through torrential rain in Garston – and she wasn't even wet.'

'But she looks as real as you, mate,' said Wrigley, 'how could she be a spook, like?'

'Well, we might know ourselves one day,' replied the sergeant, 'death comes to us all. I always thought ghosts were see-through and went about wrapped in sheets with clanking chains.'

A month later, PC Wrigley was driving home from the station one morning after a long night shift. His car was cruising along Springwood Avenue when he spotted the distinctive form of Miss Parker with her white hair and pink attire as she walked into Allerton Cemetery. PC Wrigley slowed the car and he ever so slowly followed the enigmatic lady in his car, keeping a distance of about a hundred yards between himself and the woman. She made a sharp turn right behind a hedge, and when the car reached that corner seconds later, the off-duty policeman could see no one. He'd lost sight of her. He turned the car around, intending to leave Allerton Cemetery the same way he had entered the resting grounds of the dead, but when he got to the end of the road – about thirty feet from the gateposts, Wrigley received quite a shock. Standing by the right gatepost was Miss Parker, and she was looking straight at him. As he passed her in the car, he thought that her eyeballs looked completely black – as if she had two hollows in their place, and her face was a deathly white. He drove quickly out of the cemetery and swung the car right onto Springwood Avenue. After that encounter with Miss Hilda Parker, PC Wrigley never set eyes on her again, but he often heard about the woman in pink. I mentioned the case once on a radio programme about hauntings in Liverpool and received an enormous amount of feedback. Some listeners said Miss Parker had died from a heart attack when she was assaulted by burglars at her Mossley Hill home one night, while other people claimed she was an Avon lady who had been knocked down by a stolen car. The ghost was said to have been active as late as 1989, and then she was seen no more.

A SIGN FROM THE DEPTHS

The following strange story took place in 1963. An 18-year-old girl named Victoria – who came from a well-to-do family on Prenton's Forest Road, Wirral – started to mix with the 'wrong sort of people' (as her banker father put it) – meaning beatniks and other odiferous denizens of the counterculture. Victoria had started to stay out late to frequent night clubs and coffee bars with some strange people, and her mother had recently found cigarettes made from Indian hemp and a copy of *Lady Chatterley's Lover* in the girl's bedroom. Victoria was qualified for admission to the prestigious Sorbonne but instead she preferred to live with four strange young Liverpool men – all redheads with the same Beatle haircut – in a tumbledown squat in Birkenhead discussing existentialism, nihilism and the promise of a peculiar cult concerning the amalgamation of Germanic and Aztec paganism that was on the rise in post-war West Germany. By January 1963, fifteen people were living in the squat and police finally charged the dwelling and only Victoria and the four redheads escaped; the rest were charged with various offences under the Vagrancy Act. On 17 January that year, the four redheads obtained five tickets for the Beatles gig at the Majestic Ballroom on Conway Street, and they took Victoria to see the Fab Four. After the show the 'quartet of carrot-tops' as they were nicknamed by Victoria, took her to a dark corner table of an all-night coffee bar where they persuaded her to share their "prellies" (slang for phenmetrazine pills) – a stimulant drug and appetite suppressant. Then, around two in the morning, after the consumption of countless cups of black coffee and the smoking of innumerable Senior Service cigarettes, Giles, the intellectual member of the four redheads told Victoria he wanted her to take part in an occult ritual in the cellar of a derelict house just a stone's throw from Birkenhead Park. Although she was always on the lookout for new kicks, Victoria wanted to know what this ritual was about.

'We have contacted the spirit of King Arthur,' said Giles spiritedly, 'and he wants to reincarnate.'

'And where do I come into this?' Victoria wanted to know.

'You, my dear, are now pregnant, and he wants to be reborn as your child,' Giles replied, all matter-of-factly.

'I am not in the club you vulgar beast,' laughed Victoria, 'wherever did you get that one from?'

'Oh yes you, are, and I am the father,' Giles asserted, and he drew on a cigarette and raised his eyebrows till they vanished into his overhanging fringe.

'How on earth would you know if you're the father,' chortled Victoria, 'it could be any of you here now, couldn't it?'

'Just trust me, Vicky,' said Giles, nodding slowly and smiling with smug self-assurance. 'Now, are you up for the ritual or are you going to be an actual square?'

'What on earth have you been taking, Giles?' asked a bemused Victoria. 'Mescaline? Morning Glory flower seeds? Or just too much blue stilton?'

'You'll see - if you've got the pluck m'lady!' a

confident Giles told her.

'Right, come on then, off to Camelot!' said Victoria, waving an imaginary sword in the air, and she got up and left the coffee bar and accompanied the four red-haired clones in black through a jade fog until they reached the empty shell of what had once been a three-storey Victorian house. There were about a dozen candlesticks down in the musty cellar, and three burlap sacks. The candles were lit and now Victoria could see the peculiar graffiti on the mildewed walls; what looked like runic glyphs and strange circles and crosses daubed in white paint. The redheads opened the burlap sacks and Victoria saw them take out pale green robes with matching pointed hoods with eye-holes in them. They looked like the "glory suits" worn by Ku Klux Klansmen. The four redheads donned the disturbing attire and stood in a perfect square, facing the wall. Victoria was in the centre of them. Giles began a very strange-sounding prayer: 'Hear me, my Father, come forth from the boundless light. Send me a sign from the depths! Join us today or we shall meet you in the pit.'

Then he started to sing the words and it sounded like some Gregorian chanting, a very eerie incantation to the ears of Victoria – and then she saw a figure come out of the wall of the cellar which really gave her a start! It was the glowing form of a man in a long pale robe and he wore a hood. He had a black moustache, and a pair of pale blue eyes. He spoke, but it sounded like German, then all at once, Victoria recognised him; she had been thrown by the moustache – it was usually much shorter – a toothbrush moustache. 'This isn't Arthur! This is Hitler!' Victoria cried out, and the apparition looked at her. She turned and ran, and Giles and the other three ran after her up the stairs, and when Victoria got out of the house, Giles dived onto her and threw her to the pavement, but at that moment two policemen on their beat saw the bizarre men in their costumes, and the lawmen dragged Giles off Victoria and the other three redheads ran off into the fog. Drugs and the beatnik lifestyle were blamed for what was deemed as a "silly ritual", but then Victoria came down with a morning sickness and discovered she was pregnant. The child was put up for adoption when he was three because he was uncontrollable and violent — and what became of him is unknown.

THE CLOCK OF OWLS

When the Chase family moved into the cottage in the green wilds of Ince Blundell in the summer of 2015, 16-year-old Belle claimed the loft as her make-up room. Pearly blonde Belle Chase stood at five feet and two inches and her father warned her that she'd have to crouch in her make-up room soon because she seemed to be growing inches by the week, but Belle said that was good because she *was* going to be a supermodel by the time she was nineteen and you had to be five feet and nine inches tall or over to be a proper model. The walls and ceiling of the loft was painted baby pink and at one end of the loft there was a 6-foot-long mirror set into the gable wall. The gable wall at the other end of the loft had a small round window put in which gave a fine view of the patchwork of fields, the mazy muddled network of lanes and bridlepaths, and to the extreme left of this splendid view there was a dark mysterious-looking wood, and from the moment Belle noticed it, she sensed there was something otherworldly about it, and that was in the daytime; at night, the girl couldn't even bring herself to look at that wood. Belle had the round window open all the time because it was one of the hottest summers that year, and she would yelp and call for her father every time a moth flew in.

Belle Chase took the first selfie in the new make-up

room at the long wall-mounted mirror and posted it on her Instagram account. She videoed the room and uploaded the footage to her YouTube account and planned a series of videos that would show her installing all the furniture and knickknacks in the place over the coming weeks. But then she noticed the clicking sounds in the wall. Her father said she was imagining the noises at first but her 9-year-old sister Libby could hear the faint clicks. Libby pressed her ear to the wall and calmly said, 'They're humming.'

'Oh my God! What?' said a melodramatic Belle, poised with the iPhone, ready to film the potential drama.

'Yes it's going hummmmm...' said Libby, and her huge brown eyes swung around as she listened to whatever was generating the sound.

Belle held the phone out and filmed herself. 'Oh my God, there are things living in the wall of my make-up room and only my sister Libby here believes me. She can hear something humming.'

George Chase came up into the loft in a very irritated state and told Belle to stop videoing him. His knee was playing up and he had to climb a set of steep steps to get into the make-up room. He listened at the spot on the wall indicated by Libby, and this time he heard the humming sound too. 'Yes, I can hear it.'

'Oh – my – God – ' Belle was saying to her phone's camera when her father snapped: 'Shut up, Belle! I think we might have a wasp's nest.'

'Oh my frickin' God, I'm going to be sick!' Belle said to the phone, all wide-eyed with her left hand clamped over her mouth. 'There are like insects living in this wall,' she said, her words muffled somewhat by her fingers. She added a fake retching sound.

George went outside and looked up at eaves of the cottage. There was a small gap in the brickwork near the roof and he could see a few wasps going in and out of the breach. Libby read up about wasp's nests on the web and visited Belle as she was trying to film a make-up tutorial about Barbie Pink Lipstick when Libby came into the shot and tapped her left shoulder.

'Oh my God, I don't believe this – my little sis is being a pest,' Belle told her iPhone, which was mounted on a mini-tripod on her dresser. 'Go away Libby, I'm doing a tutorial. Go and play Minecraft or something.'

Oblivious to her sister's words, Libby said: 'Belle, er, did you know that the wasps living in your wall won't harm you and the wasps only last a season and they are feeding their little baby wasps?'

'Libby, I am doing a tutorial!' Belle went to the iPhone and stopped the video.

'Belle don't kill the little babies,' Libby pleaded, 'they have as much right to life as we do.'

As she watched the video on the phone at the point of the interruption, Belle chided her sister. 'Libby – two things: stop coming into the make-up room – it's my room, yeah? And secondly, if those wasps sting your arse you won't be talking crap about letting them live! Now get out and stay out!'

That night at around 11.30pm Belle lay in bed, texting her friend Akari when she suddenly noticed the hum from the wasp's nest. She ended the text conversation about La Prairie Skin Caviar Foundation and coloured contact lenses and told Akari how she could now hear the wasps from her bedroom, and half an hour later, Belle switched off the light and sat up against a pillow for a moment in the darkened room. Strands of moonlight created by the blinds lay on the Zara wool rug, and an owl hooted somewhere in the distance. The girl adjusted the pillow and lay on her side. She heard the faint hum and thought of Libby's plea to her about sparing the lives of the baby wasps. And with that sad recollection Belle Chase drifted down the Black Nile of sleep into that strange desert wilderness of dreams, and the last sound from waking reality the teenager heard was the echoing of a village clock in the depths of the night chiming the midnight hour, and then the girl heard one of those nonsensical surreal hypnogogic phrases people have often reported as they descend into sleep. This one was "Some things are not meant to be known."

Sometime after that, Belle had a vivid dream of little baby wasps that looked as if they were in their larval stage, and yet they had little heads like human babies, and they were all smiling with their eyes closed as they slept in the hexagonal honeycombed cells of the hive. The Queen Wasp was hardly visible in the dream but Belle could sense her concern about the babies as she doted on them. The humming sound had a soothing effect on the sleeping babies, and during the dream the hum turned into some soft melody which sounded like a lullaby. Someone told Belle, 'They have their whole lives ahead of them. They haven't had a chance to feel sunlight on them yet.'

There were other dreams that night, mostly about make-up, clothes, YouTube videos and Belle's friends, and when the girl woke up she heard a clatter against her wall. Her mother had been into the room and opened the blinds and for some reason she'd closed the window, despite the summer heat.

'I've sprayed the nest, mate,' shouted an unknown's man's voice outside the window, and Belle heard him descend with rhythmic clangs from the rungs of the ladder.

It was the 'pest' controller Belle's father had mentioned last night. Belle suddenly experienced a mixture of sadness and anger as she recalled the dream of the wasp babies. She hurried from her bed to the window and looked out at the shaven-headed exterminator. He was saying that he shouldn't be using a ladder but had to because the nest was in an unusual place in the wall cavity. Belle listened with a feeling of dread as the man said: 'They're all as good as dead now with the poison on them, and the ones that flew off are covered in powder as well and they'll die later on from asphyxiation, like. As I said before, keep your windows closed for now, just to be safe.'

Belle's father smiled and nodded as he looked up at the man descending with a yellow tank on his back and a hose from it which led to a gun.

'No! Oh no, you've murdered them,' gasped Belle, and she left the room and climbed the steps to the make-up room. She pushed her ear gently against the pink silken wall and listened, and she heard cries. The hum was very faint and it stopped now and then and she could hear it increase in pitch, as if the wasps were distressed. She heard a thump as the pest controller closed the door of his van, and then he drove off.

When Belle's mother Jennifer came upstairs to the make-up room to warn her daughter about opening the round window because of the poison spray, she was startled to find Belle sitting in a corner with her face in her hands, sobbing.

'Belle! What's the matter, love?' her mum asked, closing in on her.

Belle kept her hands to her face and gently shook her head.

'Why are you crying?' Jennifer Chase asked, kneeling at her daughter's side.

'The wasps,' said Belle in a choked voice, 'they'll never see summer now. I should have stopped it – '

'The wasps?' Mrs Chase was baffled at the reply. 'Should have stopped what?'

'The man from killing them,' Belle removed her hands from her face and her mother saw her eyes screwed up as if she was in great pain. 'They weren't doing any harm.'

'Have you been talking about all this crap to Libby?' Mrs Chased asked with harshness in her voice. 'She's blanking me and your father over the wasp's nest thing!'

'Just go away and leave me alone,' sniffled Belle and her nettled mother stormed out of the make-up room in such a state of irritation, she almost fell down the steep steps.

Belle refused to come down to have lunch with her family, and at teatime her father had to bring up her meal on a tray. Again he complained about his rheumaticky knee and when he went back downstairs Belle heard her parents having a row over her 'spoilt behaviour'. Belle placed her ear to the wall and heard nothing. No sound now because all of the wasps were dead.

Akari Facetimed Belle around 8.30pm and saw that

her friend had been crying, and had no make-up on, which was so unlike her. When Belle told her friend she was depressed over the death of the wasps, Akari said, 'Girl, you are a directionless mess. You need retail therapy; you need to go shopping with me asap.'

'There's some change coming over me,' said Belle, and she noticed the full moon peeping in at her through the round window. The steadily shining lunar disk had a hypnotic pull on Belle's eyes, and Akari, four miles away at her home in Liverpool, saw Belle's eyes distracted by something on the screen of her phone. 'Earth to Belle – what are you looking at?' she asked.

Belle didn't reply. She had this bizarre feeling that the moon was feminine – a mistress of the night – and this odd notion was completely foreign to a mind that rarely thought beyond make-up and clothes. The ancient markings on the moon seemed to change into a silver feminine face for a moment, but a voice from the mundane area of Belle's life snapped her out of the strange reverie.

'Belle I am going if you're not gonna even talk to me,' sulked Akari.

'Sorry Akari, I was just looking at the moon and I came over all weird,' said Belle and she could see the coin-sized after-image of the moon on Akari's annoyed face as she looked at her phone screen.

'I think you need to go and see your doctor, Belle,' a worried Akari told her. 'Getting all upset over wasps dying and now you're looking at the moon; you might be heading towards a breakdown.'

'No, I'm just worn out,' said Belle, 'worn out and that.'

Akari started suggesting bands they should go and see at the Manchester and Echo Arenas but Belle's heart didn't seem in it, whereas she would normally become hyper and discuss what she'd wear at forthcoming concerts and arrange meet-ups with other "mutuals" - girls who were into the same bands. And so, Akari made an excuse to sign off and Belle lay there on the bed, looking at the moon making her slow climb through the skies beyond the round window.

A change occurred in Belle Chase that night; she felt as if she had suddenly discovered her real self. She turned off the lights in her make-up room and with the soft blue light of the full moon shining through the window, she walked to the full length mirror, and she stood there looking deep into her own eyes. An owl hooted outside somewhere in the night, and at that exact moment Belle wanted to belong to the night side. She recalled that her real hair colour was black, and her skin was naturally pale; she had never been one of those people who tanned easily, unlike Akari, whose golden tan never faded because she was constantly topping it up on a sunbed. It would take forever to grow the pearly blonde out of her hair, so Belle Chase decided she'd have to have it dyed black. The Oompa Loompa face foundation had to go, along with the garishly coloured clothes...

On the following day – the last day of her father's week-long holiday – Belle begged him to take her to a certain hairdresser in Liverpool, and when father and daughter returned home, Mrs Chase didn't recognise Belle at first as she got out of the car. Her hair was straight and coal black, and it contrasted strongly against her pale skin which was now devoid of any foundation.

'What's she done to her hair?' Libby asked her mum, and she watched her sister walk with six carrier bags from the SEAT Alhambra. Mr Chase walked behind Belle, smiling at his wife.

'Talk about a change in image,' Jennifer Chase said to her daughter as she passed her without an iota of acknowledgement. Belle went to the fridge, took a swig from a large bottle of Smart water, then went up to her make-up room with Libby following close behind asking question after question, none of which were answered.

'Another phase,' George Chase told his wife as he pressed the Alhambra's remote key fob.

'What's in the bags she had?' Mrs Chase wanted to know.

'She dragged me to every alternative clothing store in Liverpool, and my knee is still achy,' said Mr Chase, patting his patella. 'Every dress and top she got is black, and she got these big boots and a corset.'

'A corset?' Mrs Chase seemed aghast at the mention of the foundation garment. 'What does she need a girdle for? She's only sixteen!'

'As I say it's just another phase, you know what Belle's like,' said Mr Chase reassuringly, 'so when you get a minute love can I have a nice strong coffee?'

Akira called just after teatime when Belle was in her make-up room but she rejected the call – something she had never done before; she had even taken calls from Akira when she was in the bath. Akira called the landline at Belle's home and Jennifer Chase shouted up to her daughter, informing her that her friend was on the line, and Libby came down with a message: 'Belle is busy doing her make-up and she said she'll phone Akira around eight.'

Jennifer passed on the message to Akira, and then in a low voice she told the girl: 'She's gone all Goth. I suppose you know all about it.'

There was a pause, and then Akira gasped, 'What?'

'Didn't you know?' said Mrs Chase.

'Goth? But why?' Akira was never a conversationalist with people over thirty and usually spoke in monosyllabic utterances when she communicated with Belle's mother, and even in shock the girl kept muttering permutations of 'Goth?' and 'Belle?' and 'Why?'

At eight, Akira called her friend and it was a Face Time session to remember as far as Akira was concerned. 'Belle, you've been Gothified – is that really you?' she asked, because she could vaguely make out her friend's features now that the orange foundation, pink lipstick and false eyelashes had gone – and that almost platinum blonde hair was now as black as night. 'How much mascara and eyeliner have you got on?'

'This is who I *am*,' said Belle, confidently – and even the timbre of her voice seemed different – it was no longer squeaky. 'Take it or leave it.'

'Why?' Akira asked.

Belle gave a phoney-sounding chuckle and replied: 'What do you mean – "why?" – do you mean why am I no longer one of the sheep?'

'You've gone from a chav to a Goth,' said Akira, 'let's see the rest of you.'

'There are no such things as chavs and Goths,' said Belle, her eyebrows furrowed, 'they're just labels made up by morons and people in the media.'

'Will you be getting a tattoo next?' Akira asked with a painful imitation of a smile on her face.

'I dunno, I might,' Belle held the phone aloft then angled it so Akira could see her short black velvet flared dress, fishnet stockings and a pair of New Rock biker boots.

'What the f – ' Akira was saying when her phone notified her of incoming call. 'Hope's calling – be right back,' Akira said and her face vanished from the iPhone's screen.

Belle knew Akira would be telling their mutual friend Hope about the change to the Gothic, but she was surprised to find herself not even caring what *anyone* said about her – even friends. Belle thought about her other friends, and how they'd see what would be perceived as a change in image when she returned to school in September. It would also mean wearing the uniform, but after school she could don the clothes she identified with. Her friend Hope was so predictable; she hadn't called for weeks but now she wanted to Face Time Belle just so she could see her 'new look'. Belle rejected the call.

At one in the morning, Belle Chase sat in her darkened room on a chair that had been pulled to the round window. She watched the squadrons of clouds sliding past the face of the moon, and her eyes kept wandering down to that wood which she had first regarded as being sinister, but now, in the silvery lunar light there was something magical about it, and some indefinable atmosphere that was almost inviting about the place. She decided she'd go for a walk to that wood. She knew that if her mother or father should happen to look in on her and see the bed empty, they'd become hysterical and call the police, so Belle left a simple note written with a pink Sharpie pen which stated: 'Mum/Dad, Went to the wood for a walk.'

She decided against bringing her phone – simply because it was pink with blingy Swarovski crystals and it had her name emblazoned across the back of it in gold. She had no black iPhone cases to replace the pink one so she threw the iPhone on the bed, then left the house ever so quietly, and only the click of the Yale lock was the loudest thing to be heard. Belle set off on her nocturnal ramble and headed for the wood, which was about half a mile away. Soon she had left the few sodium street lamps behind and only the light of the moon remained to give some feeble silvery blue illumination in the fields of Ince Blundell, and to Belle Chase, who hailed from an urban upbringing in the Speke area of Liverpool, this terrain was the Central Africa of Night. The muddy-coloured clouds had moved on to the north where they covered the "Frying Pan" constellation of Ursa Major, and now nothing obscured the ancient lamp of the moon except for a colony of bats that crossed the lunar disk in a heartbeat.

'What am I looking for?' Belle whispered to herself, 'What do I expect to find out here in the dead of night?'

Her eyes adjusted to the moonlit vista; there was Ince Blundell Hall about a quarter of a mile off, barely visible as a ghostly apparition in the gossamer night mist. Belle's father had told her that this old country house had been built in the 18th Century and was now a nursing home. And what was that? A person!

Belle froze – then told herself it was a scarecrow. She kept walking and it remained still; yes, it had to be a scarecrow, just a dressed lifeless effigy of a man filled with straw and nothing more, but then she had an overwhelming urge to look behind her – and she did – and there was another scarecrow! This one was much nearer than the other one – about a hundred yards away, and this one was *moving* - and her mind registered this disturbing fact. Belle remembered leaving her mobile phone in the house and her heart literally skipped a beat and palpitated. She thought about running to the north, but when she looked in that direction she saw another figure, only this one was much further away than the other two, but it looked pale. There was only one direction to flee – south – and her heart pounded when she saw a fourth figure obstructing that escape route! The four figures slowly closed in on Belle Chase, and she ran diagonally between two of the stalking men, hoping to reach the wood. As the four menacing men drew nearer, Belle saw that they didn't seem solid – as if they were made of smoke – as she could see the distant lights of a motorway through two of them. They were ghosts! By the time she had reached the wood, the four pursuers were advancing in a row, separated from one another by just a few feet. They suddenly halted, and Belle slowed down, looked back, and began to walk backwards, wondering if she should scream for help or simply run through the wood and find a way home.

'Umph!' Belle backed into what she perceived as a tree trunk covered in hair, as it was immovable, hard and furry, and she bounced off it, winded somewhat and fell to the floor.

'Sorry!' said a rich deep and very masculine voice.

Belle was on her knees looking up at the man, but the moon was behind his head so she couldn't see his face – but she *could* see that he had a pair of horns and long pointy ears!

He reached down – apparently to help Belle up – but she drew away from him because his hand was grey in the moonlight and covered with hairs and his nails were long black claws.

Belle shrieked, stood up, backed away, then saw the four vaporous men standing there, and when she looked back, she saw that the entity she had bumped into was covered from head to foot with thick hair, and he had large expressive eyes, a van dyke style of beard, and fangs in that sinister smile of his. He reminded Belle of the mythological creature Pan, only this figure had normal – but hair-coated – legs, and not the legs of a goat. He was either someone in a very elaborate costume playing a bizarre prank – or he was something unearthly, and Belle's senses told her that it was definitely the latter.

'What's your name young lady?' the thing asked her, and his smile turned into a grin.

'What are you?' Belle said, stumbling backwards.

'My name is Hongertue,' said the bestial being, and he did not advance after Belle. He pressed his clawed hands together as if he was about to pray and added: 'They call us satyrs sometimes. Don't go – you're beautiful.'

'Who are they?' Belle asked, and she turned to glance at the four ethereal figures.

'The moonlight people – ghosts – spectres,' said

Hongertue, 'they can't harm you, but they get bored and they like to scare living folk. They won't come near you while I'm here because I can disperse them.'

Belle just sensed the satyr was harmless, and she stood there, took deep breaths, and wondered what to do next. She didn't want to run; after all, what would she be running back to? A world of mind-numbing normality she could no longer stomach.

'So, what is your name fair lady?' Hongertue asked again, and he clasped his hairy hands together and angled his horned head sideways as he grinned.

'My name's Belle,' she said, 'what's yours again?'

'Hongertue,' he told her.

She asked him to spell it, and he did, and then he said, 'Just wait there a moment,' and he ran at a phenomenal speed towards the moonlight people, charging them with his horned head bowed like a bull – and the four figures tried to separate and run but he went straight through them and they dispersed like glowing blue steam.

Belle had a feeling that Hongertue was showing off, and when he ran back to her she was ready to jump out the way in case he rammed her, but he stopped dead about six feet in front of her and straightened up.

'Do you have a mate?' he asked.

'You mean a boyfriend?' said Belle, noticing now at closer quarters that he was not clothed, and she blushed. 'No, I split up last year.'

'May I love you?' he asked in an indifferent tone, as one might ask someone the time.

'What? What did you just ask?' Belle was dumbfounded by the question.

Hongertue's eyebrows rose and with an expression

of expectancy, he said: 'May I love you and be your mate? You are so beautiful Belle and you'd suit me down to the ground as a lover.'

'I hardly know you,' said Belle, and if a human had posed the outrageous question she would have wanted to tell them where to go, but this was not a human, so she just backed away and said, 'and it's late; I better be going home.'

'It's late by your clock yes, but not by the clock of owls,' said Hongertue, and he walked after Belle.

'The what?' she asked, and noticed him walking closely behind her.

Hongertue looked up at the moon and said, 'That – the clock of owls.'

'I'm going home, Hongertue,' said Belle, turning away from her strange admirer.

'Belle! Don't be such a cold fish!' cried Hongertue, and he ran ahead of the girl and barred her way. 'Have you got a heart of stone?' he asked, and he held his clenched hairy fist to his chest.

'I'll scream,' she warned him, 'and I can really scream, believe me!' Belle walked around him, and she heard him burst into tears. She halted and looked back, and he had his back turned to her, but he was shaking as he cried with his head bowed. 'What's wrong?' she asked.

'It's because I'm not one of your lot, isn't it?' he asked in a broken voice.

'No it's not,' said Belle, feeling a little guilt creeping up on her now. 'We've only just met; it's not normal to just make love to someone like that. Even prostitutes introduce themselves first.'

Hongertue turned quickly and he was smiling – so

had that crying been nothing more than crocodile tears? 'Belle, just a kiss! Just a single little kiss!'

'Just a peck - on the cheek,' she said, and could not believe she was going to allow him to touch her with his lips; those lips that framed his fearsome fangs.

'Oh thank you Belle!' Hongertue almost knocked her over as he lunged forward and embraced her. He was a little over six feet in height and had to stoop to hold her.

It was *not* a peck on the cheek. It was *not* a peck. It was a full-blown French kiss, and Belle tried to push herself away from him but her hands felt as if they were pushing against fur-covered concrete. His hold was like a bear hug and she thought she'd faint at one point because she couldn't breathe. He withdrew his lips and she saw his eyes roll up into his forehead as if he was about to faint, but he had a strange smile on his face and she could feel his heart pounding against her chest. Somehow she managed to duck down and slip from his grasp. She turned and ran off in her new Goth boots, and she stumbled as she made her getaway but managed to stay upright. She heard him shouting her name as she ran back the way she had come. Belle did not dare look back once because she expected Hongertue to pounce on her from behind, but by the time she reached the first street lamp, she discovered to her pleasant surprise, that she had somehow enjoyed his rather brutal kiss. When she saw the cottage in the distance, Belle immediately noticed the light on in her room, and when she got nearer she could see her father in a tee shirt and tracksuit bottom walking to his car on the drive. Her mother and Libby were silhouetted against the hall light in the doorway's yellow rectangle. Belle just reached the driveway as her father was about to take off in search of her. The teenager had some explaining to do but she didn't mention Hongertue as she had not even fully convinced herself that he existed yet.

'You're a downright selfish diva, Belle!' the girl's mother branded her. Libby had been crying and Mr Chase was so incensed at his daughter's vanishing act, he couldn't get his words out.

'Belle! You stupid idiot!' a sobbing Libby yelled at her big sister.

'Oh get a grip all of you!' shouted Belle, ascending the stairs, 'I only went for a walk because I couldn't sleep! And I left a note saying where I'd gone!'

'We didn't see any note!' Her father yelled and took a pink phone out the right pocket of his tracksuit trousers and thrust it at Belle. 'You went for a walk in the middle of nowhere in the middle of the night and left your phone behind! Very clever, Belle!'

Her mother noted the strange way the brickbats were going over her daughter's head and the curious faint smile on her face. Mrs Chase wondered if Belle had been out on some romantic rendezvous. She voiced this suspicion to her husband later that morning as they lay in bed. 'I don't think she even knows anyone around here so I don't think she's seeing anyone, love,' he told his wife.

Mrs Chase snuggled into her husband and in a harsh-sounding whisper she said: 'George, this is 2015 – they meet people now on social media and arrange a rendezvous – he could be a serial killer.'

'I'll have a word with her later, love,' said George, 'and as I'm back at work in the morning can I try and get some sleep?'

Meanwhile, in Belle's room, she was looking up satyrs on Wikipedia and other internet sites. They were thought to be some form of nature spirit and were lovers of women, wine, music and dancing. They always hung around woods and had a huge sex drive. Belle's face burned when she learned that. Most of the entries about satyrs claimed they were either merely nonexistent mythological creatures or something that really did exist once but had now become extinct – a bit like the dodo. In the mind of the confused teenager there was no question about the reality of Hongertue – he existed alright, and his hug could have crushed her ribs. That kiss though – she had never experienced anything like that. Her last boyfriend Connor had never kissed her like that.

On the following day, Belle revisited the fields and the wood, and these places looked so different in the light of day. Libby followed Belle to the wood and asked her why she had come here.

'I don't know, I just felt like,' said Belle. The words of Hongertue echoed in her mind from last night under that huge moon: *'May I love you and be your mate? You are so beautiful Belle and you'd suit me down to the ground as a lover.'*

Libby suddenly told her something random: 'I think Dad's going to get you a new phone for your birthday and Mum's getting you a big Mac make-up set.'

'I'm not into phones and make-up now – ' Belle replied, then smiled and paused. 'Hey yes, it's my birthday on August 12 – I'll be seventeen.'

'That's old,' said Libby, 'you should be settling down with someone.'

'You're right for once Libby – I should be settling down with someone,' said Belle, 'not your normal someone but – '

'But what?' Libby was curious as to who her sister was referring to. She was a very perceptive kid.

'Libby, you've got a really big nose,' said Belle, and she playfully slapped her hand on her sister's head and ran off giggling. Libby sensed that her sister was in love.

'I know you're almost seventeen, Belle,' George Chase told his daughter as he sat on her bed that evening at 9pm, 'and I know you're not an idiot regarding the internet and all that, but if you ever do meet up with someone you've met online, I'd appreciate knowing a little about them. The news is full of horror stories about – '

'Dad, you're repeating yourself now,' said Belle, rolling her eyes as she lay on her side on the bed, facing away from her father. 'I'm not a kid and I am not meeting anyone off the web. Now Dad, I want you to paint the walls of my make-up room black. I hate pink with a vengeance.'

'No way – I've just had that room painted, but if you can pay for the decorators out your own pocket, be my guest.' George Chase told her and left the room. Belle wanted to go and see Hongertue so badly after midnight but she had to resist the powerful urge, and she thought she might seem more desirable to him if she played hard to get. She wondered if she'd cave in at midnight and go and see him, though.

At 11pm Belle's mother called her – six times. Eventually Jennifer Chase had to come up the stairs and she asked, 'Why are you ignoring me?'

'Oh what do you want?' groaned Belle.

'Well,' her mother gave a wide smile and said, 'Come down and hear the good news – you'll like this.'

Belle buried her face in her hands. 'Oh stop being cryptic will you? Just tell me – this is pathetic.'

'No, you'll have to come down,' Jennifer Chase insisted, and she turned and left the bedroom.

Belle seemed to be taking agonised steps down to the living room as she grimaced, and as she walked through the hall, Libby ran out and said, 'We're going to live in America!'

'What?' Belle was shocked by her little sister's claim. Hopefully she'd gotten hold of the wrong end of the stick.

'Libby, let your father tell her, blabbermouth,' shouted Mrs Chase.

George Chase seemed unable to contain his excitement. 'Belle, how do you fancy living in San Francisco?'

'They have earthquakes there,' said Belle flatly.

'What's she like?' said Mrs Chase, and then she told Belle: 'Your father's boss called him before and said he's been promoted because he's worked so hard this last year, and he's asked him to move to San Francisco to be the vice president of the company there.'

'Well can't you just move there and we can stay here?' Belle asked her father.

Mr Chase laughed, thinking she was joking, and then seeing she was serious, he became rather irate. 'Well you can stay here if you can pay the mortgage and we'll all go to the States and leave you to it!'

'But why leave here when we've only just moved in?' Belle asked, and then she realised she had tears in her eyes. Libby watched the mascara run down her sister's face.

'Because I have been offered the bloody opportunity of a lifetime, that's why, Belle!' roared her father. 'I've always wanted to live in America – I'm sick of the weather in this country – that's why my knee's in this state!'

'Well when are we supposed to be moving?' asked Belle, wiping her dark tainted tears with the back of her fingers.

'In the New Year,' said Mr Chase, 'why the hell are you crying? I thought you'd be chuffed at the news!'

And so that night, Belle went to see Hongertue again, and this time she kissed him as hard as he kissed her, and they ended up embraced on the ferny floor of the wood.

'Do you satyrs have marriage?' she asked Hongertue.

'Yes, we do – why do you ask?' he replied, and began to kiss her earlobe.

'I'd like to marry you,' said Belle.

Hongertue froze. 'You would?'

'Yes,' Belle stroked his face. 'The age of consent is sixteen where I come from, and I'll be seventeen soon – and I'd like to marry you – or am I being silly?'

'Well, as you said, we've only just met,' said Hongertue, sitting up, 'maybe in time as we get to know one another more – '

'Oh I see!' Belle sat up and started to put on her tee shirt. 'You've had your way with me now! You're not so different than my "lot" after all!'

'No! It's not that, Belle!' Hongertue actually seemed afraid when his lover started to raise her voice.

She got dressed and ran off crying, but when she

reached her home, she turned and went back to the wood – and she saw a strange red glow in the heart of that wood, and figures moving about in the crimson radiance. Belle hid behind a tree and peeped at the peculiar goings-on. Hongertue had told her about the "crack" between his world and hers in the middle of the wood, and how it allowed him to visit, but only of a night. He called Belle's reality 'the nightside.'

Belle ran to another tree nearer to the red glow and saw that the light was coming through some sort of fissure – almost as if there was a wide jagged opening in mid air, and pure blood-red light was seeping from it. The girl heard voices coming from within the crack but they spoke in a language unknown to her. Something cold touched Belle's leg, just behind her knee, and she let out a yelp and turned to see what looked like a childish version of Hongertue. A little smiling satyr, but his fur was blonde, and he had huge green eyes.

A familiar voice somewhere near shouted something that sounded like 'Altic!'

'Dadda!' said the little satyr, and he ran to two figures that came out of that glowing crimson crevice. One was Hongertue, and the other satyr was a bit smaller than him, and looked quite feminine. She bent down and the little satyr ran into her arms.

Belle stepped out from behind the tree and confronted Hongertue. 'Is that your child?' she asked.

Hongertue's eyes were wide with shock when he turned to look at Belle, and the female beside that satyr hugged him and acted as if she was afraid of Belle.

'And is that your wife, Hongertue?' Belle asked, her heart breaking.

Without a word of reply he turned his back on her and the family of satyrs rushed into the glowing red irregular opening, and then it closed over, and the light went out and Belle found herself alone in the wood. Above, watching her through the gaps in the branches was the moon, and she seemed to have a sympathetic face tonight, perhaps because she'd seen so many lovers turn untrue over aeons undreamt of. Belle left the wood, head bowed, wiped her eyes, and headed back to the cottage.

SOME STRANGE OMENS OF DEATH

One evening around 8pm in September 1971 at a semidetached house on Childwall Priory Road, Richard Taylor a 42-year-old marketing manager with a well-known pharmaceutical company, was enjoying a dinner cooked by his wife Eve when they both heard distant music. It sounded like a brass band playing *When the Saints Go Marching In* – and it seemed to be coming from upstairs.

'Have you left a radio on up there?' Richard asked his wife and she shook her head, so he got up, intending to see just what was making that music when it stopped. Eve decided that they'd merely heard the music from someone's turned-up TV set next door.

The couple retired around 11pm, and for the second night running, Richard couldn't sleep. He re-read the *Liverpool Echo* from its banner headlines to the "Finishing Touch" feature on the back page of the broadsheet, and then he perused numerous magazines – even his wife's magazines, but still he couldn't get to sleep. He asked Eve – a science teacher – to explain the Riemann Hypothesis, a complicated mathematical conjecture – as that had bored him to sleep in the past when she had talked about it, but instead, Eve dozed off fifteen minutes into her description of the hypothesis. Richard was considering taking one of the sleeping pills his company manufactured, when he decided to close his eyes and count backwards from a hundred in an effort to get some much-needed shut eye. He reached the number 72 when he suddenly heard that music he and his wife had heard earlier, and he opened his eyes. This time the music was accompanied by the appearance of a little glowing green skeleton in a top hat! This creepy apparition danced to the unseen band and kicked its bony legs in the air as it walked across the blankets. Richard estimated that the dancing skeleton was about 16 inches in height, and he lay there, frozen with fear as the thing removed its topper and waved it in the air. Richard reached out to wake Eve and instantly the glowing manikin of bones vanished and the music ceased. When Richard told his wife what he had seen she said it was probably a hallucination brought on through lack of sleep. In the morning, Eve received bad news; her brother had died in a freak car crash in Wiltshire. On five more occasions over the next two years, Richard Taylor woke in the night to see that radiant skeleton dancing on his bed, and he'd always hear that music - *When the Saints Go Marching In* – and without fail he would hear of the death of a relative or friend not long afterwards. He and Eve moved to Calderstones in 1974 and he never saw that frightening omen of death again.

Another bizarre omen of doom was seen in Liverpool from the early 1960s to around 1980, and this was a "dancing tree" in the so-called Spanish Garden on Catharine Street in the city centre. The

Spanish Garden was created on a WWII bombsite which adjoined the Catholic Byzantine-styled St Philip Neri Church on Catherine Street in the early 1950s. Dr John Garvin, an innovative parish priest with a great sympathy for the poor of the city, was the architect of this beautiful Mediterranean oasis in the middle of a grey post-war Liverpool. The garden incorporated marble columns and a pool, and was often referred to by its Spanish name, 'El Jardin de Nuestra Senora' – 'The Garden of Our Lady'. One of the saplings planted in the Spanish Garden was seen to act quite strange one night in June 1962. It was a calm summer night and yet several members of a family living in a second storey flat in one of the terraced Georgian houses facing the garden saw the tree sway from side to side and lift up to prominent branches on either side of the thin trunk in a bizarre 'dance'. All of the other trees and plants in the garden remained stock-still while the young tree performed its eerie dance, and it always happened after midnight but never after 1.30am. The tree was seen to dance six times by the family, including an occasion when it was seen by a bachelor who lived in the top flat of the house, and on each occasion those who saw the tree dance received news of the death of a family member. The bachelor saw the tree on the sixth occasion and that same night his mother suddenly died of natural causes, aged 53, and that same night a relative of the family on the second floor of the dwelling who had seen the dancing tree received a visit from a policeman to inform him of the death of his brother. The family kept their curtains drawn in the end and the bachelor subsequently moved out of the house. I assume that the terpsichorean sapling grew into one of the fine substantial trees that stands sentinel today in the garden. Was it all a series of morbid coincidences or did a young tree really perform some sinister *danse macabre*?

Ghoulish coincidences may explain away the dancing tree of Catharine Street but they cannot explain the following dark mystery. A Mr Williams – a musician with the Royal Liverpool Philharmonic Orchestra came into a Liverpool police station in July 1958 and before the bemused eyes of the desk sergeant he unwrapped a brown paper parcel to reveal a little shiny lacquered black coffin, about 2 feet in length with four silver-painted wooden handles upon it. The lid of the coffin was removed to reveal the realistic doll of a woman who was laid out in a shroud. 'That thing's the double of my wife,' said the musician, 'and she's ill with worry. Here's the letter we received inside this ghastly box.'

'This is Grim,' the letter started, 'Mrs Williams will be enormously improved by death. She will make an excellent corpse. Bye-bye. Yours solemnly, Mr G.'

'Someone's just playing a joke on you sir,' opined the sergeant, looking at the weird doll, 'and it's in very bad taste and they've gone to quite a bit of trouble to make all this.' The policeman saw that the postmark on the parcel was smudged. There wasn't much he could do, but the incident was routinely filed and the musician stormed out saying his visit had been a waste of time.

Three days later, that musician's wife died in her sleep from natural causes at the age of 33. Two more people visited the city centre station – each with dolls in coffins they'd received. Mr Clarke, a well-known conman from Toxteth with a lengthy criminal record, and an unscrupulous Wavertree landlord named Neville Culross, had each been the recipient of those little coffins containing dolls that looked just like them, and the covering letters with the disturbing packages were from the mysterious 'Grim'. According to the postmarks, the parcels had been sent from the post office on Monument Place off London Road, but no one there could recall Mr Grim posting the sinister packages. A week later, Mr Culross died of a massive heart attack, possibly brought on by intense stress because he was known to be very superstitious and believed the coffin was some omen of approaching death. Mr Clarke lost two fingers in an accident with a paper-cutting machine. He believed he had survived Grim's fatal curse by carrying a pocket Bible everywhere, and he subsequently donated a small fortune to his church.

There were a few more miniature coffins sent out by Grim – both to shopkeepers who had premises on Dale Street, and a Mr Krivanek, an anthropologist and expert on curses, was consulted by detectives. He said that hair on the head of the doll representing Culross was the victim's actual hair, possibly taken from the floor of a barber he had visited. Krivanek also said the dolls would be baptised in the names of the victims in a church font to reinforce the power of the curse. Krivanek suspected an occultist in his seventies named Mr Grorud of being Grim, and he visited the man at his carpentry workshop on Pomona Street with one of the coffins – and Grorud seemed shocked, but nothing was ever proven, although no more coffins were sent through the post after Krivanek's visit to Mr Grorud. I mentioned this case on a local radio programme some years ago and a woman rang the station to say how she recalled seeing one of the ominous coffins - and the lifelike doll of its victim – in a second hand shop in Walton in the 1960s.

TWO HAUNTED SLEEPOVERS

This chapter is about a couple of strange goings-on which have taken place during sleepovers – also known as pyjama parties and slumber parties, and earlier on in the 1960s and 1970s, sleepovers were usually referred to as 'staying over' wherein the child, usually around twelve years of age, would ask his parents or guardian: 'Can Tony stay over tonight?' or conversely 'Can I stay over at Tony's tonight?'

Sociologists have regarded the sleepover as some rite of passage, and that children sleeping away from their homes are asserting their independence. That might be so, but there's a more likely chance that the child simply wants to have fun staying up beyond his or her normal bedtime in the company of friends. The sleepover in the second story of this chapter is more adult in nature and the people sleeping over are not out to assert independence; they just want to have a good time via those old bacchanalian past times – drink, dancing and sex!

I have had many letters and emails over the years from people who have experienced all sorts of supernatural happenings during these sleepovers, and I will start with a case that took place at a house on Fairfield's Holly Road on the cusp of the Kensington area of the city, in 1990. In October of that year, a 13-year-old girl named Beth invited two schoolfriends –

Lexy and Lily – to stay over at her house one night while her parents were out on the town. Mobile phones were almost unheard of in 1990, but Beth's father had paid a fortune to obtain a mobile called the DynaTac 8000X – which weighed 1.75 lbs, and on the night of the sleepover at 10.30pm he called Beth on the landline of his home with the state-of-the-art mobile "brick" and told her he was in a place called Birdys Bar on Leece Street and that he'd be home no later than half-past midnight. Beth's mum then came on the mobile phone and sounding a little tipsy she said, 'I hope you and your friends are behaving. Don't open that front door to anyone, and if you use that cooker make sure the knobs are all turned off afterwards.'

The girls sniggered at the vague sexual association in the mention of 'knobs' and then Beth's mum said to her, 'I love you, babe,' but Beth went red because Lexy and Lily had their ears pressed against the phone's earpiece, listening in. Beth didn't say 'And I love you,' to her mum like she normally did because she'd look so uncool to her friends She hung up instead.

Not long after this, Lexy left the living room and said she was going to the toilet, but she returned with one of Beth's old dolls, which meant that Lexy had been upstairs mooching in Beth's bedroom. Beth told her friend off for snooping about in her room and Lexy stuffed the doll up her skirt, wedged it between the waistband of the skirt and her tummy under her pullover, and in a put-on crying voice she said, 'Stop picking on me, I'm pregnant!'

Beth and Lily laughed at the line and then Lexy, who was highly prone to role-playing games said to Beth in a rapid machine-gun way of speaking: 'You're my boyfriend Richard and you tell me you're leaving me even though I'm having your baby! Yes! Beth, you're Richard, and you want to walk out on me and I try to stop you but you push me on the sofa and walk out and I beg for you to come back!'

Beth rolled her eyes and then she got into the spirit of the play-acting by pushing Lexy backwards with both hands to her chest and with such force, the girl was thrown onto the sofa and landed with a mighty thump. Lily shrieked with laughter at the way Lexy landed on her back, but Lexy really got into her role and after letting out a yelp, she moaned: 'Oh Richard, you can't just walk out on me and our baby! It's your baby too and if you walk out that door I'll kill myself!'

Beth giggled, then put on a fairly serious face and told Lexy in a ridiculously-sounding affectation of a deep voice: 'Shut up you bitch, I don't give a crap what you do! Go and kill yourself for all I care, and kill that damn baby too! I'm going out tonight and I'm going to shag the world!'

Lily giggled and chipped in with another daft voice. She tried to sound American as she placed her hands on her face, gesturing that she was shocked, and she said: 'Ooh, Richard, don't talk to your girlfriend like that you beast! And don't you dare get me pregnant too or I'll chop it off!'

'Richard, don't walk out on me honey!' Lexy said, and she grimaced and told him, 'Oh no Richard! I'm going into labour!' Lily burst out laughing at the antics of her fantasy-prone friend on the sofa and Beth smiled as she walked to the living room door and said, 'I don't give a damn Lexy, you'll have to bring up the child on your own! I'm leaving for LA!'

And then Lexy let out a scream that seemed a little too realistic for her make-believe romance. She seemed to be in agony for real, and Lily and Beth stared in shock as their friend cried out, 'I really *am* having a baby! Oh God! It hurts!'

What looked like blood and water poured from under Lexy's skirt and stained the beige cushions of the sofa.

'Lexy, are you okay?' asked Lily, looking on in shock, and simultaneously Beth gasped: 'Oh my God!'

Lexy threw her head back and kept crying and groaning as more blood and water came from under her skirt. 'Help me! Help me, Beth! Oh!'

At first Beth and Lily thought it was the doll's head peeping from under Lexy's skirt, but it was the head of a baby – a flesh and blood baby with curly dark hair matted with something that looked like a greasy white substance. Beth felt so weak with shock, she grabbed hold of Lily to steady herself and Lily was trembling and kept taking alternate glances between Beth and her friend who was apparently giving birth on the sofa. Lexy's face was flushed, and coated with sweat. Her eyes rolled up into her forehead as if she was ready to pass out and her fingernails were embedded in the sofa cushions as she seemed to be going through the agonising throes of childbirth – and although Beth and Lily knew it was impossible, they could not doubt their eyes. Lily started to cry, and Beth swayed, feeling she was going to faint at any moment.

'Help me! Oh please make it stop!' begged Lexy, her face distorted with pain. She looked at the ceiling as she lay there on her back. 'Oh God, why is this happening to me?'

And then the baby was out, covered in that revolting substance called Vernix caseosa - a cheesy protective coating on newborn babies after they leave the amniotic sac. None of the girls had ever seen a baby being born before and yet they described the waxy vernix coating upon the infant and the breaking of the waters. Beth stumbled to the telephone and picked up the handset, then dropped it, picked it up again, clumsily knocked the mouthpiece against her front tooth, and dialled 999. The operator asked her what emergency service she required, but Beth was so traumatised by witnessing a birth, she was stuck for words, but eventually managed to say, 'Ambulance. My friend has had a baby.'

Because Lily was now crying quite loudly, the operator asked Beth to speak up, and Beth told Lily to shut up, and again told the woman at the other end of the line how her friend had just given birth.

'I want to go home,' sobbed Lily, and Beth told her to be quiet again as she chatted to the operator.

Lexy got up off the sofa, looked at the water and blood and traces of vernix on her thighs and knees, and then she glanced at the sofa and softly said, 'The baby's gone.'

And it was true – there was no sign – not a trace – of that newborn baby. Lily lifted a cushion where Lexy had lain and let out a shriek – but it was just the doll Lexy had brought down from Beth's room, and it had traces of blood on it. The ambulance men were soon at the door, and Beth wouldn't answer the door at first because she knew the men out there wouldn't believe her story, but in the end she opened the door and told them it had been a mistake, and she gave a garbled story about some girl – she didn't know her name – who had come into the house and dialled 999 to frame her and get her into trouble. The ambulance men were furious and left in a huff.

Lexy said that she had felt the baby moving around inside of her and the pain had been so excruciating she had come close to passing out. She examined herself in the toilet and expected to find a gaping hole where the baby had 'popped out' but she was intact, but her underwear was soaked from watery blood.

Beth's parents came home at a quarter to one in the morning and they were understandably livid when they saw the bloodstained sofa cushions, and by now, Lexy and Lily had returned to their respective homes. Beth told her mother and father exactly what had happened and when her parents said they didn't believe her she screamed that she wanted to be legally emancipated from them and called her father an idiot. She then ran upstairs to her room and lay face down on her bed in tears. Beth and her friends often talked about the strange pseudo-childbirth incident over the years as they grew up, and then in 2007 when Beth was thirty, her mother told her something that not only shocked her – it also seemed to throw some light on the weird trauma suffered by Lexy. In the early 1970s, the previous owner of the house on Holly Road raped his 13-year-old niece, and the girl became pregnant. Because the girl's family were Catholics, the niece did not have an abortion, and she gave birth to a baby boy at home, but sadly the baby later died. There were rumours that the girl later committed suicide, and the house was said to 'have an atmosphere' – meaning it was haunted, and the owners had to sell the place at a knock-down price. Beth's father bought the place and when neighbours told him and his wife about the chequered history of the house the couple had the place blessed. So, had Lexy somehow been possessed by the spirit of the raped niece? How did a real carnate baby appear – and then disappear – leaving bloodstains behind? It's a bizarre case, but typical of the stories concerning sleepovers in this chapter. Here's another one.

At a 3-bedroom semidetached house on Halewood's Woodland Road in July 1977, two sisters – 14-year-old Eloise and 16-year-old Carmen – punched the air with joy as their mother and father set off for a five-day break down in Cornwall. The girls had invited their boyfriends and some friends to stay over at the house and tonight there was going to be a party, and the girls were determined that it would be a party to remember. Just after the sisters had finished their tea, they went to their bedrooms and started to put make-up on and try out different outfits they had in mind for the party. There was a knock at the door at 6pm, and Carmen answered it to see it was Dennis, a former boyfriend of her sister Eloise. He was fifteen – a year older than Eloise, but he looked taller than when Carmen had last seen him, and he'd also grown a fluffy moustache. He stood there in a green Army surplus jacket, flared jeans and a pair of tennis shoes, and he had a cigarette in his mouth. Eloise was now going with a 17-year-old lad named Kevin, so she asked Dennis what he wanted.

With a barely-suppressed smile, Dennis said, 'I just called to say that Kevin's gone into ozzy [slang for hospital] with appendicitis, and his Mam told me to tell

Eloise.'

'Why didn't Kevin's mum telephone Eloise to tell her?' asked Carmen with a suspicious look in her almond-shaped eyes.

'She couldn't find her number,' said Dennis, and he removed the ciggie from his mouth, exhaled smoke down his nostrils, and then he added: 'but anyway, er, can I come to the party?'

'No, you can't,' Carmen decided instantly, and she screwed her face up and waved the cigarette smoke back towards the caller saying, 'what do you take Eloise for?'

'Nothing would happen like,' said Dennis, 'I'm just good friends with Eloise now.'

'Nothing will happen because you're *not* coming – bye!' Carmen told him and closed the door in his face.

Dennis walked off down Woodlands Road, but stopped and turned around when he heard a voice call his name.

'Denny! Denny!' shouted Eloise, standing in her bare feet at the gatepost of her home. She had on a denim skirt and just a bra, and she had yellow, green and blue rollers in her hair and one false eyelash glued to her eyelid.

Dennis flicked the cigarette into the road and smiled, then slowly walked to his ex as if he had all the time in the world. He didn't want to appear to be eager.

'Look, you can come to the party but there can be nothing between us, have you got that?' Eloise stipulated.

'Hey, that's fine,' Dennis replied, 'and I mean like, I wouldn't start making a move on someone when their fellah's in ozzy like; that's bad, man.'

'Did they say when Kevin will be coming home?' Eloise asked nonchalantly as if the question was just some afterthought.

'It might be tomorrow – you hussy!' shouted Carmen from the doorway of her home. 'I just phoned his mum.'

'Carmen this is 1977,' Eloise told her sister, 'girls can associate with their exies nowadays. Stop being a fuddy-duddy.'

'So when does the fun start?' asked Dennis, looking Eloise up and down.

'Half-past seven,' said Eloise, 'but can you get some drink in or anything for the party? We want it to go on all night.'

In a futile attempt at a suave voice, Dennis said: 'I've just been paid,' meaning he'd just received pocket money from both his father and the man his mother was living with, but he made out he had a part-time job somewhere, just to impress Eloise. 'I'll get a few tins of Watneys Party Seven and we've got loads of sausage rolls left over from our kid's birthday party yesterday.'

Eloise didn't look impressed. 'Can you get a few bottles of Martini as well Dennis?'

'Martini?' Dennis laughed, and felt the pound notes in his pocket.

'Or won't they serve you at the off-licence?' Eloise asked with a smirk.

'With this?' he pointed to his feeble moustache with a look of pride, 'They'd give me a barrel of rum.'

And so Dennis went off to get his contributions for the party, and he returned at half-past six with opened bottles of whiskey, Martini, Bertola Cream Sherry, an unopened bottle of Black Tower wine, and two big seven-pint tins of Watneys bitter. He explained how he had to take the bottles from his mum's drinks' cabinet because the man at the off licence had been funny with him. 'As promised though, here's the grub.' Dennis held up a plastic carrier bag bulging with sausage rolls wrapped in foil.

'Kevin will go spare when he finds out *he* was here,' Carmen told her sister, nodding at Dennis in the hallway.

Carmen's 18-year-old boyfriend Rob arrived a few minutes later in his Hillman Minx and he enlisted the help of Dennis to take seven crates of beer from the boot and back seat of the vehicle. Rob preferred Dennis to Eloise's present boyfriend Kevin, finding Dennis to be unintentionally amusing with his elaborate lies about fights he'd never had and his innumerable stories about heroic acts he'd supposedly carried out – saving dogs from ponds and his classic yarn about rescuing two kids who had climbed up an electricity pylon somewhere in Cheshire. He was just a harmless fibber, whereas Kevin had been very possessive with Eloise.

By 7.30pm about a dozen friends of the sisters had turned up at the house in Halewood, and Eloise put on a hit from the previous year on the record player: *I Love To Love (But My Baby Loves To Dance)* by Tina Charles, and soon most of the guests were dancing. Dennis had brought a 45 single of *God Save the Queen* by the Sex Pistols but Eloise – who was in charge of the record player – refused to let him play it.

Just after 8pm there were three loud knocks at the front door and Eloise turned down the stereo and said,

'Here we go – complaining neighbours!'

'I'll get it,' said Carmen's boyfriend Rob, and he went into the hallway and opened the front door. There were two old smiling ladies standing there, holding hands.

'I know,' said Rob, slowly nodding, 'we'll turn it down a notch.'

'Do you mind if we come in, young man?' said one of the elderly women in a well-spoken voice. She had a blue rinse and her hair was tied up in a bun, and the woman holding her hand had white hair done up in a similar style.

'My name's Essy, short for Esther,' said the woman with the blue-tinted hair, 'and this is my friend Norah.'

'Hello!' said Norah in an almost musical voice.

Essy continued: 'Now, the thing is this: I used to live here, a long time ago, and Norah, being my best friend, almost spent as much time here as myself, and well, I was wondering if we could come in and have a look around while we can still move about.'

'Oh! So you're not here to complain about the noise?' Rob asked, a little relieved.

'We're allowed to make as much noise as we want up to eleven o'clock,' said Carmen, appearing behind her boyfriend. She'd left the lounge to see who the party-poopers were.

'No, they're not complaining, love,' explained a smiling Rob, 'this lady used to live here and she and her best friend would like to have a look around.'

'Just a *quick* look around if it's not too much bother – we can always come back,' said Essy, clutching her friend's arm.

Carmen was a little taken aback by the purpose of

the visit, and Rob beckoned the old ladies in, and as they passed him he nodded at their backs, informing Carmen, 'That's Essy, and that's Norah.'

When the women entered the lounge, they looked at the young people dancing, then looked at one another giggling.

'They your grandparents?' a young man asked Eloise, eyeing the two old dears.

Eloise slowed her dance then stopped and shot a puzzled look at Carmen. 'Who are they?' she silently mouthed to her sister, and Carmen shrugged.

'We had a piano there,' said Norah, pointing to the wall of the lounge where a couple was kissing. 'And the radiogram was over there,' said Essy, pointing to a corner where a young girl was sitting cross-legged rolling a cigarette.

'Oh, they've taken the fireplace out,' said Norah, pointing at a bookshelf. 'Remember when I walked in on your father when he was in the tin bath in front of that fire?'

'Oh yes,' said Essy, and she emitted a strange high-pitched tittering sound like a hyena's giggle, then added: 'And if my memory serves me right, you had your dog Booty with you and he jumped all over father in that bath!'

The two old ladies went into the kitchen, and pointed to remembered cookers and mangles and traced out a wooden table with their hands as they reminisced about heavenly cakes and accidents with boiling kettles.

Carmen went to get a drink for Rob and when she returned to the lounge she saw him escorting the aged visitors to the stairs. 'Rob!' Carmen cried, 'Leave them to it, they'll be alright! I don't think they're going to steal anything.'

'I know but it seems bad manners just leaving them,' Rob shouted back over the loud music, and he went upstairs with them, and he showed them around the three bedrooms, then led them back towards the top of the stairs.

'Can Norah go to powder her nose?' Essy asked Rob, and smiled behind her hand, which was pressed over her lips.

'Yes, of course, the toilet's down there,' replied Rob, pointing to the pale green toilet door – but the old couple walked past the door and went into the bathroom. 'No, that's the bathroom!' Rob shouted after them, and he hurried along the landing but the two women went into the bathroom and closed the door behind them. Rob knocked at the door and said, 'Essy, Norah? That's the bathroom!'

Carmen appeared at the top of the stairs with a Martini in one hand and a pint glass full of Watneys bitter filled to the rim in the other. 'Rob, come and have a drink – leave them alone, they'll be alright.'

'Norah wanted to go the toilet but they've gone into the bathroom instead,' Rob explained with a concerned look.

'Oh for God's sake, Rob,' fumed Carmen, 'this is some party when we're running around doting on old biddies!'

Rob tapped meekly on the bathroom door and said, 'Essy, Norah, you're in the bathroom; the toilet's next door.'

'Mind out the way – hold these!' Carmen said, and she handed him her Martini and the pint she'd poured for him. Carmen turned the handle and barged into the bathroom. She saw the old woman with the blue rinse – Essy - leaning over her friend Norah in the bath, and straight away Carmen saw that Essy's left hand was coated with wet blood, and then she saw the crimson handprints on the white enamel of the bath – and the knife in the other hand; it looked like a carving knife. Essy didn't even look at Carmen. She was too occupied cutting the throat of Norah with a sawing motion and arterial blood shot upwards and hit the ceiling with some force. Tiny droplets of the blood landed on Carmen's hand as she lifted it to her face in shock. She backed out of the bathroom and blundered into Rob, who asked: 'What's wrong?'

Carmen rushed past him screaming, 'Murder! There's been a murder!'

Rob put the drinks down on the floor and went into the bathroom and saw Essy trying to remove Norah's head. She had cut through the woman's double chin as far as the vertebrae and she was hitting the cervical vertebrae of the neck with the blade of the knife. She turned to a horrified, frozen Rob, and smiled. 'Her head won't come off – typical,' she chuckled, and then she turned back to look at the half-decapitated corpse and seemed to lose her temper. 'See how you like that!' Essy growled, and stabbed the body of Norah in the breasts and with each plunge of the knife she muttered, 'And that!'

'Oh – oh my God! Oh!' Rob suddenly couldn't feel his legs – he was numb with shock.

'And that! And that!' Essy exclaimed, and the blade went in so far, her fist thumped the dead woman's chest and blood was driven up out of the sliced-open oesophagus and it ejaculated onto the white tiles of the bathroom wall.

Rob regained movement in his legs and he turned and ran out of the toilet, his feet smashing into the glasses of bitter and Martini, and he ran along the landing, trying to get his words together but making nonsensical noises, and he knocked a drink clean out the hand of a guest, and then he almost fell down the stairs but clutched the handrail. When he reached the lounge he asked Dennis where Carmen was, and Dennis said, 'She's all freaked out over something; she went outside with Eloise. What's up?'

Rob went into the hall and he saw the front door ajar. Already he could hear the sounds of vomit on the driveway. It was Carmen, bent over and being sick as Eloise stroked her back.

'Call the police!' Rob urged Eloise, 'there's a murder going on up in the bathroom.'

'What?' Eloise asked, 'Carmen just told me that – but I thought she was messing about!'

'No, Eloise, no one is messing about,' said Rob sternly, and he looked shaken. He stooped down and asked Carmen if she was okay, but she started to cry. He looked up and saw Eloise gazing down at him, looking stunned, or perhaps a bit tipsy. 'Phone the police now!' he roared at her.

'And tell them what?' Eloise asked.

'Oh for God's sake - tell them you want to report a murder! Hurry up!' yelled Rob.

Dennis came out and said, 'What's all that about a murder?'

'Those old women who came in to have a look around – ' said Carmen, and she took a deep breath and held her stomach as she straightened up, 'they went in the bathroom and one of them was trying to cut the other one's head off with a knife!'

'Go way!' was Dennis's dismissive reply. He smiled, obviously thinking it was all some weird wind-up.

Rob shot a grave look at Dennis and nodded. 'It's true,' he said, and his eyes seemed to be protruding on stalks.

'Rob! Rob!' Eloise shouted from the hall, and Rob went to see what she wanted. She handed the telephone handset to him and said, 'the woman asked me who is being murdered.'

Rob talked to the operator and explained the virtual decapitation in the bathroom and within minutes he heard approaching sirens. Police officers poured into the house and stormed the bathroom – but there wasn't a trace of blood in there. Essy and Norah had vanished into thin air. Rob saw them, Carmen and Eloise saw them and most of the guests at the party – and now they had vanished like a couple of *ghosts*. The police were naturally a little annoyed at being called out to deal with a non-existent murder, and Dennis did not help by his constant laughing during the cross-questioning of the guests until a policeman snapped, grabbed him by the throat slammed him up against a wall, where he glared at him for a moment, and then through gritted teeth he said: 'You look a bit familiar, mate. Aren't you that idiot who was on the roof of the social club firing an air rifle at the seagulls?'

Dennis looked terrified. The words came out raspy because of the choke-hold. 'Me? No, no officer, I haven't even got a seagull – I mean air rifle; honest. I love birds – I keep birds like.'

A detective tapped the irate constable on the shoulder and walked to the hallway. Before he left he warned Rob: 'We may still press charges for wasting police time. We'll probably be in touch very soon.' And then he left with the rest of the police, and Carmen held Rob's hand. 'You alright?' she asked. 'I knew they wouldn't believe us.'

'So that's the end of the party I suppose,' said Dennis, holding his throat.

'No, ' said Carmen, 'I'm determined to have this party, so come on everyone, let's get drinking.'

'They won't be in touch mate,' Dennis said to a worried-looking Rob, 'the coppers have got enough on their plate with the crime rate, honest. You won't hear from them again.'

'Thanks mate,' said Rob with a faint smile, and he tried to get into the party spirit, but it took quite an intake of alcohol for the teenager to do that. The police never did press charges. Rob and Dennis slept over with Carmen and Eloise and six years after this these two couples were married on the same day in a double-wedding ceremony.

I have researched the history of the house on Halewood's Woodland Road into quite some depth, and can find no record of any murder on the premises, nor have I found any record of an Esther living at the address in question. People do get away with murder of course, so perhaps the grisly incident witnessed by Rob and Carmen did take place, but that would mean the careful disposal of dismembered body parts, or at least the dumping of a headless body and its head. Then the mystery deepened even more when I gave a sanitised version of this story on a BBC radio programme. A listener in her seventies named Margaret told me she had lived on Woodland Road in the 1970s, and one evening – around 6.20pm - in the spring of 1972 (Margaret cannot remember the exact date) there was a knock at the door and Margaret's 19-year-old daughter Karen answered to see two old women on the doorstep. One of the women told Karen she had lived at her house 'many years ago' – and she wasn't specific – and then she asked the teenager if she could possibly have a look around the house for sentimental reasons. Karen shouted for her mother, who was in the kitchen cooking the tea for her husband Ken, who was due home any minute. Margaret told the old woman it was inconvenient for her to have a look around now because she was cooking the tea for her husband. The old woman seemed very sad when she was told this, so Margaret said, 'You're more than welcome to have a look around tomorrow if you like.'

The old woman looked at her friend and said nothing, and Margaret felt so guilty at refusing her entry into her home. 'When did you live here?' Margaret asked the woman, but the elderly visitors just turned around and without a word of reply they walked away and Margaret and her daughter never set eyes on them again.

One wonders if the same weird and macabre re-enactment of the murder in the bath would have taken place, and if so – why? It really is a baffling and disturbing case and it has continued to haunt me over the years.

THE UBIQUITOUS NIGHT MAIDEN

When a ghost is seen by one person it's easy to dismiss it as a product of an overtired mind, a trick of the light, and even an overactive imagination, but when a ghost is seen by a number of people, rationalizing it becomes more problematic. When the ghost is seen by a number of people over a wide geographical area, the apparition becomes even harder to comprehend, but sceptics will usually blame that convenient but vague phenomenon of mass hysteria and claim that if a story about a ghost does the rounds, it becomes a type of urban myth which gets embellished along the way. The mass hysteria angle may be true in some cases, but not in the case of the Ghostly Night Maiden – my term for what I perceive to be a nocturnal entity which is seen all over the Wirral and parts of Liverpool and Cheshire, mostly around the autumn season for some reason. In September 1969 a Birkenhead man named Ian Grant went to stay over at his friend Rod's house on Rock Ferry's Highfield Grove after the two men – both in their early twenties – had enjoyed a night out drinking and catching up on one another's lives. They reached Rod's house around midnight with three fish and three portions of chips, and they had their ad hoc supper in the kitchen with Rod's girlfriend Elaine. Elaine went to bed around 1.30am but Rod and Ian talked until around three in the morning, mostly about old friends of theirs and the usual subjects of politics and sport. By 3.15am Rod was in bed and Ian was settling down on the sofa under a woollen blanket with a pillow at his head. Ian was soon fast asleep, but he was awakened by the sound of someone shouting for help upstairs. Ian realised it was Elaine – Rod's girlfriend. Ian got up, fumbled for the light switch, then went into the hallway and climbed the stairs asking, 'What's wrong?'

When Ian went into the bedroom he saw a young woman of about eighteen sitting at the end of the couple's bed. She had long black hair, a very pale face, huge staring eyes, and she wore an old-fashioned night gown that went from her neck down to her bare feet. The stranger was leaning forward slightly with her hands on her lap. Ian flicked the light switch but the bulb blew.

From beneath the blankets of the bed, Ian heard Elaine's muffled voice cry out: 'Get rid of her!'

Ian somehow knew the girl was something supernatural, but he shouted, 'Who is she?'

'She keeps appearing! Make her go away!' Elaine screamed, and she peeped over the blankets and let out a shriek when she saw the weird figure seated at the end of the bed. Ian could not bring himself to approach the weird figure, never mind touch her and attempt to remove her from the room – and why wasn't Rod doing anything to send her on her way? It later transpired that Rod had experienced some sort of seizure after seeing the girl at the end of the bed.

As Ian stood there, ready to make the sign of the cross and say the Lord's Prayer, the girl with the huge bulging eyes vanished into thin air. Rod regained consciousness and almost punched Elaine as he fought for air, saying he couldn't breathe. He told Ian the ghostly girl had visited twice before a week back. Ian was that spooked by the incident he never returned to Rod's house and Rod and his girlfriend later moved over to Liverpool.

Readers with a good memory might recall a strikingly similar story about a girl in an old-fashioned nightdress sitting on the bed of a Wavertree couple in the very first volume of *Haunted Liverpool*. That story concerned a 20-year-old man named Rob, who hailed from Berbice Road, just a stone's throw from Penny Lane. In the autumn of 1970 Rob bumped into a friend named Jimmy at the Tudor nightclub (also known as Dutch Eddies) on Upper Parliament Street. The two men enjoyed a few drinks together, and had a lot of catching up to do so around 1.30am, Jimmy invited Rob back to his house on South Drive in the Victoria Park area of Wavertree. The two men jumped into a Hackney cab, reaching Wavertree in around fifteen minutes. Throughout the cab journey, Jimmy told bachelor Rob how great married life is and how he loved his wife dearly.

Even in the daytime South Drive has a gothic eerie atmosphere hanging over its leafy lane, possibly because the Victorian buildings that line the winding drives there are dark and rather tall, and they admit little light into their narrow tree-shaded roads. Some locals in Wavertree even believe the uncanny ambience is something to do with the ancient Neolithic urns and other prehistoric artefacts that have been unearthed in the neighbourhood over the years. The two young men left the taxi and went into the impressive suburban house. Jimmy's wife Gladys cooked a fine supper for her husband and his friend Rob, and around a quarter to three, Rob said he felt tired and asked if he could possibly sleep on the sofa. Jimmy wouldn't hear of this, and he told Rob he'd get a proper night's sleep in the old spare bed in 'the master's chamber' as he jokingly called his bedroom. The bed in question had been there when Jimmy and Gladys had moved into the house (which dated back to 1850) several years back and the couple still hadn't gotten round to moving the heavy cast-iron bedstead out of the place. Not long after Jimmy and Gladys got into bed, the couple fell fast asleep, and Rob got into the spare bed and tried to settle down, despite Jimmy's loud snores. After a few minutes, he fell into a deep dreamless sleep.

Around four in the morning, something awakened Rob. To this day he does not know whether it was a sound or something touching him, or whether it was a case of his unconscious mind simply detecting the presence of someone in the room; all Rob remembers is that *something* roused him from his slumbers, but what that something was he still cannot say. The young man turned in the old bed and happened to take a bleary-eyed glance over at the bed where Jimmy and Gladys were sleeping. What Rob saw over there sent an icy shiver down his spine. A young woman of around eighteen was sitting on the couple's bed, eyeing Rob intensely. The pale-faced girl just sat there in a peculiar posture, leaning forward, gazing directly at Rob without blinking. By the faint amber light of a sodium street lamp that filtered into the room through the net curtains, Rob could see that the silent watcher's hair was raven-black and long, and that she was wearing an old-fashioned nightgown – but what really unnerved Rob were the girl's huge and dark lifeless eyes.

Rob rubbed his eyes and took another look at the female. He sensed something very unsavoury about the girl, and ducked under the blankets for a few moments, before looking back at the couple's bed, hoping the creepy girl had gone - but she was still there, still watching Rob with that blank expression that made his flesh crawl. Again, he took refuge under the blankets. After a while, with sweat pouring from his brow, and his lungs gasping for air, he reluctantly resurfaced and peeped out to see, to his horror that the ghostly girl was still sitting over there, concentrating on him. Rob closed his eyes and prayed for morning to come, expecting the girl to approach, but she never came near him. He dared not open his tightly-shut eyes and miraculously he somehow managed to fall into a sleep, albeit light and uneasy.

In the morning, while Gladys was making breakfast in the kitchen, Rob told Jimmy about the weird girl in the 'antwacky' nightdress, but his friend just laughed and jokingly said he wished a girl of eighteen *would* sit on his bed. Rob insisted that she had been real and described her ghastly dark lifeless doll-eyes, but, knowing how superstitious his wife Gladys was about such things, Jimmy asked Rob not to mention the incident to her. Not long after I wrote about the ghostly girl in *Haunted Liverpool 1*, I speculated she was perhaps the spectre of a girl who had died in the house in the 1930s from meningitis, but literally hundreds of readers from Walton to Wirral subsequently contacted me after the publication of my book to tell me they had encountered a very similar ghostly girl in their own bedrooms and I asked many of them to sketch what they had seen. All of the sketches showed what seemed to be the same girl – the exceedingly long black hair, the enormous dark eyes, and the long white nightgown. Many witnesses mentioned the way she sat leaning forward slightly as she stared at them. All but three of the accounts of this ghost placed her squarely in the autumn season, with a majority of the visitations occurring close to Halloween. I soon began to suspect that this night maiden was a wayfaring entity who wandered the night for dark reasons known only to herself.

One dark morning in October 2003 at around 4am, a 54-year-old woman we shall call Liz (not her real name) returned to her luxurious home on Gateacre's Oakfield Avenue. She'd been out all night in the company of a friend from her workplace named David – a man who was thirty years her junior. Liz had been having a passionate affair with David for three months, and on the last occasion when she returned home she had found her husband waiting up for her, sitting on the sofa in the lounge in his dressing gown, smoking a cigarette. This time she found a note from her husband telling her to sleep in the guest bedroom as he intended to initiate divorce proceedings soon. Liz had a few drinks then went to the spare room, but being unable to sleep, she sat in an old chair in the spare room and watched the moon through the window. At one point she dozed off in the chair, but awoke around 4.30am. She saw a woman who looked to be in her early twenties, perhaps younger, sitting at the foot of the empty bed, leaning forward with both hands on her lap. This woman had long dark hair, and she wore an old fashioned high-collared night dress down to her bare feet. What unnerved Liz the most about the unexpected 'intruder' was the huge dark eyes – they were fixed upon Liz and the unknown woman wore an expression of astonishment, as if she was amazed to see her. Liz got up off the chair in a state of fright and left the room. She got into bed with her husband (who was snoring) and tried to shake him awake, but he remained asleep and Liz could smell whiskey on his breath. The weird wide-eyed woman came into the room. Liz ducked under the blankets and moments later she felt the entity sit on the bed close to her feet. The weird intruder remained there until Liz's husband woke up and in a slurred growling voice he told her he wanted a divorce. When Liz told him about the ghostly girl he didn't believe her, but on the following night, the same owl-eyed girl in white was seen in the bedroom of a neighbour.

I mentioned this latter case on a local radio programme some years ago and discovered from listeners that a ghostly girl with 'owl-like' eyes had been seen in places ranging from Crosby to Widnes over the years, and she had also been seen many times across the Mersey in the Metropolitan Borough of Wirral, as well as in Ellesmere Port and other parts of Cheshire. She always appeared in the bedroom and sat on the bed, always in the months of September and October, mostly between the hours of 3am and 4am and after being seen in one house, she'd often appear in another dwelling in the same street, sometimes on the same night. This ghostly night maiden is something of a rarity in the world of the supernatural – she is a ghost that gets about. Most ghosts haunt a specific place, but this one – and it does seem to be the same entity on each occasion – wanders the night, flitting from street to street, district to district, and her reasons for doing so are as mysterious as her nature. There's a good chance that *you* might receive one of her bedside visits soon...

Liverpool One

Shopping complex that covers part of St Thomas graveyard, parts of the old water front community know as Sailor Town. Were the seamen use to drink, and blow a size of of their wages on prostitues when they had their shore leave